This is the first book in the new series *Constitutional Systems of the World*, and as such launches what is set to become an invaluable resource for all students and teachers of constitutional law and politics. The book provides an outline of the principles and doctrines which make up the United Kingdom constitution. The chapters are written in sufficient detail for anyone coming to the subject for the first time to develop a clear and informed view of how the constitution is arranged and how it works. The main themes include: a description of the history, sources and nature of the constitution; later chapters deal with: constitutional principles, the role of the Crown, Parliament and the electoral system, government and the executive, the constitutional role of courts including the protection of human rights, the territorial distribution of power between central, devolved and local government and the European Union dimension. Secondly, the book offers an analytical discussion of the development of the constitution, its strengths and perceived weaknesses, and the on-going reforms aimed at modernising the UK constitution. The book is written in an accessible style, with an emphasis on clarity and concision. It includes a list of references for further reading at the end of each chapter.

Constitutional Systems of the World: Volume 1

Constitutional Systems of the World
Co-edited by Peter Leyland and Andrew Harding

In an era of globalisation, regimes of constitutional law and good governance may be regarded increasingly as vital issues in all types of society. Since the end of the cold war there have been dramatic developments in democratic and legal reform. Post-conflict societies have been faced with the challenge of establishing systems of law and governance. In addition, societies already firmly based on constitutional governance and the rule of law have undergone recent constitutional change and experimentation with the introduction of modified institutions and new forms of governance. Equally, comparative analysis reveals that constitutional systems worldwide have been subject to varying degrees of cross-fertilisation. Constitutional texts for practically every sovereign state are now easily available on the internet. However, texts which, rather than offering detailed description, provide an understanding of the true context, purposes, interpretation of a constitutional system are much harder to locate. This series seeks to provide scholars and students with accessible introductions to the constitutional systems of the world, supplying both a road map for the novice and, at the same time, a deeper understanding of the key historical, political, and legal events which have shaped the constitutional landscape of each country. Each book in this series deals with a single nation, and each author is an expert in their field.

Forthcoming titles in this series

The Constitution of the People's Republic of China
Michael Palmer

The Constitution of South Africa
Heinz Klug

The Constitution of Australia
Cheryl Saunders

The Constitution of France
Sophie Boyron

The Constitution of the United States of America
Mark Tushnet

The Constitution of Vietnam
Mark Sidel

The Constitution of India
Pratap Bahnu Mehta

The Constitution of the United Kingdom

A Contextual Analysis

Peter Leyland

·HART·
PUBLISHING

OXFORD – PORTLAND OREGON
2007

Published in North America (US and Canada) by
Hart Publishing
c/o International Specialized Book Services
920 NE 58th Avenue, Suite 300
Portland, OR 97213-3786
USA
Tel: +1 503 287 3093 or toll-free: (1) 800 944 6190
Fax: +1 503 280 8832
E-mail: orders@isbs.com
Website: www.isbs.com

Hart Publishing, 16C Worcester Place, OX1 2JW
Telephone: +44 (0)1865 517530 Fax: +44 (0)1865 510710
E-mail: mail@hartpub.co.uk
Website: http://www.hartpub.co.uk

British Library Cataloguing in Publication Data
Data Available
ISBN-13: 978-1-84113-666-0 (paperback)
ISBN-10: 1-84113-666-2 (paperback)

Typeset by Hope Services, Abingdon
Printed and bound in Great Britain by
TJ International Ltd, Padstow, Cornwall

Constitutional Systems of the World: Series Editors' Preface

Since the end of the cold war there have been dramatic developments in democratic reform the world over. Societies already firmly based on constitutional governance and the rule of law have undergone constitutional change and experimentation in fields such as devolution and human rights, and their constitutional systems are increasingly subjected to comparative analysis and transplantation. In most regions of the world there are emerging democracies and post-conflict societies which are undergoing a great deal of institutional and public law reform. Constitutional ideas have certainly never been as important as they are at the beginning of the 21st century. Scholars of several disciplines, students, policy-makers, activists and politicians study them avidly. While there is clearly a need for information and insights regarding constitutional systems of the world, there is currently a lack of publications designed to meet this need. Constitutional texts for practically every country in the world are now easily available on the internet. However, texts which enable one to understand the true context, purposes, interpretation, and incidents of a constitutional system normally exist only as part of a national literature which is not designed for international or comparative purposes, and usually make assumptions about history, political culture, legal traditions and points of controversy which are not apparent to those unfamiliar with the country in question.

'Constitutional Systems of the World' is a new series which introduces, interprets and analyses the world's constitutional systems, taking a comparative law approach and dealing with themes common to all the countries covered. These books seek to enable us to understand the true context, and nature of changing constitutional systems in the 21st century. The first tranche of books in the series covers the United Kingdom, Australia, France, India, the People's Republic of China, South Africa, the United States and Vietnam. The authors are all noted experts in their field. Each book is a concise introduction to the main features of the constitutional system, aiming at contextual analysis rather than comprehensiveness. Themes related to political and legal accountability as part of the constitutional order will be the most prominent.

The General Editors of the series are Professor Andrew Harding of the University of Victoria in Canada, and Professor Peter Leyland of London Metropolitan University in the United Kingdom. While it is the editorial policy to commission books for the series, the General Editors will be pleased to receive proposals from prospective authors, who are encouraged to write to us at harding@uvic.ca or p.leyland@londonmet.ac.uk.

Preface

This project originates from an approach to contribute a volume on the United Kingdom constitution to an Italian series of books on World constitutions edited by Professor Nino Olivetti Rason and Professor Lucio Pegoraro and published by G Giapichelli of Turin*. The brief from the editors was clear, namely, to produce a concise account of how the UK constitution currently operates which would obviously make sense to an overseas audience of students and scholars. As well as gratefully accepting the offer to write the Italian version which was published in 2005, it immediately struck me and my friend and colleague Professor Andrew Harding that no such series was available in English for comparative constitutionalists to draw upon. This book is the first volume in a brand new series which seeks to fill what was perceived by us as a serious gap in the literature.

In preparing the original Italian version and in extensively re-writing the volume for an English language audience, this original brief, which insisted on concision, has continued to provide a guiding principle. There are a substantial number of recognised texts on constitutional law which provide a comprehensive overview of the UK constitution and, in addition, there are some scholarly accounts which as well as providing an overview address theoretical questions, but these works may assume too much prior knowledge for someone coming to the subject for the first time. The attempt here has been to produce an accessible analytical study which not only describes the main constitutional processes, but seeks to offer a critical overview, and, at the same time, answer some of the fundamental questions about the nature of constitution. It has proved a considerable challenge to write. This is not only because the United Kingdom has an uncodified constitution with no obviously agreed boundaries to it, but because it was necessary to adopt an organising principle which, to some extent at least, might be suitable for studies on other constitutional systems. The approach has been to consider the historical context, sources, and principles before moving on to address central aspects of the institutional framework concentrating on the Crown, Parliament, government and executive, the constitutional role of the courts, and the territorial division of power between central government, devolved

* P Leyland, *Introduzione al diritto costituzionale del Regno Unito* (G Giapichelli, Torino, 2005)

and local government. European Union law has ever increasing prominence as part of the UK constitution, but the discussion of EU institutions and law in this account is integrated into chapters where it is deemed relevant, rather than forming a separate topic in its own right. Important issues are introduced and discussed in context, sometimes more than once to make it easier for readers to follow; and there has been an attempt to write a summary or conclusion at the end of each chapter to draw together the strands of the discussion.

I have many people to thank for their help and support in producing this book.

I would like to start with the Italian connection and express my gratitude to Lucio Pegoraro and Nino Olivetti Rason for getting me involved in the first place. I would also like to acknowledge the help and support of Justin Frosini, Tania Groppi, Luciano Vandelli and Sandro Torre.

I have had tremendous help and support from my co-editor Andrew Harding and from Gordon Anthony who have been kind enough to comment on many chapters and make countless invaluable suggestions. Thanks also to Terry Woods, Nicholas Bamforth, Dawn Oliver, Bill Bowring, Richard Turney and to other colleagues and friends.

I would particularly like to thank Richard Hart for his encouragement and for his enthusiasm for the project and Mel Hamill at Hart Publishing for her hard work on the text of this book.

Most of all, I would like to acknowledge Putachad for her wonderfully original presence, her innovative and beautiful cover design, and generally for her love and support.

Peter Leyland
London
January 2nd 2007

Contents

Table of Cases

European Court of Human Rights

European Court of Justice

United Kingdom

United States

Table of Legislation

European

India

Malaysia

Nigeria

South Africa

United Kingdom

Primary Legislation

Secondary Legislation

United States

Zimbabwe

1

UK Constitution:

Context and History

—⇒•◦•←—

PART I: CONSTITUTIONAL CONTEXT – Introduction – What is Liberal Democracy? – Freedom of Expression, and the Broadcasting and Print Media – The UK Constitution, Constitutionalism, and Good Governance – **PART II: HISTORY** – The Importance of History – Qualifying Absolute Monarchy – The Emergence of Parliament and the Path to Democracy – Defining the Nation: What is the United Kingdom? – Empire, Commonwealth, and Europe – Conclusion

PART I: CONSTITUTIONAL CONTEXT

INTRODUCTION

OUR DISCUSSION BEGINS by explaining why the unwritten UK constitution is unusual. In general the constitution is *the* text which sets out the fundamental and superior law of the nation. It not only describes the main institutions of the state, but also provides a framework of basic rules which determine the relationship between these institutions. In addition, it will usually provide in outline the legal and non-legal rules and procedures that define the system of central and local government. At the same time, the constitution normally places limits on the exercise of power and sets out the rights and duties of individual citizens. Tom Paine explained that it is the property of a nation, and not of those who exercise the government: 'A constitution is a thing antecedent to the government, and always distinct therefrom.'[1] In nearly every other state the term

---

[1] T Paine, *Rights of Man* (London, Penguin, 1791: 1969) p 213.

constitution refers to this document (or series of documents) which contains this *fundamental* and *superior* law of the nation. The constitution of the United Kingdom is unwritten/uncodified in the sense that it is not contained in any single document. Furthermore, a codified constitution, as a form of *higher order* law, will generally be entrenched. A specified procedural device (eg a referendum or a higher majority plus federal ratification) must be followed to introduce changes, which makes a codified constitution relatively difficult to amend. In contrast to most others, the UK constitution is not entrenched. In consequence, it is relatively flexible, in the sense that any aspect can be changed by way of ordinary legislation and certain aspects can be modified by convention (discussed in chapter two).

The next point to stress is that constitutions will often be designed to deliver a particular system of government, and, at the same time, respond to prevailing local conditions. The founding fathers who drafted the constitution of the United States were keen to include strong institutional inhibitions on the exercise of anything approximating to kingly powers, while also creating a federation with a territorial division of authority between central government and state governments. On the other hand, the Soviet constitutions in Russia under Lenin and Stalin following the revolution in 1917 were conceived to deliver an ideological commitment to a socialist state of workers and peasants. The capitalist system of economics and individual property is expressly rejected in the text of these constitutions. We might compare the South African constitution, which followed a protracted struggle to overturn a previous regime based on apartheid. The 1996 constitution seeks to achieve a reconciliation between ethnic groups, and it is intended to create a democratic state committed to non-racialism and non-sexism and to the advancement of human rights and freedoms and the achievement of equality. The United Kingdom lacks a written constitution which has been custom-built to achieve particular goals, but rather the nation has acquired in piecemeal fashion over the span of several centuries a constitution which supports a liberal democratic system of government.

WHAT IS LIBERAL DEMOCRACY?

Next, we need to be clear about what is meant by *liberal democracy*.[2] In setting out a model of democracy Professor Sunstein has recently opined that 'the central goal of a constitution is to create the preconditions for a well

---

[2] For further discussion see J Morison, 'Models of Democracy: From Representation to Participation' in J Jowell and D Oliver (eds), *The Changing Constitution*, 5th edn (Oxford, Oxford University Press, 2005).

functioning democratic order, one in which citizens are genuinely able to govern themselves,'[3] and he advocates a form of deliberative democracy which is marked out by political accountability and a high degree of reflectiveness and a general commitment to reason giving. More commonly, this term *liberal democracy* refers to the fact that power and legitimacy are reached through the indirect consent of the population as a whole. The consent to be governed is achieved after an electoral process delivers representatives to a Parliament. The majority in Parliament vote for laws which, to some extent at least, reflect the will of the majority. However, when looking at constitutional systems, it would be a mistake to believe that a system of majority rule, in itself, satisfies the credentials of liberal democracy. This is because, while it may be accepted that in some matters the will of the majority should prevail, in regard to others, a crucial feature of 'liberal democracy' is that there are limitations on majority rule. For example, the interests of minorities must always be protected to some degree. In practical terms, this means that political parties may offer policy choices to the electorate regarding say, higher or lower levels of taxation, the role of the public sector, and particular policies to pursue in education, health, social services, and law and order. However, the constitutional arrangements in a liberal democratic system must prevent the tyranny of the majority from prevailing by establishing strong constitutional guarantees. This is normally achieved in the field of civil liberties by means of a charter or bill of rights, which will set out the extent of rights which will be protected (eg freedom of speech and religion, freedom to demonstrate, freedom from arbitrary arrest, and so on). However, the United Kingdom with its uncodified constitution has relied on ordinary laws, and a tradition of restraint demonstrated by the executive organs of the state, until the Human Rights Act (HRA) 1998 incorporated the European Convention on Human Rights into domestic law.

FREEDOM OF EXPRESSION, AND THE BROADCASTING AND PRINT MEDIA

A key hallmark of liberal democratic systems is the recognition of basic freedoms and, in particular, freedom of expression. It is worth briefly pausing to see how the role of press and broadcasting media operates and is regulated under the UK constitution. First, as we just noted, this right to free expression, included under Article 10 of the European Convention on Human Rights, has become integrated as part of domestic law since the enactment of

---

[3] C Sunstein, *Designing Democracy: What Constitutions Do* (Oxford, Oxford University Press, 2001) p 6.

the HRA 1998 (which is discussed in chapter seven). Although this freedom might be limited under specific laws (eg incitement to racial hatred, or defamation) freedom of expression must allow for a general right to project opinions through the publication of newspapers, pamphlets, and magazines and through access to television, radio, and cinema. The magnification of the political function of the media might be understood in terms of its 'capacity to discover and publish what authority wished to keep quiet, and to give expression to public feelings which were not, or could not be, articulated by the formal mechanisms of democracy.'[4] It was this potential which turned the broadcasting media into major actors on the public scene. Politicians employ the mass media to further their ends, but they are also extremely wary of the capacity of the press and broadcasting media to bring the mighty down by rooting out incompetence and wrongdoing. The demise of Richard Nixon as President of the United States, following the exposure of the Watergate break-in, and its cover-up, is a classic example of investigatory reporting providing the basis for subsequent official action, eventually resulting in the President's resignation. Ministerial resignations in recent years have been attributable in part at least, to campaigns pursued in the press and broadcasting media.[5] In other words, in a positive way the media is capable of acting as an important counterweight to government in a system where, as we shall see, the executive organs of the state are strong.

This capacity of the media to act as a check on the democratic process is clearly very important. Recent experience in Italy draws attention to the potential problems if the independence of the broadcasting media is undermined: 'In a country resting on universal suffrage, . . . the corruption of information—through the overwhelming control of the media, especially television, both private and state—is a pre-condition for the debasement of democracy.'[6] The Italian state institutions operating under the constitution were not able adequately to withstand the conflicts of interest that arose with the election of a Prime Minister who was not only in a position as the owner of national TV channels to manipulate opinion in his favour, but also, as Prime Minister, capable of using his influence to make appointments to the state broadcasting channels to suit his interests.

Perhaps surprisingly, there are no specific constitutional safeguards in the UK, but it is unlikely that a comparable situation could arise. First, as Members of Parliament, ministers already have a duty to act in the interests of the nation as a whole, as well as special duties to their constituents. Second,

---

[4] E Hobsbawn, *The Age of Extremes* (London, Abacus, 1994) p 581.

[5] One such example was the resignation of the Secretary of State for Transport, Stephen Byers, in May 2002.

[6] M Jacques, 'The Most Dangerous Man in Europe' (2006) *The Guardian*, 5 April.

under the ministerial code of practice (referred to in chapter six) all ministers, including the Prime Minister, must ensure that no conflict arises, or appears to arise, between their public duties and their private interests. The list of declared personal interests must cover all kinds of financial interests, as well as relevant non-financial private interests, such as links with outside organisations (including broadcasting organisations).

There have never been any formal restrictions on private ownership of the print media, and the press is subject to a form of self-regulation carried out be the Press Complaints Commission. Many national newspapers continue to be strongly partisan. For example, the *Daily Telegraph* and *Daily Mail* have consistently supported the Conservative Party, while the *Daily Mirror* has endorsed Labour. Newspapers reflect the views of their owners in their editorials, and they seek to influence the political opinions of their readers, especially at election times. However, by way of contrast, cinema, radio, and television have been subject to varying kinds of statutory regulation. Technical progress has made the media increasingly difficult to control. Such regulation has to address the conflicts of interest that inevitably arise in the quest to open up markets by allowing bidding for broadcast channels. The Communications Act 2003 lays down the conditions for the granting of licences and, in doing so, it sets limits on cross-media ownership (eg combining print media with broadcast media).[7] Equally, the legislation seeks to protect a wider public interest by controlling the editorial line. It sets out special impartiality requirements relating to elections and referendums.[8] Further, it requires that the news generally on broadcast television and radio is reported with due accuracy.[9] Moreover, the Office of Communications (OFCOM) as regulator is under a statutory duty to ensure that its licensees do not project their own views on politically controversial matters. In a democratic system there needs to be a strong public interest dimension to state regulation in this field.

In addition, there are mechanisms in place to safeguard the relative independence of the BBC as state broadcaster. The BBC is required to be impartial. It must refrain from expressing its own opinion on current affairs or on matters of public policy.[10] The corporation operates under a renewable Royal Charter which requires the governors of the BBC to act as regulators and makes them ultimately responsible for its management (the director-general appointed by the governors is responsible for the day-to-day running of the organisation). To minimise political manipulation, the appointment

[7] Communications Act 2003, c 5.
[8] *Ibid.*
[9] Communications Act 2003, ss 319 and 320.
[10] G Robertson and A Nicol, *Media Law* (London, Penguin, 2002) p 826.

process for BBC governors is conducted under certain guidelines (the Nolan principles)[11] by the Office of the Commissioner for Public Appointments (OCPA). After the interviewing process, recommendations are put forward to the Secretary of State for Media and Culture, and then to the Prime Minister.[12]

In sum, in the domain of broadcasting the BBC and other broadcasters can act as a conduit for criticism of politicians as long as this criticism is not part of an agenda set by the broadcaster. Despite the absence of a constitution, citizens are generally able to express themselves, and the freedom of the press and broadcasters to disseminate information in the United Kingdom is constrained by an intricate combination of formal regulation and informal safeguards.

THE UK CONSTITUTION, CONSTITUTIONALISM, AND GOOD GOVERNANCE

The UK constitution has evolved in the sense that the rules which have come into being have been accumulated as a response to circumstances, and they can be regarded as the residue of a historical process with particular laws and conventions incorporated following significant events. Apart from describing institutions and procedures, the starting point in drafting a codified constitution or modifying an existing constitution is to come as close as possible to reaching a consensus on any limits imposed on the majority. As we observed above, each constitution reconciles these issues in its own individual fashion. Unlike most other constitutions, the UK constitution has not been designed according to any ideology or theory to deliver a particular system of government. Despite lacking any guiding principle, the UK system could also be said to display the characteristics of what might be described as *constitutionalism.*

The vast majority of constitutions set out a framework of rules which, if applied and interpreted in the spirit intended, would produce if not a version of liberal democracy, at least conditions of good governance. The point to stress is that the constitution needs to be supported by mechanisms which allow the commitments in the text to be implemented. In many constitutions there is a significant gulf between the statement in the constitution and

---

[11]   These are: selflessness, integrity, objectivity, accountability, openness, honesty, leadership.
[12]   The Hutton Inquiry (2004) into the death of government scientist David Kelly in 2003 exposed the tension which often exists between the BBC and the government over the reporting of news and current affairs. See A Doig and M Phythian, 'The Hutton Inquiry: Origin and Issues' (2005) 58(1) *Parliamentary Affairs* 104–8.

actual compliance. In the majority of cases it is achieving substantial conformity with the rules that becomes the crucial issue. Indeed, as one well-known commentator puts it: 'The fundamental notion of the *Rechtsstaat* or the rule of law was . . . not conceived out of the blue and introduced without resistance. It was, in fact, the fruit of political conflict and scholarly disputes stretching over many centuries.'[13] Rather than compliance with strict constitutional rules, in the United Kingdom the interpretation of some of the important constitutional conventions may arise as a matter of debate and controversy (see the discussion of individual ministerial responsibility in chapter six).

The first point would be to note that any exercise of political power will be bounded by a system of higher order rules which will usually be set out clearly in the constitution. The second point is to recognise what these rules are likely to concern. For example, in virtually every case these rules will specify the procedure for making valid legislation, and a distinction will often be drawn between what can be the permissible content of ordinary legislation as opposed to law relating to the constitution itself. Further, the higher order rules contained in the constitution will outline the method for the formation of the government, and the rules may place limits on the action taken by the executive organs of the state, including the civil service and the police, in the implementation of law. Finally, the constitution may provide that a court (often a constitutional court) has the capacity to invalidate legislation or executive action which fails to comply with the law of the constitution. Constitutionalism is defined in terms of adherence to the rules and to the spirit of the rules. As Professor De Smith has observed: '[this] becomes a living reality to the extent that these rules curb arbitrariness of discretion and are in fact observed by the wielders of political power.'[14]

A genuine constitution for reformers in the eighteenth century, such as Tom Paine, restrained and regulated the exercise of absolute power. Apart from its positive aspects, namely, dealing with the generation and organisation of power, a constitution may be taken to comprise a series of devices designed to curb discretionary or unlimited power. It seeks to establish different forms of accountability[15] not simply through a system of freely elected government, but by placing restrictions on the power of the majority. This accountability is reliant on transparency, and it is acted out in a number of

---

[13] R Van Caenegem, *An Historical Introduction to Western Constitutional Law* (Cambridge, Cambridge University Press, 1995) p 17.
[14] S De Smith, 'Constitutionalism in the Commonwealth Today' (1962) 4 *Malayan Law Review* 205.
[15] See C Harlow, *Accountability in the European Union* (Oxford, Oxford, University Press, 2002) ch 1, 'Thinking about accountability'.

familiar ways[16]: an obligation for the government to be responsible to the elected Parliament; legal limits established by the courts (often including a constitutional court) on the exercise of public power; formal financial accountability in public affairs; accountability through contractual agreement where public services are provided by private organisations; and, additionally, accountability through the intervention of constitutional oversight bodies such as parliamentary select committees, ombudsmen, and courts (discussed in later chapters).

Moreover, the constitution also results in further ground rules in the form of laws, codes of practice, and conventions being adopted to ensure fair play at every level.[17] Finally, an equally significant characteristic of constitutionalism is a degree of self-imposed restraint which operates beyond the text of the constitution, and its attendant rules, especially on the part of political actors and state officials. The point to stress here is that all nations have a constitution of some kind, but constitutionalism is only established in a true sense where political behaviour is actually contained within certain boundaries. In the first place, the rules need to embody a defensible constitutional morality which accords with principles of good governance[18] but the constitution also represents a sufficiently widely accepted political settlement. In the second place, there must be a general adherence at all levels to the constitutional rules and the wider body of law and conventions associated with them. In the United Kingdom we will soon discover that there is a debate about the adequacy of constitutional safeguards, especially in relation to the exercise of executive power, but although the rules are often embodied in informal conventions, there is generally a high degree of compliance by the main political actors.

PART II: HISTORY

THE IMPORTANCE OF HISTORY

In general, constitutions are formally adopted as a specific text of special importance introduced at a decisive moment in a nation's history to achieve

---

[16] For a discussion of the development of such mechanism in the United Kingdom, see: D Oliver, *Constitutional Reform in the UK* (Oxford, Oxford University Press, 2003) chs 1, 2, and 3.

[17] Loughlin points out: 'Like all representationational frameworks, a constitution is a way of organising, and hence also of generating, political power . . . and orchestrating the public power of the state': see M Loughlin, *The Idea of Public Law* (Oxford, Oxford University Press, 2003) p 113.

[18] For a discussion of 'good governance' from a global perspective, see Francis N Botchway, 'Good Governance: The Old, The New, The Principle and The Elements' (2001) 13 *Florida Journal of International Law* 159–210.

obvious goals. For example, the constitution of the United States was approved after the success over the British in the American War of Independence. The 'Bill of Rights' was adopted as the first 10 amendments in 1791, but apart from a further 17 amendments the constitution has remained in its original succinct form. The First Republic in France was introduced shortly after the revolution of 1789, and the most recent Fifth Republic was introduced in 1958 to redress the instability of previous constitutions by bolstering the presidential role. In modern times there has been no single domestic event that has required a comprehensive revision of the UK constitution and so the United Kingdom has no constitutional text with this special status. Rather, the constitution is comprised of a variety of sources including statute law, common law, and constitutional conventions (the sources of the constitution are discussed in chapter two). The constitutional arrangements for the United Kingdom have evolved in phases reflecting the political, social, and economic experiences of many centuries. The events selected for coverage are dealt with thematically rather than in chronological sequence, and they are intended to set the scene for the discussion that follows in subsequent chapters.

QUALIFYING ABSOLUTE MONARCHY

The first recurring theme worth mentioning involves certain qualifications which have been placed in the exercise of the absolute authority of the monarchy. An obvious starting point looks back to medieval times, and relates to the dispute between the King and his barons which culminated in the drawing up of the Magna Carta of 1215.[19] The feudal system originally operated on the basis that the King's barons or nobles held their lands from the King in exchange for an oath to him of loyalty and obedience, but with the obligation to provide a fixed number of knights whenever these were required for military service. By the reign of King John this feudal obligation for service was expressed through the imposition of arbitrary financial payments determined by the King and his entourage of royal officials, which were often used to maintain an army. The barons were dissatisfied with what they regarded as a form of unjust taxation, and they were sufficiently united to prevail over the King. The Magna Carta itself has been seen by historians as a response to a wide-ranging catalogue of grievances. For example, as well as acknowledging the freedom of the Church and recognising that London and other cities should enjoy their own liberties and customs, the charter

---

[19] http://www.bl.uk/treasures/magnacarta/translation.html; C Breay, *Magna Carta: Manuscripts & Myths*, London, British Library, 2002.

refers to the navigation of rivers and looks towards the standardisation of weights and measures. However, the charter set out some fundamental rights by recognising that no one should be denied justice or punished except by judgment of their peers or by the law of the land. As one commentator has observed: '[A] common core was an undertaking by the crown to observe a precisely formulated code of behaviour towards their subjects or, in other words, to respect their rights and liberties as specified in the charters.'[20] Although only selected provisions of the Magna Carta were later confirmed by the English Parliament, certain rights and liberties may be traced back to the original document, which amounted to a catalogue of restrictions on the power of the King.

The limitation on royal authority by constitutional means was achieved in stages. The Tudor monarchs, notably Henry VIII and Elizabeth I, were very powerful, and they were personally active in the affairs of government, but by this period Parliament also became increasingly important. While these Tudor monarchs were able to dominate Parliament, they also ruled through Parliament in order to legalise their actions: 'the sixteenth century had a concept of the supremacy of law, embodied in the rule of the common law and sovereignly controlled by statute, which limited the free power of monarchy and was so recognised, in theory and practice by the Crown.'[21]

The seventeenth century was of great constitutional significance. The Stuart Kings, particularly Charles I (1625–49), sought to claw back the initiative from Parliament by re-asserting the divine right of kings to govern. An obvious problem for the King was that Parliament had to be summoned when he wished to raise taxes, for example, to pursue foreign policy, to fight wars, or to crush insurrection. The Petition of Right in 1628, which arose after a person had been imprisoned for refusing to pay a loan imposed by the King (see *Darnel's Case* 1627, also known as 'the *Five Knights' Case*[22]) had already signalled dissatisfaction, because Parliament rejected the idea of taxation without its consent, and it questioned the Crown's authority to impose arbitrary imprisonment and martial law. The struggle between the Crown and Parliament came to a head with the Civil War (1642–49). As well as contesting the right to impose taxes without Parliament's consent, mentioned above, the King's authority to summon and dismiss Parliament at will was also called into question. The resistance of MPs to the King's demands when Parliament was recalled culminated in an event of symbolic importance. The King entered Parliament in person with soldiers at his side in order to arrest five dissenting MPs. The Speaker of the House of Commons refused

---

[20] R Van Caenegem, above n 13, p 17.
[21] G Elton, *England Under the Tudors* (London, Methuen, 1974) p 483.
[22] 3 *State Trials* 36–7.

to co-operate with the King's demands in an act of open defiance. At this point factions within Parliament were prepared to resort to armed insurrection to resist the King's demands. In the struggle that followed parliamentary forces prevailed over those of Charles I, and the King was tried and executed in 1649. Oliver Cromwell's Commonwealth under the Instruments of Government lasted only a few years before the restoration of the monarchy with the accession of Charles II in 1660.

Charles II's reign was relatively uneventful in regard to constitutional matters. However, he was succeeded by his brother James II, who was not only a Roman Catholic, but, like his father Charles I, was prepared to disregard the will of Parliament. The use of his royal authority to promote Catholics to prominent positions in what had become a strongly Protestant nation sparked a strong backlash with far-reaching constitutional implications. With the prospect of revolt on the horizon, James dissolved Parliament in 1688 before fleeing the country. In the meantime the opponents of James II invited William of Orange (a Dutch Protestant), who was married to James's daughter Mary, to take up the throne on certain conditions. The position of the King in relation to Parliament was set out in the Bill of Rights of 1689, later enacted as the Parliament Recognition Act of 1689. This landmark document was not a charter of citizens' rights in the modern sense, because it was not concerned to define comprehensively the rights of citizens. Nonetheless, it is extremely important for setting in place certain fundamentals of the contemporary constitution. In particular, it confirmed that it was illegal for the Crown to execute laws, raise taxes, or keep an army in peacetime without the consent of Parliament (Articles I, IV, and VI). It provided not only that a freely elected Parliament should meet on a regular basis, but it gave formal recognition to the privileges of Parliament, which included a right to free speech and debate for MPs, and it gave them the right to regulate their own proceedings without limitation or interference either from the Crown or from the courts. Shortly afterwards, the Act of Settlement 1700 regulated the succession to the throne and it also established the security of tenure of judges. In sum, as Hill observes: 'The men of property [were] secure and unfettered in their control of local government; as taxpayers they determine government policy . . . [they] won freedom—freedom from arbitrary taxation and arbitrary arrest, freedom from religious persecution, freedom to control the destinies of their country through their elected representatives, freedom to buy and sell.'[23] (The constitutional role of the Crown is considered further in chapter four.)

---

[23] C Hill, *The Century of Revolution* (London, Abacus, 1978) pp 263 and 265.

THE EMERGENCE OF PARLIAMENT AND
THE PATH TO DEMOCRACY

As has just been stressed, the UK Bill of Rights of 1689 established that ultimate Sovereignty was vested in the King in Parliament, not in the King alone.
The power of the Crown and the prerogatives of the Crown were thereafter
restricted. In theory at least, unlimited authority had been granted to
Parliament as the body with unrestricted law-making capacity. However, this
change was only a limited step towards parliamentary democracy in a modern
sense. The problem was that Parliament represented elite groups and it
mainly protected property rights. The idea of a representative Parliament had
been in evidence at least from Edward I's Model Parliament of 1295, whose
membership was based on the principle of two knights from each county,
two burgesses from each borough, and two citizens from each city. Further,
by 1341 the House of Commons was meeting separately. In fact, the composition and powers of Parliament re-emerged as an issue of great constitutional importance during the course of the late eighteenth and early
nineteenth centuries. As well as the development of political ideas associated
with popular 'revolutions' in America and France which recognised citizen
rights, the nation itself was experiencing rapid transformation. There were
new pressures associated with industrialisation, the growth of population,
and the rapid expansion of towns and cities. While the complexion of the
nation and the distribution of its population was in the course of changing,
only a small minority had the right to vote, and the geographical division into
constituencies sending members to the House of Commons no longer
corresponded to where the centres of population were now located in the
industrial cities and towns of the Midlands and the North. Reform Acts in
1832, 1867, 1883, and 1884 went some way towards extending the right to
vote, and to redistributing seats more evenly but it was not until 1918 that
universal suffrage for men and votes for women over 30 were secured, with
women securing equal voting rights in 1928.

At the beginning of the twentieth century, the extension of the franchise
had far-reaching constitutional consequences. More representative political
parties (eg the Liberal and Labour Parties) were given a mandate from the
wider electorate to introduce programmes of social reform, and, having
obtained a majority in the elected House of Commons, the government in
power claimed authority to achieve its political goals. On the other hand, the
House of Lords (sometimes referred to as 'the Upper House') comprised
the titled nobility (titles were originally granted directly by the King, but by
the nineteenth century candidates were nominated by the Prime Minister)

who originally derived their wealth and influence from the ownership of land. Peers were able to pass on their titles to the next generation by heredity, and as members of the House of Lords they had a traditional right to sit and vote in Parliament. During the nineteenth and early twentieth centuries the landed aristocracy began to use this voting power in the House of Lords first to delay the process of parliamentary reform, and later to oppose the manifesto commitments and budget proposals of the elected Liberal Government. This opposition precipitated a constitutional crisis. The House of Lords as the unelected legislative chamber was expected to defer to the House of Commons in financial matters and when it not only blocked legislative proposals but refused to pass a budget in 1909 it was eventually forced to agree to having its powers significantly qualified by way of the Parliament Acts of 1911 and 1949. The composition of the House of Lords remains unresolved, but a category of peers appointed for their lifetime only (life peers) was introduced in 1958, and in 1999 the majority of hereditary peers were excluded from participating in the business of the House (the role of Parliament is discussed in chapter five).

DEFINING THE NATION: WHAT IS THE UNITED KINGDOM?

Another dimension to domestic constitutional evolution has concerned the formation of the United Kingdom, comprising England, Wales, Scotland, and Northern Ireland. In chapter eight we will consider the constitutional implications of recent devolution provisions, but at the outset, it is useful to be familiar with the territorial reach of the sovereign nation. In the case of Wales, conquest of the principality by England was completed under Edward I between 1272 and 1307. Royal authority over Wales was later set out in Henry VIII's reign, first by an Act of 1536 'for laws and justice to be ministered in Wales' which also allowed Wales to return MPs to Westminster, and second, the details of the political and legal assimilation of the union between England and Wales were contained in another statute of 1543.

Edward I and other English kings ultimately failed in their attempts to overwhelm Scotland by force, but the thrones of Scotland and England were eventually united, when in 1603 James VI of Scotland succeeded Elizabeth I as James I of England. James had been unsuccessful in his attempt to effect a union of the two kingdoms in an administrative sense. Under the restored constitutional monarchy of William III and Mary, which was set in place by the Bill of Rights of 1689, it was not long before the Scots were faced with a choice. In essence, either the Parliaments of England and Scotland would have to unite, or there would have to be a separation of the monarchies.

Taking account of the economic advantages of fusing the two nations, the Scottish Parliament opted for union. The Treaty of Union and the Act of Union with Scotland 1707 were of enormous significance. This agreement was recognition that England and Scotland were to come under a single Parliament of Great Britain and that the rule of succession for the two thrones would be the same. However, as part of the deal Scotland retained many of its national institutions (church, legal system, and educational system).

The relationship between England and Ireland has been both turbulent and complex. In brief, England had assumed direct rule over Ireland in 1534, and Henry VIII was recognised as King of Ireland in 1541. The Catholic majority (later to generally support the Nationalist cause) were hostile to British rule, which tended to favour Protestant settlers (termed 'Unionists' as they remained loyal to the Crown and favoured maintaining close association with Westminster) introduced into Ireland mainly from Scotland by the English. There were many periods of rebellion, which were sometimes brutally suppressed. Following resolutions by the Parliaments in Westminster and Dublin, Ireland was eventually united with England at the beginning of the nineteenth century. This union was achieved by the Act of Union of 1800, which also confirmed the place of Irish MPs at Westminster. However, the prevailing arrangements were not acceptable to Irish Nationalists (who formed a substantial majority, particularly in the South of Ireland), some of whom resorted to intermittent violent struggle. Apart from repressive measures to confront the unrest, the political response of the Liberal Party (pioneered by W.E. Gladstone) was to attempt to introduce a considerable degree of Irish self-government in domestic affairs, but each of the Home Rule Bills of 1886, 1893, and 1912 was unsuccessful. This was largely because they failed to satisfy the competing claims of Nationalists and Unionists. To accommodate deep-seated differences, the Government of Ireland Act of 1920 was based on partition between the six counties in the North, comprising Northern Ireland with a Parliament in Belfast, and the remainder of Ireland with a Parliament in Dublin. However, the 1920 Act was only implemented in the North. A form of devolved government based at Stormont was set up in 1921 and Unionists secured a promise to allow the North to give its consent before any future assimilation with the South. The situation concerning devolved government in Northern Ireland will be discussed further (in chapter eight). Almost at the same time, the British Government reached an agreement with representatives of a provisional government of Ireland to allow an Irish Free State to be established. The Irish Free State (Agreement) Act of 1922 excluded the 26 counties of the South from jurisdiction of the UK Parliament under the Act of Union of 1800. The current Irish constitution dates from 1937, and the Republic left the Commonwealth under the Republic of Ireland Act 1948, which paved the way for the formation of an independent Republic of Ireland in 1949.

In sum, the term *United Kingdom* now refers to a sovereign state which includes England and Wales, Scotland, and Northern Ireland.

EMPIRE, COMMONWEALTH, AND EUROPE

At the beginning of the twentieth century the United Kingdom was a powerful imperial nation. A quarter of the world's population was ruled directly or indirectly from Westminster. Despite victory in World War I (1914–18) and World War II (1939–45), the diminution of Britain's military, economic, and political influence was reflected in the transition from this vast empire to a self-governing Commonwealth. Viewed from a constitutional perspective this transition occurred in phases. First, there were self-governing colonies, referred to as dominions, which included Canada, Australia, South Africa, and New Zealand. The Balfour Declaration of 1926 later enacted through the Statute of Westminster 1931 established that the Westminster Parliament would not legislate for the dominions without their consent. In the words of one commentator: 'Its main effect was to end the Empire-wide writ of the United Kingdom Parliament.'[24]

After World War II, the British withdrew from India in 1947 and the Indian Independence Act of 1947 created independent dominions of India and of Pakistan. Malaysia was granted independence under the Federation of Malaya Independence Act 1957. The rapid decolonisation of Africa began with Ghana gaining independence in 1957. In the West Indies, Jamaica and Trinidad were granted independence in 1962. Withdrawal from Africa was completed when, after a protracted dispute and civil war, the Zimbabwe Act of 1979 formally granted independence to Zimbabwe (formerly Southern Rhodesia). In each of these nations the Westminster Parliament gave up its local jurisdiction, and a new constitution was adopted usually featuring prominent elements of the Westminster model, together with a system of law based on the common law. The British Commonwealth has continued as a club of nations of ex-British colonial status with the Crown symbolically at its head. The nations co-operate in the common interests of their peoples and in the promotion of human rights, international understanding, and world peace.[25]

---

[24] R Holland, 'Britain, Commonwealth and the End of Empire' in V Bogdanor (ed), *The British Constitution in the Twentieth Century* (Oxford, Oxford University Press, 2003) p 638.

[25] For a fuller statement of principles, see http://www.thecommonwealth.org/Internal/ 20723/key_declarations/ and the Harare Commonwealth Declaration, 1991.

As the influence of empire and Commonwealth waned, and UK economic involvement with the United States diminished after World War II, so the importance of Europe has increased. The Treaty of Rome 1957, which set up the Common Market (EEC) without UK inclusion, was a first step towards Churchill's vision of a 'United States of Europe'[26] which would be able to avoid the recurrence of war by featuring a close partnership between France and Germany together with other nations. The United Kingdom eventually joined the EEC (now the European Union (EU)) on 1 January 1973 after protracted negotiations. Although the United Kingdom signed up to a mainly economic treaty, from a constitutional perspective, membership of this supra-national organisation resulted in a sacrifice of sovereign power in a number of areas. A new hierarchy of law was recognised which meant that a set of European institutions were capable of making laws which could override the authority of the UK national Parliament and UK domestic courts (this issue is discussed in chapter three). Despite being highly controversial across the major political parties (Conservative, Labour, and Liberal Democrat), EU membership was entered into without consulting the electorate. The *post hoc* 1975 referendum settled the issue of association with Europe decisively in favour of continued EU membership after a passionate campaign during which otherwise strict rules of party loyalty (including collective Cabinet responsibility discussed in chapter six) were suspended. In recent years there have been significant changes to the EU, with successive Treaties granting membership to many more nations (from 9 in 1973 to a current total of 25 states) and extending the range of policy areas which are subject to EU law[27] (see chapter nine for discussion of the European constitution).

CONCLUSION

In this preliminary discussion we have seen that the most distinctive feature of the UK constitution is the fact that it lacks formal codification. Nevertheless, it displays the broad characteristics of what has been termed *liberal democracy* and achieves this without having guarantees set out as part of a set constitutional framework. Moreover, the constitution has been presented as a product of history, in the sense that many crucial aspects relating to the monarch, Parliament, the protection of rights, and the territorial extent and organisation of the nation have evolved in response to significant events.

---

[26] Winston Churchill set out these ideas in a speach delivered in Zurich in 1946.

[27] See I Ward, *A Critical Introduction to European Law*, 2nd edn (London, Butterworths, 2003) ch 1.

The next chapter will reveal that, in the absence of the authority provided by a single text, the constitution can only be approached by reference to a range of disparate sources, including formal law, but also including many pivotal constitutional conventions.

FURTHER READING

Bagehot W, *The English Constitution* (London, Fontana, 1963).

Barendt E, *An Introduction to Constitutional Law* (Oxford, Oxford University Press, 1998).

Barnett H, *Britain Unwrapped: Government and the Constitution Explained* (London, Penguin, 2002).

Holland R, 'Britain, Commonwealth and the End of Empire' in V Bogdanor (ed), *The British Constitution in the Twentieth Century* (Oxford, Oxford University Press, 2003).

Loughlin M, *The Idea of Public Law* (Oxford, Oxford University Press, 2003).

Maitland F, *The Constitutional History of England*, 10th edn (Cambridge, Cambridge University Press, 1946).

Marshall G, 'The Constitution: Its Theory and Interpretation' in V Bogdanor (ed), *The British Constitution in the Twentieth Century* (Oxford, Oxford University Press, 2003).

Morison J, 'Models of Democracy: From Representation to Participation' in J Jowell and D Oliver (eds), *The Changing Constitution*, 5th edn (Oxford, Oxford University Press, 2005).

Mount F, *The British Constitution Now* (London, Heinemann, 1993).

Oliver D, *Constitutional Reform in the UK* (Oxford, Oxford University Press, 2003).

Sunstein C, *Designing Democracy: What Constitutions Do* (Oxford, Oxford University Press, 2001).

Van Caenegem R, *An Introduction to Western Constitutional Law* (Cambridge, Cambridge University Press, 1995).

2

The Sources of the Constitution

Introduction – PART I: SOURCES OF THE CONSTITUTION –
Statute Law – The Common Law – European Union Law – European
Convention on Human Rights – Legal Treatises – The Law
and Customs of Parliament – The Royal Prerogative – PART II:
CONSTITUTIONAL CONVENTIONS – Defining Conventions –
The Practical Importance of Constitutional Conventions –
Conclusion

INTRODUCTION

THE UNITED KINGDOM has a constitution but it is not a codified constitution. In other words there is no single document (or
series of documents) that is known as *the* constitution. The lack of a
codified constitution also means that there is no body of rules which is
antecedent to the institutions of state and government and which could
therefore be said to form an act of foundation. Despite the fact that there is
no fundamental law relating to the constitution, it is possible to approach a
description of the constitution by reference to a number of key constitutional
sources. To take an obvious example, the Human Rights Act 1998 makes the
individual rights defined under the European Convention on Human Rights
(ECHR) of central constitutional importance, but, at the same time, many
other statutes may be of relevance to constitutional practice in the field of
human rights: for instance, the Police and Criminal Evidence Act 1984 deals
more specifically with police powers and the rights of the individual.

In many nations today the constitution is linked to a system of representative government, but in the United Kingdom in particular, there is much
less reliance on legal *rules* and safeguards, and much more reliance on constitutional conventions which are underpinned by a commitment to a

democratic system of government. The evolution of the constitution has been possible because conventions are capable of being easily modified to accommodate changing circumstances. All constitutions are to some extent uncodified, with their own conventions, but a distinguishing feature of the UK constitution is that so much of its constitutional practice is governed by conventions. In consequence, particular attention in this chapter is devoted to discussing conventions as a source of the constitution and their significance in relation to constitutional practice. First of all we will consider the other sources of the constitution.

PART I: SOURCES OF THE CONSTITUTION

STATUTE LAW

In the United Kingdom the basic principle of the constitution is the doctrine of parliamentary sovereignty. Since the Bill of Rights of 1689 the courts have recognised Acts of Parliament as the highest source of law. In one sense it might be true to say that all statutes passed by Parliament which have not been repealed are part of the constitution. This is because each one has been passed to set out or refine particular areas of law and there is a coincidence between ordinary law and the constitution. However, in practical terms, it is obvious that certain statutes are of special *constitutional* importance. The Petition of Right 1628 concerned the principle of no taxation without representation. The Bill of Rights 1689, although not a modern Bill of Rights, as discussed in chapter one secured a Protestant succession to the monarchy (a position that was confirmed by the Act of Settlement 1700). The Bill of Rights also formally confirmed that the seat of power had swung towards Parliament as part of a constitutional monarchy.

The nature of constitutional statutes was considered in *Thoburn v Sunderland City Council.*[1] While Laws LJ did not set out any special test to determine the question of what would qualify, it was explained that constitutional statutes are pieces of legislation which condition the legal relationship between citizen and state in some general, overarching manner, or which enlarge or diminish the scope of what might be regarded as fundamental constitutional rights. A number of important constitutional statutes which will be the subject of discussion in later chapters were recognised by Laws LJ as falling into this category (constitutional statutes are discussed at greater length in chapter three). The Acts of Union with Scotland in 1707 and with Ireland in

---

[1] [2003] 3 WLR 247.

1800 dealt with arrangements for combining the English Parliament first with the Scottish Parliament and then the Irish Parliament. The Parliament Act 1911 set limits on the powers of the House of Lords in regard to legislation. The Representation of the People Act 1918 extended the vote to all men over 21 and women over 30, and the Representation of People Act 1969 reduced the voting age so that all adults over 18 could vote. The European Communities Act 1972 incorporated the Treaty of Rome and in so doing placed important limitations on the sovereignty of the Westminster Parliament. The Scotland Act 1998, the Government of Wales Act 1998, and the Northern Ireland Act 1998 set out the principles for devolution. The Human Rights Act 1998 had the effect of incorporating the ECHR directly into English law and in so doing provides the United Kingdom with what is, in effect, a bill of rights.

THE COMMON LAW

In a system where judicial precedent applies, judicial decisions are binding and are used to develop the law on a case-by-case basis. The common law has always been an important source of the constitution. Certain aspects of private law, particularly concerning contract and tort, are comprised of rules originating from judicial decisions. There are particular landmark cases which have expanded the common law in a constitutional context. These decisions remain of constitutional significance. For example, the case of *Entick v Carrington*[2] concerned trespass and placed limits on powers of the Crown and Secretary of State to interfere with the person or property of the citizen without lawful authority. More recently, the UK Home Secretary was found to be in contempt of court for ignoring an order of the High Court in *M v Home Office*[3] (discussed in chapter three). However, it is important to note that decisions of the courts (including the House of Lords) may be amended and overridden by later statutes, eg the decision in *Burmah Oil v Lord Advocate*[4] prompted the UK Parliament to pass the War Damage Act 1965, which had retrospective effect. The courts accept the validity of Acts of Parliament and thus validate the concept of parliamentary sovereignty. Although they do not directly challenge legislation, part of their role is to interpret statutes under established rules of statutory interpretation (see chapter seven).

[2] (1765) 19 State Tr 1029.
[3] [1994] 1 AC 377.
[4] [1965] AC 75.

EUROPEAN UNION LAW

The European Communities Act 1972, which came into force on 1 January 1973, made the law of the European Community (now the European Union (EU)) an important constitutional source. In *Van Gend en Loos*[5] the European Court of Justice had explained the implications for member states of becoming a member:

> The Community [now EU] constitutes a new legal order of international law for the benefit of which the States have limited their Sovereign rights . . . Independently of the legislation of member states, Community law therefore not only imposes obligations on individuals but is also intended to confer upon them rights which become part of their legal heritage.

Some categories of EU law have direct effect, which means that any rights or obligations enjoyed by or imposed on any individual under the Treaties can be enforced in the English courts. This body of law is confined to those areas covered by the Treaty of Rome 1957 and subsequent Treaties. Each Treaty (ie the Maastricht, Amsterdam, and Nice Treaties) has been incorporated into UK domestic law by statute. The law emanating from Europe which applies in the United Kingdom includes regulations, directives, and decisions. EU membership also means that rulings from the European Court of Justice can be binding on domestic courts within the United Kingdom. The importance of the EU was recognised by Lord Denning in *Bulmer v Bollinger*,[6] when he famously described the Treaty of Rome as being 'like an incoming tide. It flows into the estuaries and up the rivers. It cannot be held back, Parliament has decreed that the Treaty is henceforth to be part of our law.' Where it applies, EU law operates as a higher order law and will have the effect of overriding domestic legal provisions. The proposed European constitution has not been proceeded with after it was rejected in referendums held in France and Holland in 2004, but if a European constitution is adopted and incorporated into UK law by statute, it will further define the domestic role of community law and of community institutions.

EUROPEAN CONVENTION ON HUMAN RIGHTS

Since the Human Rights Act (HRA) 1998 came into force in October 2000 the ECHR is incorporated as part of UK law. The ECHR can be regarded as amounting to a constitutional charter of rights. As we shall see in later chap-

---

[5] Case 26/62 [1963] ECR 1 at 12.
[6] [1974] 2 All ER 1226.

ters, the ECHR is an international treaty setting out basic individual rights including: right to life; liberty and security; prohibition of torture and slavery; right to fair trial; no punishment without law; right to respect for privacy and family life; freedom of thought, conscience, and religion; freedom of expression; freedom of assembly and association; and prohibition of discrimination. All public bodies, including the courts, are legally required to act in a way which is compatible with the above rights, and a remedy may be sought if these citizen rights are breached (see chapter 8).

LEGAL TREATISES

The lack of a codified constitution has meant that academic and legal treatises which describe and analyse the nature of the constitution as it has evolved assume special status. For example, there are classic works that may be cited with authority when seeking to establish how the constitution operates. Walter Bagehot's *The English Constitution* provided an influential account of parliamentary democracy during the mid-Victorian period. It was famous for making a distinction between the 'efficient' and 'dignified' parts of the constitution. The book was published at about the same time as the Second Reform Act of 1867 extended the right to vote to 1.5 million male householders and distributed more parliamentary seats to the main industrial towns. Probably the most influential contribution has been *An Introduction to the Study of the Law of the Constitution* by AV Dicey, which was first published in 1885. Although this study was and still is controversial, for instance in the sense that it might be characterised as hostile to modern forms of democracy, Dicey nevertheless provides arguably the most persuasive explanation of the core concepts of parliamentary sovereignty and the rule of law. Parliamentary practice and procedure, which is obviously an important part of the contemporary constitution, is frequently determined by reference to *A Practical Treatise on the Law, Privileges, Proceedings and Usage of Parliament*, now in its 23rd edition. This work is referred to simply as '*Erskine May*' after the constitutional theorist who produced the original volume. Contemporary studies by constitutional experts are also relevant where there is a lack of clarity over aspects of constitutional practice. However, relying on academic sources is apt to present problems, since experts may differ in their interpretation of how constitutional doctrine applies. For example, the studies by the late Professor Sir William Wade and Professor Paul Craig on the subject of administrative law adopt markedly different approaches.[7] Constitutional

---

[7] See W Wade and C Forsyth, *Administrative Law*, 9th edn (Oxford, Oxford University Press, 2003); P Craig, *Administrative Law*, 5th edn (London, Sweet & Maxwell, 2003).

treatises should be regarded as *subordinate* sources, which are only resorted to by the courts and other constitutional players when there is no other established authority.

THE LAW AND CUSTOMS OF PARLIAMENT

The law and customs of Parliament refers to the resolutions of the two Houses of Parliament which establish parliamentary practice (standing orders of the House). This body of rules is of great political importance and it ranges from the regulation of debates to the functions of the leaders of the government and opposition. These rules can be changed by MPs and peers. For example, the recommendations of the Select Committee on Procedure (1978) were adopted following the 1979 general election resulting in the introduction of the House of Commons Departmental Select Committees to scrutinise the work of government departments. It is important to note that as parliamentary rules and procedures are established by standing orders, they fall outside the scope of both legislation and common law.

THE ROYAL PREROGATIVE

Many powers are exercised by ministers and officials under primary or secondary legislation, but the *royal prerogative* refers to those powers which have been left over from the period when the monarch was directly involved in the process of government. These remaining powers, now mainly exercised by ministers, include: making treaties; declaring war; deploying the armed forces; regulating the civil service; and granting royal pardons. The prerogative powers continue to be important for the operation of government in these areas, and the prerogative powers have been recognised by judges in developing case-law. (The nature and extent of prerogative powers are discussed in more detail in chapter four.)

PART II: CONSTITUTIONAL CONVENTIONS

Conventions are a particularly important source of the UK constitution and they are also crucial to understanding how the constitution functions. In the remainder of this chapter conventions will be discussed in more detail. An observer of the UK constitution would build up a very incomplete account of its workings if attention was given only to legal rules, since conventions, in the words of one commentator, 'provide the flesh which clothes the dry bones of the law.' It is evident that: 'The legal structure of the constitution is everywhere penetrated, transformed and given efficacy by conventions.'[8] Conventions are the source of the non-legal rules of the constitution. They may be characterised as being associated with laws but at the same time they are distinct from them. They lubricate the formal machinery of government and assist in making government work. In this sense they have an important *practical* dimension. It is very difficult to settle constitutional disputes without understanding them. Moreover, conventions allow what would otherwise be a rigid legal framework to be kept up to date with the changing needs of government because they are capable of evolving. In subsequent chapters we will be looking in detail at a number of conventions, but first we need to understand why conventions have been difficult to define and note the different areas in which they apply.

DEFINING CONVENTIONS

The difficulty in defining conventions is mainly because they encompass a wide range of practices, some of which are a lot more certain than others. The important thing to remember is that they determine many of the practices of government and aspects of conduct of state institutions. They are not the result of a legislative or a judicial process but rather often arise from what Professor Turpin calls 'the hardening of usage' over a period of time. A failure to adhere to an important convention might lead Parliament to cast a disputed practice into legislative form.

Perhaps the most influential definition derives from AV Dicey, who explained that[9]

> the 'conventions of the constitution' consists of maxims or practices which, though they regulate the ordinary conduct of the Crown, of ministers, and of other persons under the constitution, are not in strictness laws at all.

In recognising that conventions were mainly the customary rules which determined how the discretionary powers of the state were exercised, Dicey drew a special distinction between laws, which he explained were enforceable in the courts, and conventions, and he maintained that conventions were 'rules intended to regulate the exercise of the whole of the remaining discretionary

---

[8] Sir Ivor Jennings, *The Law and the Constitution*, 5th edn (London, University of London Press [check OK], 1959) pp 81 and 113.

[9] A Dicey, *An Introduction to the Study of the Law of the Constitution*, 10th edn (Basingstoke, Macmillan, 1959), p 24.

powers of the Crown.' It is important to recognise that for Dicey the key characteristic is that conventions, unlike laws, are not enforceable in the courts. Conventions consist of the understandings, habits, practices, maxims, and precepts which are necessary to regulate the conduct of the sovereign, the Prime Minister, ministers, and officials, and also that of other constitutional players. It is true to say that conventions are not directly enforced in quite the same way as laws, but that the existence of conventions has been recognised by the courts as part of judicial reasoning. For example, in *Attorney-General v Jonathan Cape Ltd*[10] the Attorney-General on behalf of the government was unsuccessful in getting the court to enforce in the public interest the confidentiality requirement which forms part of the convention of collective Cabinet responsibility by getting the court to issue an injunction to prevent a former Cabinet minister from serialising his memoirs. However, as one commentator notes: 'The Attorney-General may be said to have been victorious in this case in gaining judicial acceptance of the principle that a legal obligation of confidentiality attaches to Cabinet proceedings, even though the court decided that the Crossman diaries no longer . . . retained their confidential character, and so fell outside the protection of the law.'[11]

Sir Ivor Jennings, approaching the task of definition from a different perspective, suggested that three questions should be posed in order to identify a valid convention. The first task is to determine whether there is a precedent for the practice. Finding this out involves ascertaining how often and how consistently a practice has been observed previously. The second question asks whether those operating the constitution have accepted the convention as binding. Could it be said that an obligation is created by the practice under consideration? While the first question merely requires a descriptive response, this second question is much more problematic. Some conventions are both relatively easy to identify and to follow and they are accordingly regarded as binding, for example, the requirement that the Prime Minister must be a member of the elected House of Commons. However, this is not always the case. For example, the convention of individual ministerial responsibility is of enormous constitutional importance. It concerns the accountability of the executive to Parliament, but there is considerable uncertainty over the exact way in which it applies. As we shall see in chapters five and six, there is debate among experts concerning how ministers are accountable to Parliament for shortcomings in their department, and, in particular, the circumstances when resignation by a minister is required. The final question posed by Jennings acknowledges the strong pragmatic dimen-

---

[10] [1976] QB 752.
[11] C Turpin, *British Government and the Constitution*, 5th edn (London, Butterworths, 2002) p 109.

sion to the constitution. It asks whether there is a good *political* reason for the existence of a convention. By taking another example we can see what Jennings had in mind. The deference of the House of Lords to the House of Commons is very important. The legitimacy of the Commons has increased because it is the democratically elected House of Parliament. This approach also illustrates that many conventions have arisen because of usage over a period of time. During the constitutional crisis that followed the rejection of the budget in 1909 (explained further below) Prime Minister Asquith reminded King George V that it had been established that the Sovereign acts upon the advice of his or her ministers. He asserted respectfully that there was no longer any doubt that the final decision-making power rests with the elected government enjoying the confidence of Parliament.

In some situations it may be difficult to know whether a practice has actually been recognised as a convention. Determining the validity of a convention may come down to establishing whether the actors regard the conduct as binding upon them. Dicey believed that conventions formed part of a constitutional morality which is positive. Conventions are followed because a failure to obey them would lead to *legal* difficulties. For example, Parliament must assemble each year to pass financial resolutions and make a budget to raise taxes and pay for the government, armed forces, local government, etc. Dicey's account does not explain why parliamentary sessions continue beyond setting a budget. In contrast, Jennings believed that disregarding conventions would result in *political* rather than legal problems. The refusal of the House of Lords to pass the budget in 1909 serves as an excellent illustration. This action by the Lords was in clear breach of a convention, and this failure to pass a Finance Bill prompted a political crisis for the obvious reason that a government without a budget to pay officials and the armed forces, and so on, could not govern. From the moment of the budget's rejection a stalemate existed between the elected House of Commons and the mainly Conservative hereditary peers in the House of Lords. After protracted negotiations, King George V agreed to create sufficient peers to secure the passage of a Parliament Bill, curbing the powers of the Upper House, but only if there was a mandate from the electorate for the reform. After the general election in December 1910 returned a Liberal-dominated coalition committed to reform, the Conservative peers in the House of Lords backed down and passed the Bill. Apart from removing the general veto over legislation exercisable by the House of Lords, the Parliament Act of 1911 placed in statutory form what had been regarded as a convention, namely, that the House of Lords could not veto or delay money Bills.

We can conclude this brief discussion by recognising that there is no way of knowing with certainty what an established convention is, except from the behaviour of the sovereign, politicians, or other officials responsible for operating it as part of the constitution. At least, it might be said of some conventions that they are rules of political practice which are regarded as binding by those to whom they apply. In this sense it could be claimed that they therefore provide a *prescriptive* view of what should happen in a range of given situations. However, Professor Griffith has rejected an approach to the constitution which is over-dominated by backward-looking conventions and he takes a much more pragmatic view—'the constitution is what happens'— and goes on to suggest 'if it works, it's constitutional.'[12]. Since it is difficult to reach a satisfactory definition beyond this discussion, it will be informative to introduce some of the main conventions applying to the respective state institutions. Their constitutional importance will become more fully apparent as we proceed with this discussion in subsequent chapters.

THE PRACTICAL IMPORTANCE OF CONSTITUTIONAL CONVENTIONS

Before discussing the various elements of the constitution in more detail, it is important to be familiar with some of the main constitutional conventions.

(1) The Crown

Most of the important conventions that operate in relation to the sovereign bear witness to the passage of authority away from the Crown, and in the majority of cases there is very little discretion left with the monarch. For example, it has long been established that the royal assent to Bills that have completed their passage through the House of Commons and the House of Lords is never refused by the reigning monarch. To do so would undermine the capacity of a representative Parliament to pass legislation. By way of contrast, there are conventions where some discretion may have to be exercised. It is a well-established convention that the sovereign appoints the leader of the majority party in the House of Commons to form a government and become Prime Minister. Assuming one party enjoys such a majority, the leader of that party will always be chosen to form a government. However, if no party emerges from a general election as a clear winner (as occurred after the 1974 general election) the monarch will have to decide whom to call upon to form a government. Advice may be taken from experts, but the final

---

[12] J Griffith, 'The Political Constitution' (1979) *MLR* 1 at 19.

decision rests with the monarch. The lack of clarity on such an important question has led to calls for statutory procedures to be set in place which would determine the outcome should this situation recur.[13]

One of the most important constitutional conventions requires the Sovereign to act upon the advice of the Prime Minister and his or her ministers. In practice, although the business of government is conducted in the name of the Crown the key decisions are taken at ministerial level. Also, the sovereign's speech given from the throne in the House of Lords at the opening of each session of Parliament setting out government policy is always written by the Prime Minister. Further, it has been recognised by convention that, upon the request of the Prime Minister, a dissolution of Parliament will be granted by the sovereign allowing a general election to be held. Finally, it has long been established that the sovereign in person cannot sit as a judge in his or her own courts.[14]

(2) Prime Minister, Cabinet, and Executive

Turning next to conventions in relation to the government and the executive, the roles of the Prime Minister and Cabinet have developed and continue to develop by convention. Sir Robert Walpole, usually regarded as the first Prime Minister, depended heavily on the King's patronage and mainly operated as the King's spokesman in Parliament. Walpole, who was officially appointed First Lord of the Treasury, disliked the use of the term 'Prime Minister', which carried with it the connotation that he was royal favourite.[15] Modern Prime Ministers continue to consult the monarch by having regular meetings, but by the nineteenth century the appointment of Prime Ministers came to depend on the results of the election process. The person sent for had to be capable of forming a government commanding a majority in Parliament. It has also been established by convention that the Prime Minister and the Chancellor of the Exchequer must be members of the House of Commons and, as a result, directly accountable to the electorate.

Furthermore, there has never been any law either setting out the formal limits of prime ministerial powers, which, as we shall see later, have grown enormously, or defining with any precision the relationship between the Prime Minister and the Cabinet. For example, it has been suggested that during the course of the twentieth century the Cabinet system changed from

---

[13] Fabian Commission Report, *The Future of the Monarchy* (14 July 2003). See Fabian Society website, publications archive.

[14] See the famous case of *Prohibitions del Roy* (1607) 12 Co Rep 63.

[15] H Wilson, *A Prime Minister on Prime Ministers* (New York, Summit Books, 1977) p 8.

the Cabinet acting as the sole decision-making body to the situation which prevailed up to the late 1970s where decision-making took place within Cabinet committees. More recently, under Thatcher and Blair, the Cabinet, rather than acting as decision-making body or a principal forum for debate, meets for regular collegiate team-building and informal exchanges of views on policy matters at senior ministerial level.[16] Also, the Prime Minister's personal office of advisers and civil servants at 10 Downing Street and the role of the Cabinet Office in co-ordinating government have expanded according to the requirements of the office of Prime Minister with no formal constitutional limitation (see the proposals referred to in chapter six for a Civil Service Act).

Further conventions of central constitutional importance relating to the Prime Minister and Cabinet are discussed in later chapters. In particular, collective Cabinet responsibility requires the Cabinet to unite around a policy position or for dissenters to resign. The convention arose from the need to provide the sovereign with advice that was not conflicting (see chapter five). Individual ministerial responsibility concerns the accountability of ministers and the executive to Parliament and requires ministers to be directly answerable to Parliament for their actions (see chapters five and six).

(3) Parliament

Looking back historically, it has already been observed that the attempt of monarchs in the seventeenth century to govern without Parliament led to conflict between Parliament and the King. Since the Bill of Rights of 1689 it has been established that Parliament is summoned at least once a year. Furthermore, it is a convention of fundamental constitutional importance in the Westminster type of parliamentary system that the government should command a majority in the House of Commons, and that if it is unable to do so the government should fall. The rationale behind the convention is obvious. The government requires a majority in the elected chamber to pass the legislation it needs to govern effectively. The Prime Minister normally determines the date of an election within a five-year limit, as set by the Parliament Act 1911. However, the Prime Minister must offer to resign if his or her party loses a vote of confidence in the House of Commons. The defeat will trigger a general election.[17] The strong impetus towards party organisation and

---

[16] A Sheldon, 'The Cabinet System' in V Bogdanor (ed), *The British Constitution in the Twentieth Century* (Oxford, Oxford University Press, 2003) p 129.

[17] Such a resignation followed by a general election last occurred in 1979 when Prime Minister James Callaghan was defeated in a House of Commons vote of confidence by a single vote.

discipline within Parliament (particularly the House of Commons) has resulted from the application of this convention, which has been recognised since 1841.[18]

Also, the so called 'Salisbury convention' recognises that the House of Lords should not use its delaying power under the Parliament Acts 1911 and 1949 in respect of legislation which forms part of the electoral programme of a governing party, once again showing deference to the elected House of Commons. Many procedural questions relating to Parliament are determined by convention and these include: the time allocated in the House of Commons to the official opposition; the fact that political parties are represented on committees according to the percentage of MPs supporting them; and the 'pairing' arrangements for MPs through which government and opposition whips allow for the non-attendance of MPs for votes in the House of Commons. Finally, the Speaker is elected by members of the House of Commons to preside over the House. Although the MP selected as Speaker will have been a member of the government or opposition party, it is a convention of the highest importance that she or he will, as Speaker, act with strict impartiality.

(4) Judges and the Courts

The Bill of Rights 1689 and the Act of Settlement 1700 formally recognised the importance of judicial independence by securing the tenure of judges. But there are a number of conventions relating to the judicial role. It is generally acknowledged that the professional conduct of judges should not to be questioned in Parliament, except where there is a substantive motion for dismissal. (Senior judges can only be dismissed by Parliament using this procedure, and no senior judges have been dismissed in modern times.) Until very recently there was no clear separation of powers in the United Kingdom, as we will see when discussing the role of the Lord Chancellor in chapter seven. The Constitutional Reform Act 2005 will set up a UK Supreme Court outside of Parliament (operational from October 2009) and reformed the system of judicial appointments. Nevertheless, it was already an accepted convention that judicial appointments were made on merit (and not on the basis of political affiliation) and that serving judges should not have any active involvement with party politics. (In chapters seven and eight we will

---

[18] P Norton, 'The House of Commons and the Constitution: The Challenges of the 1970s' (1981) 34 *Parliamentary Affairs* at 266–7.

assess how the courts deal with questions of legality under the rule of law.[19]) The other side of this coin is the convention that ministers, as members of the executive branch, should avoid direct comment on specific cases under consideration by the courts during the course of litigation (particularly if the case involves the government).

CONCLUSION

In this chapter we have observed that the uncodified UK constitution is comprised of a number of different sources, but it is quite clear that statute law is the predominant source of the constitution, as is evidenced by the recent battery of legislation reforming aspects of the constitution (devolution, human rights, and freedom of information Acts have been introduced since 1997, to name but a few examples). The doctrine of sovereignty proposes that Parliament is all-powerful and, in theory at least, has the capacity to determine the nature of the constitution. The limits of this doctrine will be critically examined in the next chapter. However, a substantial part of the discussion has concentrated on conventions as a constitutional source. Conventions vary, from well-established practices which will be applied with predictable outcomes to rather vague guidelines which are open to interpretation in the way that they are applied. Failure to adhere to conventions can have far-reaching consequences. The constitutional crisis following the budget in 1909, discussed earlier, was caused because the House of Lords chose to ignore the convention which recognised the predominance of the House of Commons over the House of Lords on financial matters. Legislation in the form of the Parliament Act 1911 was necessary to prevent a similar situation occurring. It has been suggested by some writers that a more extensive process of juridification or codification would serve to clear up other ambiguities surrounding the way conventions apply. It is worth remembering, however, that all constitutions have conventions. The UK constitution has more than its fair share, because the constitution as a whole has not yet been codified.

In general conventions have served the constitution well in filling a gap between constitutional formality, in the sense of defining what the actors should do to make the constitution work, and political reality, in the sense of

---

[19] Principles of judicial review have been developed which recognise the respective roles of the executive and the courts in regard to the decisions of public bodies. In cases referred to them the courts deal with the legality of acts of public authorities and set in place procedural safeguards, but the courts do not step into the shoes of the decision-maker. See eg S Sedley 'The Common Law and the Courts' in Lord Nolan and S Sedley (eds), *The Making and the Remaking of the British Constitution* (London, Blackstone, 1997).

determining how such conduct might be modified to take account of changing circumstances. In essence, conventions provide built in flexibility which
can be regarded as a tremendous advantage. However, certain conventions,
in particular individual ministerial responsibility, are of crucial importance in
defining the mechanism for accountability and for the control of executive
power. Many writers have argued that the rules surrounding this convention
have not been modified sufficiently to account for modern conditions of
government and the emergence of what is often termed the *contracting state*
(see chapter six and the discussion of 'elective dictatorship').

FURTHER READING

Anthony G, *UK Public Law and European Law: The Dynamics of Legal Integration*
(Oxford, Hart Publishing, 2002).

Bagehot W, *The English Constitution* (London, Fontana, 1963).

Bogdanor V (ed), *The British Constitution in the Twentieth Century* (Oxford,
Oxford University Press, 2003).

Bradley A and Ewing K, *Constitutional and Administrative Law*, 13th edn
(London, Longmans, 2003).

Brazier R, *Constitutional Practice: The Foundations of the British Constitution*, 3rd edn
(Oxford, Oxford University Press, 1999).

Dicey A, *The Law and the Constitution*, 10th edn (London, Macmillan, 1959).

Griffith J, 'The Political Constitution' (1979) 1 *Modern Law Review* 1.

Marshall G, *Constitutional Conventions* (Oxford, Clarendon Press, 1984).

Munro C, *Studies in Constitutional Law*, 2nd edn (London, Butterworths, 1999),
ch 3.

Turpin C, *British Government and the Constitution*, 5th edn (London,
Butterworths, 2002).

Van Caenegem R, *An Introduction to Western Constitutional Law* (Cambridge,
Cambridge University Press, 1995).

Wilson R, 'The Robustness of Conventions in a Time of Modernisation and
Change' [2004] *PL* 407.

3

Constitutional Principles

—————◦•◦————

Introduction – Parliamentary Sovereignty – The Rule of Law –
Separation of Powers – Conclusion: Redefinitions of Power

INTRODUCTION

ANY DISCUSSION OF the British constitution depends upon a
knowledge of the sources of the uncodified constitution, allied to
familiarity with the main principles which underpin the current
workings of the constitution. These concepts can be linked to landmarks in
constitutional history mentioned earlier, but, at the same time, they are of
central importance to current practice, and they are open to interpretation in
different ways. For example, it was noted in the opening chapter that the Bill
of Rights of 1689 makes the Crown subject to the will of Parliament and that
it also recognises that Parliament (Crown, Lords, and Commons) has unlimited legislative authority. In short: 'The principle inherent in the Bill of Rights
is the supremacy of Parliament in law.'[1] It will be necessary when discussing
the sovereignty of Parliament to assess what this apparently absolute doctrine now means, given that the European Communities Act 1972 allots special status to European Union (EU) law, and the Human Rights Act (HRA)
1998 requires judges to interpret statutes according to the European
Convention on Human Rights (ECHR).

Another point worth making at the outset is that these doctrines are
related to each other. Laws may derive from a democratically elected
sovereign Parliament and gain legitimacy from the legislative process, but, at
the same time, when implementing any such laws, there needs to be a way of
protecting citizens from arbitrary treatment. Or, to put it another way, any

---

[1] C Munro, *Studies in Constitutional Law*, 2nd edn (London, Butterworths, 1999) p 128.

discretionary powers given to the police or officials must have legal bounds. Dicey was at pains to stress that: 'In England the idea of legal equality, or of the universal subjection of all classes to one law administered by the ordinary courts, has been pushed to the utmost limit.'[2] The rule of law was regarded by Dicey as *the* idea that has the potential under the common law to qualify the supremacy of Parliament, but we will soon discover that the rule of law is difficult to define and it is not a neutral concept. Rather, it must have a strong moral dimension. Professor Jowell has pointed out that it 'bears an aura of moral compulsion and over the years has been invoked to restrain the abuse of official power.'[3]

The final concept discussed in this chapter is separation of powers. Constitutions necessarily describe different kinds of powers and functions and delineating the distinction between such powers and functions is frequently a central issue in drafting a constitution. The objective is almost invariably to prevent the concentration of too much unchecked power in one set of hands. Obviously, the United Kingdom lacks a custom-designed constitution embodying a strict separation of powers. Nevertheless, the concept and language of separation of powers is still relevant. Two aspects are mentioned as a prelude to the discussion that follows later in this chapter. First, the judicial review procedure which has developed under the rule of law results in the judicial branch overseeing the activities of the executive branch to prevent abuses of power. In this regard, the issue of judicial independence has been addressed at important moments in constitutional history to allow the courts to perform such a role. For example, the Act of Settlement of 1700 (see chapter one) protected judges from summary dismissal, and the recent Constitutional Reform Act 2005 (see chapter seven) sets in place a system for judicial appointments which seeks to minimise executive interference. Second, in the United Kingdom there is no separation between the legislative and executive branches since ministers must be Members of Parliament. Such a fusion between legislative and executive functions at the heart of the system has led commentators to consider whether formal and informal 'checks and balances' which exist as part of constitutional practice are sufficient to achieve adequate constitutional accountability by ensuring the containment of a powerful executive branch.

---

[2] A Dicey, *An Introduction to the Study of the Law of the Constitution*, 10th edn (Basingstoke, Macmillan, 1959) p 193.

[3] J Jowell, 'The Rule of Law Today' in J Jowell and D Oliver, *The Changing Constitution*, 5th edn (Oxford, Oxford University Press, 2004) p 6.

PARLIAMENTARY SOVEREIGNTY

The legal sovereignty of Parliament was regarded by Dicey as the founding principle of the constitution. In his words, it meant that 'Parliament . . . has under the English constitution the right to make or unmake any law whatever; and, further, that no person or body is recognised by the law of England as having a right to override or set aside the legislation of Parliament,' and it is 'the very keystone of the law of the constitution,'[4] in the sense that the sovereignty of Parliament is a fundamental rule upon which no legal limits could be placed. This emphasis on the absolute power of Parliament is because in the absence of a codified constitution the all-powerful position of Parliament in its capacity to act as law-maker assumes special importance. In the first place, parliamentary sovereignty holds that, in theory at least, Parliament comprising the House of Commons, the House of Lords, and the Sovereign has the capacity to pass or repeal any law without any legal limits. As Blackstone remarked, it confirms that 'Parliament can do everything that is not naturally impossible.'[5]

Second, a crucial aspect of the sovereignty of Parliament is that provisions in a more recent statute will prevail over those in an older statute, and it would appear to follow from this proposition that Parliament cannot bind its successors. This limitation is because any pre-existing law can be superseded by an Act passed by a later Parliament. And it is a rule which has special importance in a constitutional context, because, on one view, if this applies strictly, it means that the entrenchment of constitutional principles/bill of rights is not possible. The capacity of Parliament to reconstitute itself and entrench basic principles has been the subject of much theoretical debate in academic circles.[6] For example, a critique by Sir Ivor Jennings of the orthodox theory argues that the rule of recognition as explained by Dicey is a common law concept.[7] It has been accepted by the courts that statute law is superior to the common law. In consequence, it follows that Parliament can enact legislation changing this rule by drafting a statute that requires the courts to accept that some Acts of Parliament are protected from repeal by simple majority vote. In other words, if judges are subordinate to Parliament then Parliament can tell the judges what rules to follow in determining

---

[4] Dicey, above n 2, pp 40 and 70.

[5] W Blackstone, *Commentaries on the Laws of England, book 1*, 19th edn (London, Sweet & Maxwell, 1836) p 161.

[6] See J Goldsworthy, *The Sovereignty of Parliament: History and Philosophy* (Oxford, Oxford University Press, 1999) ch 2, 'Defining Parliamentary Sovereignty'.

[7] I Jennings, *The Law and the Constitution*, 5th edn (London, University of London Press, 1959) p 152ff.

whether or not a statute is unconstitutional. At a practical level, following the far-reaching changes of recent years, it will be important for us to consider below whether the conference of power on other bodies has had a significant impact on sovereignty. To put it simply, has sovereignty really shrunk, as some commentators have contended?[8]

There is an influential view developed by Wade[9] and Allen which maintains that Parliament's sovereignty is itself established through judical acceptance under the common law: 'Legislation obtains its force from the doctrine of Parliamentary sovereignty, which is itself a creature of the common law and whose detailed content and limits are therefore of judicial making. Parliament is sovereign because the judges acknowledge its legal and political supremacy.'[10] The next step in this argument is to maintain that a statute which flies in the face of common law values, eg because the measure is outrageously undemocratic, might be declared invalid by the courts. (As we note when discussing the *Jackson* case below, some House of Lords judges have recently repeated the highly controversial suggestion that primary legislation *in extremis* might by challenged in the courts.[11]) One obvious objection to the common law view takes things back a stage further and questions the legal source of judicial authority to make the common law: 'The only alternative consistent with the argument is to think judges conferred authority on themselves.'[12]

Third, the sovereignty of Parliament means that there is no other body which has authority to challenge the validity of laws made by Parliament in the proper manner. This aspect of the doctrine contradicts a view held earlier that 'an Act of Parliament could be disregarded in so far as it was contrary to the law of God or the law of nature or natural justice ... [when] the supremacy of Parliament was finally demonstrated by the Revolution of 1688 any such idea has become obsolete.'[13] Article 9 of the Bill of Rights of 1689 provided that 'proceedings in Parliament ought not to be impeached or questioned in any court or place out of Parliament.' This assertion has been taken to mean that statutes passed by Parliament cannot be challenged by the courts in respect of their validity. For example, in *British Railways Board v Pickin*[14] the

---

[8] Munro, above n 1, p 149.

[9] W Wade, 'The Basis of Legal Sovereignty' (1955) *Cambridge Law Journal* 172–97.

[10] T Allen, *Law, Liberty and Justice* (Oxford, Oxford University Press, 1993) p 10. The point has been made that it could hardly, without circularity, be a doctrine based on statutory authority

[11] See Lord Steyn, Lord Hope, and Baroness Hale in *Jackson v Attorney-General* [2005] UKHL 55, [2006] 1 AC 262.

[12] J Goldworthy, *The Sovereignty of Parliament: History and Philosophy* (Oxford, Oxford University Press, 1999) p 240.

[13] Munro, above n 1, p 130.

[14] [1974] AC 765.

plaintiff was adversely affected by a private Act of Parliament, namely the British Railways Act 1968. He attempted to argue that it was invalid on the grounds that Parliament had been misled as to relevant facts during the Bill's passage through Parliament and also that certain procedural rules (standing orders) of the House of Commons had been ignored. The challenge was rejected on final appeal to the House of Lords. Lord Morris confirmed: 'When an enactment is passed there is finality unless and until it is amended or repealed by Parliament.' On the issue of the courts not being able to question the way legislation is passed, *Pickin* remains good authority. However, in *Jackson v Attorney-General*[15] (discussed in more detail below) it was unanimously held that the courts had jurisdiction to determine whether the disputed statute (the Hunting Act 2004) was a valid Act of Parliament. Had the court decided that this was not a valid statute, it would not have been able to set aside the legislation (the legislation would remain in force), but the court had the power 'to ascertain the validity of a purported Act of Parliament.'[16]

A further crucially important point about legal sovereignty which will be relevant in relation to many issues under discussion in this book is that this principle determines the relationship between Parliament and the courts. It means that although the courts have an interpretative function in regard to the application of legislation, it is Parliament, and not the courts, which has the final word in determining the law. This is markedly different from most codified constitutions. For example, in the United States, the Supreme Court held in *Marbury v Madison*[17] that it could determine whether laws passed by Congress and the President were in conformity with the constitution, permitting judicial review of constitutional powers. The situation in the United States is that ultimately there is judicial rather than legislative supremacy.

Before we further examine the current limits of sovereignty it is worth pointing out that with each of the measures of constitutional reform introduced post-1997 great care was taken to preserve the sovereignty of the Westminster Parliament (for example, in regard to devolution, see section 28 of the Scotland Act 1998). Also, the HRA 1998 is specifically designed not to undermine the doctrine of sovereignty. The courts cannot invalidate primary legislation which conflicts with rights under the ECHR; they are empowered only to make what is called a 'declaration of incompatibility' (see chapter seven for a more detailed discussion).

---

[15] Above n 11.
[16] A Young, 'Hunting sovereignty: Jackson v Her Majesty's Attorney General' [2006] *PL* 192.
[17] (1803) 1 Cranch 137.

Express Repeal and Implied Repeal

In explaining the limits of parliamentary supremacy, it is important to understand the difference between express and implied repeal. Express repeal is relatively straightforward to set out. This is when a later statute declares that the whole or part of an earlier statute is being superseded by the provisions that are being currently introduced. In *legal* terms there is general agreement among commentators that the power of the Westminster Parliament expressly to repeal legislation remains in place despite developments such as EU membership and the HRA 1998. However, it would be more accurate to say that any limitations to this power are likely to be political rather than legal. For example, if Parliament decided to remove the right to vote at elections the resulting law would be legally valid, but the attempt to take away such a basic right might, at the same time, precipitate demonstrations and civil unrest. Similarly, there would be no legal impediment to Parliament repealing, for example, the Nigeria Independence Act of 1960 with provisions that purported to re-impose colonial status. Such an Act would, however, be unenforceable, and would no doubt also result in strong condemnation from Nigeria itself.

If we turn to implied repeal, the situation in regard to the scope of Parliament's power is less clear when there is a lack of consistency between an earlier and a later statute, without any guidance as to which will apply. There was, at one time, clear judicial authority to support the idea that a later statute will always prevail over an earlier one. A seminal case on this point is *Ellen Street Estates v Minister of Health*.[18] A court had to determine what should happen where a provision (or provisions) in an earlier statute clashed with those in a later statute, and whether an attempt to bind a future Parliament was valid. This conflict concerned the construction of the Acquisition of Land Act 1919 and the Housing Act 1925. Section 7(1) of the Acquisition of Land Act 1919 was worded so that it might appear to bind later statutes, and the compensation scheme in this Act was more generous than that in the Housing Act 1925. A litigant was seeking to take advantage of the earlier scheme. However, the Court of Appeal held that, even if it had been the intention of the earlier Parliament to bind future Parliaments, the provisions of the later statute would take precedence. Maughan LJ stated: 'The legislature cannot, according to our constitution, bind itself as to the form of subsequent legislation and, it is impossible for Parliament to enact that in a

---

[18] [1934] 1 KB 590.

subsequent statute dealing with the same subject-matter there can be no implied repeal.'[19]

We need to examine why this doctrine stated by Maughan LJ has been significantly qualified by recent constitutional developments. Dicey was able to argue in the late nineteenth century that parliamentary legislation was supreme in the hierarchy of law, and that all statutes emanating from Parliament had equal authority, with the most recent prevailing. It is clear that this is no longer the case since certain Acts of Parliament have come to have special significance.

Sovereignty and European Union Law

It will be obvious that EU law emanating from the Treaty of Rome (and subsequent Treaties, and also a European constitution, should one be agreed) and developed by the European Court of Justice has fundamentally qualified the concept of parliamentary sovereignty. The EU comprises an additional institutional layer of government, operating at supra-national level. For example, it consists of the European Commission, which is formed from commissioners appointed by the governments of member states. This body is expected to represent the interests and objectives of the community and is mainly concerned with initiating proposals, decision-making, and the implementation of rules throughout the community. The Council of the EU, which comprises ministers from member states, exercises legislative and executive powers and functions. Further, there is a European Parliament, which consists of members elected in each member state. Although the European Parliament is not primarily a law-making body, it has to be consulted in the legislative process under the co-decision procedure. The important point to stress is that the European legislative process gives rise to particular forms of law which apply in the United Kingdom. Most prominently, there are regulations, which have general application in all member states, and there are directives, which are capable of having direct effect, but may require implementation by individual member states. Membership of the EU means that for as long as the 1972 Act and successive legislation incorporating later Treaties remain in force, the UK Parliament has surrendered its powers to legislate in regard to those areas covered by EU law.

The effect of EU law may be to confer rights directly on individuals which national courts must protect. As Lord Denning recognised in *Bulmer v Bollinger*[20] (see chapter two), this body of law has direct effect within member

---

[19] *Ibid* at 597.
[20] [1974] 2 All ER 1226.

states and it has to be applied by the courts. When considering the limits of sovereignty we need to be clear about the status of EU law within individual member states. The decision in *Van Gend en Loos*[21] paved the way for the establishment of the supremacy of this body of law by developing the doctrine of primacy. It was in this ruling that the ECJ held that 'the Community constitutes a new legal order of international law for the benefit of which the states have limited their sovereign rights, albeit within limited fields, and the subjects of which comprise not only Member States but also their nationals.'

For our purposes, the radical impact of Community law can be demonstrated by reference to the landmark decision in *R v Secretary of State for Transport, ex parte Factortame (No 2)*[22]. The facts concerned the granting of fishing rights. The Merchant Shipping Act 1988 (section 14) established a new register of UK vessels which was only open to those which satisfied certain conditions. One of these conditions specified that only vessels which were 75 per cent UK owned were eligible for registration. It was argued by the applicants, who were directors of Spanish companies, that this requirement infringed the anti-discrimination provisions of the Treaty of Rome on grounds of nationality. The matter was referred by the House of Lords to the European Court of Justice (ECJ) in Luxembourg.

The ECJ ruled that domestic courts were required to ensure effective protection of EU law rights. The Merchant Shipping Act 1988 obviously contravened rights recognised under Community law, and it followed that the UK domestic courts should not be precluded from granting interim relief to protect these rights. In line with its earlier decision in the *Simmenthal Case*[23] the ECJ had focused on the effectiveness principle and on the obligation of national courts under Article 5 (now 10) of the Treaty to ensure observance by setting aside obstructive national rules which precluded or limited the grant of an appropriate remedy. The ECJ did not actually specify the conditions under which a national remedy, such as interim relief, should be granted in a given case. The House of Lords was left to decide this point in accordance with national principles. However, the ECJ made clear that a rule that prohibited absolutely the grant of interim relief would contradict the principle of effectiveness.[24]

In *Factortame (No 2)* the House of Lords recognised that domestic legal systems were required under the Treaties to enforce directly effective rights under EU law. Following this ruling by the ECJ,[25] the House of Lords issued an

[21] [1963] CMLR 105.
[22] [1991] AC 603, [1991] 3 CMLR 769.
[23] Case 106/77, *Amministrazione della Finanze dello Stato v Simmenthal Spa* [1978] ECR 629.
[24] See P Craig, 'Britain in the European Union' in J Jowell and D Oliver, *The Changing Constitution*, 5th edn (Oxford, Oxford University Press, 2004) p 99.
[25] Case-213/89.

injunction preventing the minister from enforcing the nationality requirements under Part II of the Merchant Shipping Act 1988 which were in conflict with EU law. Lord Bridge stated: 'to insist that, in the protection of rights under Community law, national courts must not be inhibited by rules of national law from granting interim relief in appropriate cases is no more than a logical recognition of [the] supremacy [of Community law].'[26] This decision confirmed that, in those areas covered by the Treaties, Parliament no longer reigns supreme; it will be European and not domestic law which predominates.

UK membership of the EU represents a significant qualification to the principle of parliamentary sovereignty. The doctrine of primacy requires that Community law prevails over domestic law in all areas covered by the Treaties. Although the European Communities Act (ECA) 1972 and the legislation incorporating subsequent Treaties passed through Parliament in the same way as other statutes, these measures can be regarded as a special kind of legislation. There is general agreement that the ECA 1972 (and subsequent Acts incorporating the Treaties) could be expressly repealed by Parliament. This step would be necessary if the United Kingdom ever decided to bring to an end its membership of the Union. However, assuming that this does not happen, the effect of sections 2(1), 2(2), and 3 of the ECA 1972 is to make the European Treaties, and the legislation emanating from them, the most authoritative source of UK law. After it was established in the courts that the will of Parliament had been to make domestic law subject to EU law, a major exception to the principle of implied repeal had been established.

The wider constitutional and legal implications of such qualifications to sovereignty have become increasingly apparent. In *Thoburn v Sunderland City Council*[27] it has recently been stated that 'In the present state of its maturity the common law has come to recognise that there exist rights which should properly be classified as constitutional or fundamental . . . And from this a further insight follows. We should recognise a hierarchy of Acts of Parliament: as it were "ordinary" statutes and "constitutional" statutes.' Laws LJ proceeded to reason that the two categories must be distinguished on a principled basis. In essence, he suggests that constitutional statutes are pieces of legislation which condition the legal relationship between citizen and state in some general, overarching manner, or which enlarge or diminish the scope of what might be regarded as fundamental constitutional rights. Such legislation might do both these things. The special status of constitutional statutes follows the special status of constitutional rights. Many examples can be cited from the well-known landmarks of constitutional history. Any such list would include: the Magna Carta 1215; the Bill of Rights 1689; the Act of

26 [1991] AC 603 at 658.
27 [2003] QB 151.

Union 1707; the Reform Acts which distributed and enlarged the franchise; the HRA 1998; the Scotland Act 1998; and the Government of Wales Act 1998. After making this distinction Laws LJ controversially suggests that ordinary statutes may be impliedly repealed while constitutional statutes may not repealed in this way. There would be a requirement of express or specific words in the later statute to achieve the result. In brief, it would appear that this amounts to a recognition of a higher order of laws which is operating at a constitutional level. An area where the constitutional status of statutes will be put to the test is in situations where the government uses its power to dominate Parliament to produce legislation which undermines the rights and liberties of citizens. The Anti-Terrorism, Crime and Security Act 2001, which granted the authorities extended powers to detain terrorist suspects, is one such example, which is discussed further in chapter seven.

The Human Rights Act 1998 and Sovereignty

A limit to the doctrine of implied repeal is equally relevant to any discussion on human rights. In effect, the HRA 1998 incorporates the rights contained in the ECHR. The Act allows the courts to provide effective legal remedies for the breach of Convention rights while formally adhering to the doctrine of parliamentary sovereignty. As we shall see later (chapter seven), the effect of the Act is to put all public authorities (Parliament, government and civil service, local and devolved government, the police, and the courts) under a legal duty to uphold this charter of rights. To inhibit non-compliance, ministers, when introducing parliamentary Bills, are required to issue a statement to the effect that the proposed legislation will be compatible with Convention rights, and this statement is published on the face of the Bill. The Act appears at one level specifically to preserve parliamentary sovereignty—if a court makes a declaration of incompatibility this does not invalidate primary legislation. However, in an important sense here, too, there is no implied repeal, since the courts have been required from 2 October 2000 to interpret all subsequent legislation in a way that is compatible with Convention rights, if it is possible for them to do so. The purposive construction of subsequent statutes (the rule of construction which requires the courts to give priority to Convention rights when interpreting any statute) results in this provision under the HRA 1998 prevailing over a subsequently enacted statute. This exception to sovereignty is confined to situations where the courts are called upon to interpret the will of Parliament in respect to European Convention rights. Unlike the New Zealand model, there is no provision in the HRA 1998 to apply the doctrine of implied repeal when interpreting the Act, which means that Convention rights will be presumed by the courts to be protected, unless it is expressly stated to the contrary in a subsequent statute.

Political Sovereignty

Dicey argued that *political sovereignty* (as opposed to legal sovereignty, which rests with Parliament) lay with the electorate and it is therefore associated with representative and responsible government. Political sovereignty is based on the doctrine of the mandate. It means that manifesto policies are carried out by legislation passed by Parliament (we will be noting that the extension of franchise actually strengthened the power of government, not that of Parliament). However, the formidable powers to legislate without constitutional qualification allow a government with a popular mandate to make wide-ranging changes, including constitutional reforms. Thus, according to the *Whitehall Model* of executive dominance expounded by Birch, the government controls Parliament and not Parliament the government.[28] Indeed, the term 'elective dictatorship' was used by Lord Hailsham to explain how parliamentary sovereignty had turned into the sovereignty of the House of Commons, which in turn is dominated by the party machine in the hands of the Prime Minister and the civil service.[29]

The *Jackson* Case: A New Interpretation of Sovereignty?

Finally, we must consider *Jackson v Attorney-General*.[30] The decision by the House of Lords must be viewed in light of the wider debate over the respective roles of Parliament and the judiciary.[31] It has already been noted above that the issue of parliamentary sovereignty took centre stage when the courts were recently called upon to consider the validity of the Hunting Act 2004, which banned the hunting of foxes with dogs in the face of strong opposition from the hunting lobby. Also, we have seen how the Parliament Acts 1911 and 1949 radically modified the powers of the House of Lords.[32] The

[28] A Birch originally expounded this view in 1967; now see *The British System of Government*, 10th edn (London, Routledge, 1998) at p 163ff.

[29] Lord Hailsham, 'Elective Dictatorship' (Richard Dimbleby Lecture, 1976).

[30] Above n 11.

[31] See J Jowell, 'Parliamentary Sovereignty under the New Constitutional Hypothesis' [2006] *PL* 562.

[32] The Life Peerage Act 1958 and the House of Lords Act 1999 modified the composition of the second chamber.

Hunting Act 2004 was relatively unusual in that it had been repeatedly rejected by the House of Lords, and the House of Commons eventually invoked the override procedures set out under section 2(1) of the Parliament Act 1911 and the Parliament Act 1949 which allowed legislation to be passed into law without the approval of the House of Lords.[33] It is important to remember that by passing the Parliament Acts of 1911 and 1949 Parliament had, in effect, reconstituted itself after the settlement of 1689 by changing the method for approving legislation in circumstances specified in these Acts. The claimants attempted to argue that the 1949 Act, which had reduced the delaying power of the Upper House to one year, was made by a form of subordinate legislature,[34] and that it had not been validly enacted. In consequence, they sought a declaration that it should have no legal effect. It was possible to present such a case because the Parliament Act 1949 also depended upon section 2(1) of the Parliament Act 1911 and, therefore, it too only received the approval of the House of Commons and the Crown (and not the House of Lords). The effect of the 1949 Act was to increase the powers granted to the House of Commons, and the claimant's case further rested on the proposition that this extension by the House of Commons of its own authority ran counter to the principle that delegates are prevented from increasing their own powers.

The House of Lords (Judicial Committee) rejected this argument. Their Lordships held that the Parliament Act 1911 clearly provided that 'any' legislation passed in accordance with section 2 would be an Act of Parliament, and that such legislation should not be classified as a species of subordinate legislation. Taking full account of the historical background leading up to its passage, their Lordships preferred to view the effect of the Parliament Act 1911 as a restriction of the powers of the House of Lords rather than an extension of the powers of the House of Commons. It was also held that there was nothing in the 1911 Act which prevented the use of the procedure laid down in its provisions to amend the Act. In other words, the 1949 Act, which had the effect of doing precisely this, by restricting the delaying power to one year, was deemed to be valid.

According to Dicey, the basic rule of the constitution is that Parliament has unlimited sovereignty. Parliament is omnipotent and therefore any valid law passed by Parliament would be recognised by the courts and it would trump any previous Act, including a law modifying the role of Parliament.[35]

---

[33] The Parliament Acts have been invoked on rare occasions: the Government of Ireland Act 1914, the Welsh Church Act 1914, the War Crimes Act 1991, the European Parliamentary Elections Act 1999, the Sexual Offences (Amendment) Act 2000.

[34] According to a view expressed by W Wade, *Constitutional Fundamentals* (London, Stevens, 1980) at pp 27–8.

[35] See quote from Dicey at n 2, and *ibid*, ch 1.

On the other hand, critics of Dicey, notably Jennings, believed that legal sovereignty merely refers to the fact that the legislature has for the time being powers to make laws of any kind in the manner and form required by law,[36] implying that effective qualifications to sovereignty might be effectively included. This judgment has not resolved the academic dispute, but some *obiter* statements depart from a Diceyan position by envisaging possible limits to parliamentary sovereignty. Lord Steyn and Baroness Hale stated that new laws could be passed to change manner and form in respect to the passage of legislation, by for example introducing a two thirds majority rule applying under particular conditions. Certain limits to sovereignty were linked to the exceptions contained in the Parliament Act 1911. Seven judges (out of nine) opined that any statute not receiving the consent of the House of Lords, which extended the life of a Parliament beyond the five years stipulated in the Parliament Act of 1911, would not be recognised by the courts as valid.[37] On this view, it can be claimed that Parliament has bound its successors in regard to any Bill containing such a provision.

The Law Lords have been criticised at a technical level, perhaps unfairly, for failing clearly to resolve the conflicting legal issues raised in *Jackson*. However, it should be stressed that it is the political context which is of central importance here. In the first place, under the rules of the constitutional game as it is currently played, opening up the possibility of a successful direct challenge to legislation because of its failure to gain the approval of the unelected House of Lords would undermine the democratic process, and therefore probably precipitate a response from Parliament anyway. In the second place, as Lord Bingham recognised in his judgment, the modification to the principle in the Parliament Acts which has allowed the elected House of Commons to prevail over the House of Lords has been accepted by political players from all parties since the passage of the Parliament Acts. Reference to practice appears to confirm the famous truism that 'the constitution is no more and no less that what happens.'[38] Finally, an emerging judicial view is also implied in some of the judgments which questions the unqualified supremacy of Parliament and foresees the possibility of judicial intervention to invalidate legislation where it involves flagrant abuse of power (threats to human rights, removal of judicial review, etc).[39] It should be apparent that a significant step in the direction of challenging sovereignty

---

[36] I. Jennings, *The Law and the Constitution*, 5th edn (London, University of London Press, 1959), at p 152ff.

[37] Young, above n 16, p 193.

[38] J Griffith 'The Political Constitution' [1979] *MLR* 1 at p.19.

[39] M Elliott 'The Sovereignty of Parliament, the hunting ban and the Parliament Acts', (2006) *Cambridge Law Journal*, March, p 3.

through court decisions would fundamentally change the balance of the constitution (see chapter nine for further discussion on this point).

THE RULE OF LAW

The conception of the rule of law expounded by Dicey needs to be understood together with the doctrine of parliamentary sovereignty. This is because the related concept of the rule of law, in effect, imposes qualifications to what appears to be the unlimited nature of parliamentary sovereignty. The rule of law is formally defined in the *Law of the Constitution* as having three rather different connotations.

First, it recognises the predominance of regular law over arbitrary power. There is an assertion that no one should be punished except for a clear breach of the law established in the *ordinary* courts. In a more general sense, the rule of law means that there should be an absence of arbitrary power and suggests that government and other public bodies require lawful authority in order to act. In terms of the practice of government in a contemporary context, this would rule out wide discretion placed in the hands of the executive which is not subject to strict legal qualification. In practice, it is not uncommon for modern legislation to grant wide discretionary powers. For example, section 3 of the Security Services Act 1989 empowers the Home Secretary to issue a warrant authorising the taking of action for the purpose of assisting the service to discharge any of its functions in connection with the obtaining of information. This can be done without the need to actually specify any suspected offence. Indeed, the proliferation of discretionary powers is a characteristic of the modern state.

Second, the Diceyan approach to the rule of law requires strict equality before the law in the sense that no one is above the law and all persons are equally subject to the jurisdiction of the ordinary courts. This is a principle which, in theory, applies from the highest government ministers and top officials to the most humble citizens. It means that the government and the executive should be amenable to control by the courts. This control element was important for Dicey as it forms the basis of his criticism of the *droit administratif* (see discussion of the red light and green light perspective in chapter 7, 'The Constitutional Role of the Courts'). While the French system is characterised as affording special protection to officials, in contrast, the rule of law principle of equality was demonstrated by the famous decision in *Entick v Carrington*[40]. This was the occasion when Lord Camden made an affirmation

[40]   (1765) 19 St Tr 1030.

of the normal process of law. It was held that, in the absence of a statute or common law authority, the action by the representatives of the King were unlawful.

On closer examination, the idea of equality can be seen to be qualified in a number of respects. In the first place, certain groups enjoy legal immunity. To take some obvious examples, MPs are granted special (parliamentary) privileges, the Queen has immunity from legal proceedings, and diplomats also enjoy immunity. In the second place, inequality is present because discretionary powers are given to officials. They are granted powers that members of the public do not have (eg to raise taxes, to make compulsory purchases of land). Also, legislation frequently distinguishes one category of persons from another. To cite some examples, as part of housing law landlords are granted rights not granted to tenants, and likewise under employment law employers enjoy distinct rights to their employees.

Third, in the absence of a codified constitution, Dicey pointed out that the rights of individuals have been defined and enforced by the courts. He argued that the British constitution is a result of the ordinary law of the land, in the sense that remedies protecting the liberties of the citizen have been developed under the common law. The concept of negative liberty works on the basis that, rather than setting out rights in positive form, conduct is lawful unless it contravenes specific law. From a Diceyan standpoint, the common law principles of natural justice (see the discussion of judicial review in chapter seven) that are applied by the courts might be regarded as an expression of the rule of law. However, the view that rights in general can be protected in this way is difficult to sustain in the constitution as it functions today. In practice, there has been increasing reliance on statute law to set out rights and qualify rights. The most important recent example of this trend was the enactment of the HRA 1998. The HRA 1998 has the effect of incorporating the ECHR into domestic law, and so from 2 October 2000 the Convention became a surrogate 'Bill of Rights' for the United Kingdom.

The numerous statutory provisions that have reduced rights or qualified rights equally cast doubt on Dicey's faith in the common law as the primary legal means for protecting the citizen's liberties against the state. For example, the Criminal Justice and Public Order Act 1994 placed further restrictions on the right of citizens to demonstrate and introduced important qualifications to the right to silence in criminal trials. Faced with such assaults on individual liberty, judicial eloquence has not been backed up by effective action. In *Liversidge v Anderson*[41] Lord Atkin stated:

---

[41] [1942] AC 206.

'In this country, amid the clash of arms, the laws are not silent. They may be changed but they speak the same language in war as in peace. It has always been one of the principles of liberty for which on recent authority we are now fighting, that the judges are no respecters of persons and stand between the subject and any attempted encroachment on his liberty by the executive.'

Lord Atkin's worthy defence of freedom is found in a dissenting judgment. The minister's decision to detain persons of external origin without cause was upheld by the House of Lords. It has been suggested that the outcome might have been different in today's climate of increased judicial activism, but the point is that the courts cannot be depended upon to uphold rights, especially when there is a climate of great public fear and concern. More recently, in *R v Secretary of State for the Home Department, ex parte Brind*,[42] the House of Lords was not prepared to intervene to prevent a government broadcasting ban aimed at the IRA and other groups in Northern Ireland who were not prepared to denounce the use of violence to secure their political aims. In general, the rule of law prevents governments from legislating retrospectively because of the injustice that such measures would be likely to cause. There have been exceptions, for example, where the implications of a court ruling threaten to have far-reaching consequences for the government[43].

The Response to Dicey

Does the rule of law enable us to distinguish democratic government from dictatorship and does it provide a sound basis for setting out constitutional rights? According to Dicey's view, a society is governed under the rule of law *only* if it meets his criteria, and it ultimately amounts to a *political* judgement whether a nation achieves such standards. In Dicey's formulation an emphasis is placed on individual rights rather than social rights. The concept has the effect of excluding all but his own definition of what comprises a liberal democracy from having the rule of law. Jennings launched a substantial critique of Dicey's conception of rule of law[44] because he argued that the rule of law must amount to more than: 'law and order is better than anarchy.' It is a doctrine which must be seen to exist within a context of democratic government. The problem is that without a moral dimension the rule of law could as easily be applied to a tyranny as to a liberal democratic society. It could describe any society where law and order exists, including the German Third

---

[42] [1991] 1 AC 696.
[43] For example, the decision in *Burma Oil Co v Lord Advocate* [1965] AC 75 prompted the War Damages Act 1965.
[44] *The Law of the Constitution*, 10th edn (London, University of London Press, 1959).

Reich. Ferdinand Mount has attacked Dicey's doctrine of the rule of law as being inescapably narrow, addressing rudimentary personal rights such as free speech and assembly but overlooking 'the complex and diverse local and national bureaucracies both inside and outside the governmental system which had already become a feature of British life.'[45]

It is not surprising then that the Diceyan view has faced sustained criticism from left-of-centre advocates of progressive social reform, like Jennings, Robson, and Laski, because the rule of law overlooks the problem of addressing collective rather than individual social and economic rights.[46] Formal equality under the law means very little if a large proportion of the population suffers from economic and social marginalisation. From a left-of-centre standpoint constitutional rights need to be defined beyond the liberal agenda of freedom of speech, religion, and assembly to include basic rights to housing, health, and education. Furthermore, in the current environment, the question of access to the law itself is controversial. A reduction in the availability of legal aid means that for many people the prospect of obtaining redress in the courts is not a realistic option. As a result there has been the emergence of alternative forms of redress: eg ombudsmen, law centres, and the citizens' charter (which has been rebranded as Service First). Bradley and Ewing argue that 'it is not possible to formulate a simple and clear cut statement of the rule of law as a broad political doctrine.'[47]

On the positive side, the rule of law has left the United Kingdom with a political and legal culture with an emphasis on due process. Put in simple terms, there is an expectation that government and the apparatus of state power will be exercised by ministers and officials operating within law. In turn, this power is arbitrated by an independent judiciary. It is generally the case that rule of law principles operate as a set of institutional restraints to the exercise of executive power. The rule of law addresses certainty in decision making and it determines how a satisfactory balance between rule and discretion can be reached when putting the law into effect. The problems might arise if the courts become too intrusive, as many would argue that the judges should have a subordinate role to a democratically elected Parliament and any government formed from it.[48] Nevertheless, the judicial oversight function is very important and is closely related to the role of judicial review in its

[45] F Mount, *The British Constitution Now: Recovery or Decline?* (London, Mandarin, 1993) p 58.

[46] J Jowell, 'The Rule of Law Today' in J Jowell and D Oliver (eds), *The Changing Constitution*, 5th edn (Oxford, Oxford University Press, 2004) p 8.

[47] A Bradley and K Ewing, *Constitutional and Administrative Law*, 14th edn (Harlow, Pearson, 2006) p 105.

[48] See, eg, M Loughlin, *Public Law and Political Theory* (Oxford, Oxford University Press, 1992) p 197ff.

supervisory role under the ultra vires principle which will be discussed later (see chapter seven).

Dicey developed these ideas in a different era. The rule of law was presented as an ideal. Now it should be the basis for criticising, not admiring, our legal culture. In response to the profound changes that have taken place since Dicey, public lawyers and political theorists have been required to adapt these principles. We need to consider in the light of current constitutional practice the reality of questions about 'elective dictatorship'. Indeed, it has been suggested that the United Kingdom has witnessed the triumph of a 'Model of Governance' over a 'Model of Law' in which regulation has become the basic technique of administration, and administrative programmes are reduced to numbers and evaluated according to measures of value for money.[49] If this is the case, how can the situation be redressed? In subsequent chapters we will see the need to identify the shortcomings of the mechanisms for control at the level of the administrative state and in regard to the conferment of rights.

In a somewhat different sense, the rule of law might imply that law and order is always better than anarchy. However, the rule of law is not achieved simply by the semblance of order (eg citizens generally conforming to arbitrary and unjust law in Nazi Germany 1933–45 or in Soviet Russia, particularly under Stalin 1922–53) but it depends on restraints that apply to governments and that governments apply to themselves. Prime Minister Blair allowed the Hutton Inquiry to investigate the inner workings of government following disquiet over the justification for UK involvement in the Iraq war. Prime Minister Major set up the Scott Inquiry (discussed in chapter six) following the collapse of the Matrix Churchill trial. Both investigations were sanctioned not withstanding the potentially far-reaching implications for the government. In contrast, the Prime Ministers of Italy (Berlosconi 2001–06) and Thailand (Shinawatra 2001–06) have recently used their authority to suppress investigation of alleged abuse of the political system and ignored objections to a conflict of interest between their personal positions and their political office. The rule of law suggests that law and order and political liberty are mutually dependent, and it demands respect for what we termed *constitutionalism* (see chapter one). In the United Kingdom this will usually be associated with adherence to procedural rules and adherence to important constitutional conventions (discussed in chapter two).

---

[49] See, eg, C Harlow and R Rawlings, *Law and Administration* (London, Butterworths, 1997), ch 5, and C Harlow, *Accountability in the European Union* (Oxford, Oxford, University Press, 2002), p 189.

SEPARATION OF POWERS

The rationale behind the prescriptive doctrine of separation of powers is to avoid the concentration of power in the hands of a single person or body. The diffusion of authority among different centres of decision-making has long been regarded as a safeguard against totalitarianism and a means of preventing the abuse of power. Modern views of the separation of powers are a product of eighteenth-century thought. In 'The Spirit of Laws'[50] Montesquieu stated that all would be lost: 'if the same man or the same ruling body, whether of nobles or of the people, were to exercise these three powers, that of law making, that of executing the public resolutions, and that of judging crimes and civil causes.' Tom Paine had written in 1792:[51] 'From the want of a constitution in England to restrain and regulate the wild impulse of power, many of the laws are irrational and tyrannical, and the administration of them vague and problematical.' The constitution of the United States is heavily influenced by the idea of limiting and checking power. A clear distinction is made between legislative, executive, and judicial functions. For example, the legislative body is an elected Congress comprising the Senate and the House of Representatives. Congress is able to initiate legislation but this requires presidential approval. Equally, the President can initiate legislation, which requires approval from Congress. Another feature is that the government is formed from outside Congress. However, Congress has assumed a crucial role in keeping check on the government by a network of committees. The President has executive power and is responsible for appointing the government. However, the most important nominees for government and also for the Supreme Court require the approval of the Senate. An element of tension between the three branches is deliberately built into the system. The Watergate Affair involved the investigation by Congress of serious malpractice and a subsequent cover-up by the President, and it demonstrated that even the President could be forced to resign for a gross abuse of power.[52]

The UK constitution, by way of contrast, has no clear separation of powers. Rather, there is a limited separation of functions and a considerable number of overlapping powers. This does not mean, of course, that legal process is not employed as means of subjecting governmental power to legal control. But it might be more accurate to characterise the constitution as having a number of checks and balances. These will be considered at greater length in

---

[50] *De L'Esprit des Lois* (Book XI, ch 6, 1748).
[51] T Paine, *Rights of Man* (London, Pelican, 1969) p 217.
[52] See *US v Nixon* (1974) 418 US 683.

chapters five and six. Although the concept of *separation of powers* has not been deliberately incorporated into the UK constitution there is a long history of placing limits on the exercise of power. The Magna Carta, which was signed in 1215, was an agreement between the King and his barons that established formal limits on the exercise of royal power. In the seventeenth century the attempt by James I, and more especially Charles I, to revive the doctrine of absolute kingship based on divine right, led to the civil war between King and Parliament between 1642 and 1649. The conflict arose from the attempt to rule and raise taxes without the assent of Parliament. It resulted in a victory for Parliament and a short spell of republican rule under Oliver Cromwell.

The monarchy was restored shortly after Cromwell's death. Although Charles II was prepared to accept the throne on terms set out by Parliament, his brother James II provoked a renewed crisis by seeking to re-establish absolute rule and to favour Catholics in a nation which was predominantly Protestant. His conduct was in blatant defiance of Parliament, which was dissolved by the King in July 1688. This prompted a crisis. This attempt to rule without Parliament and then the prospect of a Roman Catholic successor to the throne in fact led to a collapse in support for the King, who fled from the country. It was at this point that the terms of a new constitutional settlement were set out by an assembly of peers and MPs that declared itself to be Parliament. William of Orange, who was married to Mary, James II's daughter, was invited by Parliament to take over the throne. Clearly, the supremacy of Parliament over the absolute supremacy of kings was demonstrated by the passage of the Bill of Rights of 1689, which engineered the change to the royal succession. However, apart from securing a Protestant succession, the Bill of Rights was primarily intended to make far-reaching limitations on the absolute power of the monarch. In the first place, it provides that Parliament cannot be suspended by the monarch except with its own consent. Second, it confirmed that the levying of taxes must be approved by Parliament, and third, it states that a standing army cannot be formed in peacetime without the consent of Parliament. The courts accepted this political settlement as law by recognising that statutes passed by Parliament, not, as previously, 'enacted by the monarch in Parliament', had to be enforced and that its enactments take precedence over the common law. In sum, Parliament had imposed conditions on the power of the King.

Fusion of Powers

It has already been pointed out several times that the UK constitution evolved gradually. It was not designed according to a blueprint which took on board the concept of separation of powers. In consequence, there has been no clear demarcation between legislative, executive, and judicial functions in the contemporary state In fact there are institutions which combine more than one of these functions. The sovereign is technically part of all three branches. From the throne in the House of Lords, the Queen opens each session of Parliament. The government governs in her name. Justice is dispensed through the royal courts. In practise however, there is a strong element of constitutional limitation on the exercise of royal power. This is to the extent that there is no active contribution to the routine workings of government. In addition to legislation such as the Act of Settlement of 1700, this has often been achieved by the recognition of important conventions in relation to the exercise of prerogative power. Also, it was confirmed in Lord Coke's landmark judgment in *Prohibitions del Roy*[53] that the King, in person, was not able to judge disputes.

The most obvious overlapping of powers is in Parliament. Rather than having a clear separation between legislature and executive as exemplified in the US constitution, the UK government is formed from within Parliament. It survives only if it is able to maintain its majority in the House of Commons. Indeed, this is what Walter Bagehot writing in the nineteenth century was keen to emphasise when he stated that 'the efficient secret of the English Constitution may be described as the close union, the nearly complete fusion of executive and legislative powers.'[54] After the majority party in the House of Commons is recognised as the government, its continuation in office depends upon being able to maintain a majority whenever there is a vote on government legislation or on major issues of confidence. The whips (party managers) have emerged to deliver this majority. As a result, there is no real impediment to the legislative competence of Parliament. This is because the government is able to count on its majority in the House of Commons to secure the passage of its legislative programme. What we described earlier as the supremacy of Parliament is, in fact, the supremacy of the executive. This feature of the constitution has been termed 'elective dictatorship'. A central concern is to prevent the abuse of power by establishing legal means of controlling power, and a key question for any student of the constitution is whether ministers as Members of Parliament are made sufficiently accountable to Parliament for their actions (see chapter six).

There has been an overlap between legislative and judicial powers in several different ways Parliament is primarily a legislative and scrutinising body, but it has contained the Judicial Committee of House of Lords, which is the highest appellate court. (The government has now passed the Constitutional

---

[53] (1607) 12 Co Rep 63.
[54] W Bagehot, *The English Constitution* (London, Fontana, 1963) p 65.

Reform Act 2005, which will introduce a Supreme Court to replace the House of Lords. The new court will have a similar jurisdiction to the House of Lords, but the methods of judicial appointment and of court administration will be modified.) The Lords of Appeal in Ordinary (the Law Lords) have been the judges that make up the highest domestic appellate court while having the right to sit as peers in the House of Lords,[55] but by convention primarily participate in debates concerning criminal justice and other technical legal matters. They act more like consultants than politicians. On the other hand, the Lord Chancellor was, until recently, head of the judiciary and President of the Chancery Division of the High Court. This position allowed the incumbent to sit personally as a judge and to determine which other Law Lords sat on appeals, as well as acting as Speaker of the House of Lords. Added to this, the House of Commons and the House of Lords can sit as courts having the power to discipline their own members. The Attorney-General is the law officer of the Crown. In this capacity he or she acts as the government's principal legal advisor, but the Attorney-General is also a minister who is able to initiate criminal and civil proceedings in the courts when this is seen as in the public interest. There is an expectation that ministerial duties will be performed independently of the government but there may be a clear conflict of interest. (For example, the Scott Inquiry was critical of the advice given by the Attorney-General over the use of public interest immunity certificates to prevent evidence going before the courts.)

The Lord Chancellor

The office of Lord Chancellor demonstrated the overlapping of powers and functions most graphically. This is because the incumbent held executive office as ministerial head of a government department and, by virtue of this position, was given a seat at the Cabinet table. Added to this, the Lord Chancellor not only had the right to participate in the legislative proceedings of the House of Lords but also presided over the House as its Speaker. In common with other ministers, the Lord Chancellor introduced legislation and participated in debates. (The other Law Lords by contrast do not take part in political activity, and Supreme Court judges will not be members of the House of Lords.) Lastly, the Lord Chancellor was head of the judiciary. In this capacity he decided which judges presided over appeals taken to the Judicial Committee of the House of Lords and to the Privy Council. The Lord Chancellor was himself able to sit as a judge on the panel, although this became

---

[55] The Law Lords, with some other senior judges, are also eligible to sit on the Appellate Committee of the Privy Council to hear appeals from mainly Commonwealth jurisdictions.

an increasingly rare occurrence as the other responsibilities became more onerous. This position produced a direct conflict of interest. First, the Lord Chancellor's Department (now renamed the Department for Constitutional Affairs) had a central role in the appointment of senior judges. Second, the appeals to the House of Lords sometimes involve political matters of controversy concerning the government, and increasing doubts were raised over the propriety of the Lord Chancellor sitting as a judge in such a court.

The Judicial Role

In the light of the overlapping of powers which is characteristic of the constitution, to what extent does the United Kingdom have an independent and impartial judiciary? With the notable exception of the Lord Chancellor, who was always a prominent supporter of the government, senior judges are not appointed on grounds of their political affiliations and they have been granted protection against summary dismissal since the Act of Settlement of 1700. The rule of law doctrine, as explained above, requires the government/executive to operate according to the law. An independent judicial branch is required to ensure that this occurs. In recent times the judicial review procedure has become the principle method of challenging the legality of the actions of public bodies, whether they are operating under statutory powers or under prerogative powers. Procedural reforms and the development of the grounds of judicial review have contributed to a heightened profile for the courts and a period of greater judicial activism. There has been an enormous increase in the number of cases coming before the courts. During the late 1980s civil servants were alerted by a general circular called 'The Judge over your Shoulder' to be aware of judicial review. In the estimation of some commentators, the courts were assuming the guise of a surrogate opposition at a time when the official party political opposition in Parliament was particularly weak. However, there is a danger that the authority of Parliament could be undermined by excessive judicial activism.

Indeed, ministers have claimed that instances of judicial activism undermine the authority of Parliament and their ability to implement policy. On the other hand, securing executive accountability to the law must equally be regarded as central to judicial review. The friction between the executive and the courts is often most obvious in areas of government competence falling under the Home Office. The examples which follow will serve to illustrate this in different ways. In *M v Home Office*[56] an asylum seeker from Zaire was

[56] [1994] 1 AC 377.

seeking judicial review of a decision by the Immigration Service (an executive agency which is part of the Home Office) to deport him, but the hearing coincided with the date set for his repatriation. The prospect of deportation before the judicial proceedings were complete led M's lawyers to make an emergency application to the court to put matters on hold. The application was successful and an undertaking to the judge was given from the Home Office not to act while the case was pending. This instruction was not adequately communicated by the Home Office to the Immigration Service. In the meantime, M was flown out of the country. Contempt proceedings were brought by M's lawyers against the Home Secretary for ignoring a court order. This boiled down to a question of whether the courts were in a position to issue coercive orders against ministers. The sovereign's courts were taking punitive action against the Crown in the guise of her ministers.

The House of Lords held that the judge in the original case had jurisdiction to issue injunctions, including interim injunctions, against ministers and other officers of the Crown. At the same time, an injunction would be binding against the Home Secretary personally, notwithstanding the fact that he was operating in an official capacity and according to advice given to him. Reaching this conclusion involved drawing a distinction between the immunity from judicial process enjoyed by the Queen in person, and making a finding against a minister in his or her official capacity (or his or her department) or against a minister personally. It was reasoned that a finding of contempt against a government department would, in circumstances such as those applying in the instant case, 'vindicate the requirements of justice' and ensure that orders of the court are obeyed. This is a highly significant outcome, since it illustrates that the courts will intervene if a government department seeks to interfere with the administration of justice.

In *Duport Steel v Sirs*[57] Lord Scarman and Lord Diplock recognised the danger of judges being drawn into politics and realised that too much discretion in disregarding a statute could lead to uncertain and arbitrary law. A steel company took an action against a trade union contesting the union's immunity from tortious liability under the Trade Union and Labour Relations Act 1974. In particular, the court had to decide whether or not secondary picketing by workers during the course of an industrial dispute was lawful. This was at a time when the Conservatives had recently won an election on a promise to curb trade union power but this proposal (including a provision to outlaw secondary picketing) was a matter of great public controversy between the major political parties. The Court of Appeal, presided over by Lord Denning MR, found in favour of the steel company. The House of Lords overturned the

---

[57] [1980] 1 WLR 142, HL.

decision and by doing so upheld the statutory rights of trade unions. Their Lordships by overruling the Court of Appeal were not supporting the political position of the trade unions in their industrial action. They were merely fulfilling their constitutional role in interpreting the statute according to the will of Parliament. Lord Scarman stated that 'the constitution's separation of powers, or more accurately functions, must be observed if judicial independence is not to be put at risk.' A few months later the Employment Act 1980 came into force and outlawed the practice of secondary picketing that had been deemed by the House of Lords to be lawful under the previous statute.[58]

In a somewhat different context there is a constitutional convention (albeit a weak one) holding that ministers should not directly criticise judicial decisions. Such attacks have the potential to undermine the role of the courts in policing the executive under the rule of law. In what we have described as a period of judicial activism, the courts have been much more prepared to intervene in judicial review cases setting limits on executive power. Government ministers (both Conservative and Labour) have responded by being much more forthright in their criticism of the courts, especially where they appear to stymie the main thrust of legislation. A good example of such a clash was the ministerial reaction to a successful challenge to the Nationality, Immigration and Asylum Act 2002. The Act was introduced to clamp down on what the government portrayed as a flood of bogus claims for asylum. In *R (on the application of Q) v Secretary of State for the Home Department*[59] there was a challenge by way of judicial review to the way the measures were being applied by the Immigration Service. It was held that the requirement under section 55 of the Act that claims must be made as soon as reasonably practicable was being interpreted in a way that was unlawful. Its effect was to deny natural justice, and the consequent withdrawal of all support to those who did not make prompt claims would leave asylum seekers destitute. In turn, this interfered with the rights of asylum seekers under the European Convention on Human Rights by being in breach of Articles 3 and 8. (Since 2 October 2000 the HRA 1998 requires the courts to interpret legislation in a manner which is consistent with Convention rights.)

The decision in the Administrative Court was strongly attacked by the Home Secretary, and the press (including *The Times* and the *Telegraph*) took their cue from the minister with accusations that the judge was deliberately overturning the will of Parliament and thereby undermining government policy. However, the conclusions reached in the Administrative Court were largely supported by the Court of Appeal, and no further appeal to the House

---

[58] See A Tomkins, 'Of Constitutional Spectres: Review of Eric Barendt: An Introduction to Constitutional Law' [1999] *PL* 531.
[59] [2003] EWHC 195 Admin; (2003) *The Times*, February 20.

of Lords was attempted by the Home Office. In other words, far from deliberately thwarting the will of Parliament, the judicial branch was merely performing its role by ensuring that executive power was being exercised according to the rule of law.[60] Judges do not personally respond to criticism by ministers and the press. It has been suggested that a convention to prevent outspoken attacks of this kind should be followed more strictly to prevent attempts by politicians to apply pressure on the courts.

The examples that have just been discussed suggest that to a considerable degree the judicial branch is prepared to follow a line which is independent of government. However, in certain policy areas the courts have been extremely reluctant to overturn decisions made by government. This has been especially true in cases involving national security, for example, *R v Secretary of State for the Home Department, ex parte Cheblak*,[61] where the court held that a statement from the authorities that their action in serving a deportation notice was for national security reasons was sufficient under the enabling Act.

To take another issue, in recent years there has been controversy over the balance struck between the roles of the executive and the judiciary in the determination of sentencing in criminal cases, as there have been attempts to introduce legislation which reduces or removes entirely judicial discretion. For example, the Crime (Sentences) Act 1997 imposes mandatory life sentences for a second serious offence and minimum seven-year sentences. In such areas this controversy has also concerned the extent to which the determination of sentences should be a judicial process, allowing judges to exercise a discretion based on broad parameters set out by Parliament, and the degree to which the Home Secretary should retain power to determine sentencing tariffs for long-term prisoners of all ages.

Overlapping powers

It has been explained that concepts of the separation of powers have often attempted to distinguish legislative, executive, and judicial functions and propose that one organ of government should not exercise the functions of another. However, if we examine the role of the executive in the United Kingdom, we find there is an overlapping of both executive and legislative powers and executive and judicial powers. The executive functions of ministers and their departments are frequently combined with powers to formulate delegated legislation. It is common for legislation to provide scope for sub-rules and regulations to be drawn up by officials. The term 'Henry VIII

---

[60] See A Bradley, 'Judicial Independence under Attack' [2003] *PL* 397.
[61] [1991] 1 WLR 890.

clause' is applied when there is wide discretion in the making of delegated legislation.[62]

Equally, the growth of the administrative state has resulted in officialdom having judicial functions in many policy areas ranging from the allocation of means-tested benefits to the determination of immigration appeals. Of course, procedural safeguards have been incorporated as part of the adjudication process operated by tribunals and other bodies. The constitutional reforms introduced by the Labour administration between 1997 and 2001 have had a far-reaching impact on the shape of the constitution and it is not surprising that there have been shockwaves which have resonated since their introduction. For example, the HRA 1998 and the devolution legislation have extended the constitutional dimension to the role of the judiciary. Recently, the government has reacted with further reform introducing the Constitutional Reform Act 2005 which, as we shall see in chapter seven, addresses the conflicts which arise from the overlapping powers and functions that were integral to the Lord Chancellor's office.

CONCLUSION: REDEFINITIONS OF POWER

It is worth asking how useful this eighteenth-century conception of separation of powers is, given the present shape of the state and taking account of the way power is currently exercised. The position has changed radically over recent years. For example, since 1979, the United Kingdom has experienced: privatisation of public utilities; complex layers of state regulation; deregulation; new public management; the creation of 'next steps' agencies; contracting in the public sector; compulsory competitive tendering in local government; public–private partnerships; the citizen's charter; and health service reorganisation (to name but a few of the most prevalent initiatives). State institutions, particularly central and local government, are increasingly tied into relationships with business, with the voluntary sector, and with consumer groups in many different ways. These modified approaches clearly have important implications in the shaping and management of our public institutions. Frequently services are publicly funded but the service is delivered under contract by the private sector (such services ranging from prisoner escort, street cleaning, and refuse disposal to school meals). It will be apparent that the term 'governance' has been used to describe the divergent patterns and tangled interweaving of public and private bodies.[63] Since

---

[62] See, eg, the Deregulation and Contracting Out Act 1994.

[63] See, eg, R Rhodes, *Understanding Governance: Policy Networks, Governance, Reflexivity and Accountability* (Buckingham, Open University Press, 1997).

Labour was elected to office in 1997, the HRA 1998 and the Freedom of Information Act 2000 have imposed additional obligations on public authorities in their dealings with the citizen. Another dimension has been the increasing prevalence of EU law as part of the domestic scene. What this really means is that the United Kingdom now has a 'multi-layered' constitution[64] comprising policy networks at sub-national (ie devolved), national, and supra-national level. On the one hand, the public have been conferred with a new sets of rights and, on the other, there are increasingly dense networks through which power is exercised. Channels of accountability and perception between the political masters and end users are often blurred (take, for instance, the hostile public reaction to many aspects of EU policy). Such complexity may even call into question the predominant role of the state, and, in particular, the capacity of any government to intervene effectively by legislative means to address contemporary problems. For example, levels of crime have remained high despite many legislative initiatives in this field by successive administrations. As the UK constitution lacks any sense of overall design, the extent to which the separation of powers should have a central future role can be questioned. The most important consideration may be avoiding potential conflicts of interest between constitutional players rather than reshaping the institutions according to a particular model. In sum, these developments suggest that it is no longer realistic to analyse our constitution in terms of a unitary, self-correcting constitution.

The idea which has been central to this discussion is that under a constitutional framework, whether formal or informal, power must have limits, and in order to achieve such limits there needs to be a division of power. In the UK constitution the separation of powers is an untidy concept. The idea certainly does not apply in the strict sense, as it does to a much more obvious extent in the United States. It is more accurate to conclude by emphasising that there are conventions that are observed which safeguard some *division* of power and functions between the various branches of government. For instance, parliamentary select committees dominated by the party that forms the government frequently criticise the government and thereby provide some check on the executive. Judges generally display caution in making judgments that are politically sensitive. Ministers usually show some reserve in their criticisms of judicial decisions. The Lord Chancellor as the minister overseeing the process has recommended judges for many years on grounds of professional competence rather than political affiliation. The idea of checks and balances rather than separation of powers conveys the import-

---

[64] See N Bamforth and P Leyland, 'Introduction' in N Bamforth and P Leyland (eds), *Public Law in a Mulit-Layered Constitution* (Oxford, Hart Publishing, 2003).

ance of creating a tension between institutions with different constitutional functions. But reaching a satisfactory balance between these considerations remains problematic and the far-reaching changes that have been introduced in recent years threaten to present further challenges (see chapter seven, 'The Constitutional Role of the Courts').

FURTHER READING

Allan T, *Law, Liberty, and Justice: The Legal Foundations of the British Constitution* (Oxford, Oxford University Press, 1993).

Bogdanor V (ed), *The British Constitution in the Twentieth Century* (Oxford, Oxford University Press, 2003).

Bradley A, 'The Sovereignty of Parliament' in J Jowell and D Oliver (eds), *The Changing Constitution*, 4th edn (Oxford, Oxford University Press, 2000).

Bradley A and Ewing K, *Constitutional and Administrative Law*, 13th edn (Harlow, Longmans, 2003).

Craig P, 'Dicey: Unitary, Self-Correcting Democracy and the Rule of Law' (1991) 106 *Law Quarterly Review* 105.

Dicey A, *Introduction to the Study of the Law of the Constitution*, 10th edn (London, Macmillan, 1959).

Ewing K, 'The Unbalanced Constitution' in T Campbell, K Ewing and A Tomkins, *Sceptical Essays on Human Rights* (Oxford, Oxford University Press, 2001).

Fredman S, 'Human Rights Transformed: Positive Duties and Positive Rights' [2006] *PL* 498–521.

Goldsworthy J, *The Sovereignty of Parliament: History and Philosophy* (Oxford, Oxford University Press, 1999).

Goldsworthy J, 'Legislative Sovereignty and the Rule of Law' in T Campbell, K Ewing, and A Tomkins, *Sceptical Essays on Human Rights* (Oxford, Oxford University Press, 2001).

Harden I and Lewis N, *The Noble Lie: The British Constitution and the Rule of Law* (London, Hutchinson, 1986).

Jowell J, 'The Rule of Law Today' in J Jowell and D Oliver (eds), *The Changing Constitution*, 4th edn (Oxford, Oxford University Press, 2000).

Jowell J, 'Parliamentary Sovereignty under the New Constitutional Hypothesis' [2006] *PL* 562–80.

MacCormick N, *Questioning Sovereignty: Law, State and Practical Reason* (Oxford, Oxford University Press, 1999).

Munro C, *Studies in Constitutional Law*, 2nd edn (London, Butterworths, 1999).

Wade W, *Constitutional Fundamentals* (London, Stevens, 1980).

4

The Crown and the Constitution

INTRODUCTION

THE UNITED KINGDOM has a hereditary monarch as head of state. The Queen performs an important role as the personification of the nation. She appears on the national and international stage and in this capacity she is often associated with occasions of pomp and ceremony that evoke memories of imperial glory. It is particularly this feature that distinguishes the British monarchy from its counterparts in Holland, Belgium, and Scandinavia. However, as we shall see in the discussion that follows, although only limited power is exercised by the Queen on her own initiative, many constitutional functions still require her direct involvement. The path to constitutional monarchy has involved both the deliberate curtailment of royal power and its gradual erosion. The terminology is somewhat misleading. The government is still described as Her Majesty's government, central government acts in the name of the Crown, and the courts are presided over by Her Majesty's judges, but in modern times the monarch, although head of state, has a greatly subordinate constitutional role to Parliament, the government, and the courts. This is now accepted by reigning monarchs without question. In this chapter we will first discuss the institution of the monarchy, the royal prerogative, and the nature of the Crown as part of the current constitutional framework.

During the Middle Ages and Tudor times kings and queens ruled through the exercise of the royal prerogative, but the idea that the powers of the monarch should be limited by law can be traced back at least as far as the Magna Carta of 1215. It was later established that general laws could not be made by way of proclamation—only Parliament could enact laws. It was also recognised that the King himself could not act as a judge, but must act through the judges in the courts. Since the *Case of Proclamations*[1] it has been recognised that the scope of the prerogative can be determined by the courts. As we noted in chapter one, the events of the seventeenth century, and in particular the Civil War 1642–49 and the 'Glorious Revolution' of 1688, are significant in English constitutional history because they signalled the decisive end of any pretensions to absolute monarchy, with most powers over legislation and delegated legislation eventually passing to Parliament. This coincided with the emergence of the doctrine of the supremacy of Parliament described by Dicey. This trend was reinforced in the eighteenth century with the Hanoverian succession to the throne (of George I in 1714), when ministers became directly responsible for the day-to-day running of government. The scope of government activity was then much more limited, with only a few Whitehall departments (such as the Treasury, the Foreign Office, and the Board of Trade), but as the foundations of the modern administrative state were laid in the late nineteenth and twentieth century, with the role of government being greatly expanded, so the monarch became increasingly peripheral to the central activities of the executive. In this sense, the influential nineteenth-century writer on the constitution Bagehot was correct when he commented in reference to Queen Victoria that '*she reigns but does not rule*'.[2]

The abdication crisis which erupted in 1936, once again, confirmed the pre-eminence of Parliament and prime ministerial government over the monarch.[3] Edward VIII shortly after succeeding to the throne decided he would like to marry his mistress, the American divorcee, Mrs Simpson. The Prime Minister, Stanley Baldwin, with the support of his Cabinet and the leader of the opposition, made it clear that, given the King's position as head of the Church of England and the marriage vows that would be entailed, this match was constitutionally unacceptable. Edward therefore had to choose between the hand of Mrs Simpson and continuing on the throne. Confronted with what amounted to an ultimatum from the Prime Minister and his government, Edward gave up the throne in favour of his brother, who became King George VI.

It will already be apparent from these examples that the evolution from a ruling monarchy to a constitutional monarchy took many hundreds of years.

---

[1] (1611) 12 Co Rep 74.
[2] C Munro, *Studies in Constitutional Law*, 2nd edn (London, Butterworths, 1997) at p 256.
[3] A Taylor, *English History 1914–45* (London, Pelican, 1975) p 490ff.

Moreover, the link with the past has special significance because, for a nation which has not experienced a recent political revolution, the monarchy represents tradition and continuity. The Queen, as a symbol of national identity, can be said to personify the state. She performs an important constitutional role but is, in fact, left with very little real political power. It is a convention of the highest constitutional importance that the monarch always follows the advice of her ministers. Many of the most far-reaching powers which formerly were exercised by the monarch, mainly prerogative powers, are now in the hands of the Prime Minister and the government. Although these powers are exercised by the government, they are still performed in the name of the monarch.

WHAT IS THE ROYAL PREROGATIVE?

The majority of issues involving the use of the prerogative are concerned with governing the country. The prerogative includes crucial areas such as the conduct of foreign affairs, defence, and national security, and when outlining the Queen's constitutional role it will be apparent that she has a major presence in many areas but exercises only limited power because the prerogative is now in the hands of the Prime Minister, ministers, or officials. The royal prerogative comprises residual powers and functions which were originally associated with the monarch. In considering the royal prerogative and its exercise it is useful to draw out a contrast between what appears to be the site of legal power as opposed to the constitutional reality of where power actually resides. In practical terms, the powers encompassed by the term 'prerogative' are of great importance for the effective working of government. They range from the conduct of foreign affairs, the making and ratification of treaties, the preservation of national security, the maintenance of the defence of the realm, and the exercise of the enormous powers of patronage available to the Prime Minister. Certain prerogatives are now regulated by constitutional conventions to enable government to function. The way these powers are exercised has recently been considered by parliamentary committees, and there have been recommendations to introduce statutory regulation in order to achieve greater clarity in respect to the scope and application of the prerogative and to achieve increased parliamentary approval and scrutiny.

The prerogative involves distinguishing between of two elements: (a) the *personal* prerogatives of the monarch; and (b) the *political* prerogatives, that is, those used by the government/executive/Crown in foreign affairs and domestic policy. Generally speaking, government operates within the parameters conferred by Parliament under statutory provisions. There are certain areas where the prerogative provides the legitimation for the use of a common law power and confers certain immunities on those using it. Considerable controversy has arisen over the definition and extent of the prerogative, particularly between the accounts of Sir William Blackstone in the eighteenth century, who stresses the 'special pre-eminence' of the King's powers, and Dicey in the nineteenth century, who was of the view that:

> The prerogative appears to be both historically and as a matter of actual fact nothing else than the residue of discretionary or arbitrary authority, which is at any given time legally left in the hands of the Crown . . . Every Act which the executive government can lawfully do without the authority of the Act of Parliament is done in virtue of this prerogative[4].

This is a broad definition embracing all the non-statutory powers of the Crown of a residual (ie leftover) nature. Judicial decisions have tended to reflect the Diceyan position.

The centrality of the concept of parliamentary sovereignty to the constitution means that, as a general rule, statutory powers prevail over the prerogative. Parliament has the capacity to curtail prerogative powers. In situations where there is a conflict between statute and the prerogative, the statute will always prevail. The leading case illustrating this principle is *Attorney-General v De Keyser's Royal Hotel Ltd*[5]. In 1916 during the course of World War I the government, acting in the name of the Crown, took control of a hotel to accommodate the headquarters of the Royal Flying Corps under the Defence of the Realm Regulations. It then denied the legal owners any right to compensation. Compensation appeared to be available to them under statute, namely, the Defence Act 1842. It was argued by the Crown that since it had been acting under prerogative power in wartime any compensation for the requisition of this hotel was a matter within its discretion. However, the court held that this was now governed by statute. The statutory power in effect superseded the prerogative. Lord Atkinson stated that 'after the statute has been passed, and while it is in force, the thing it empowers the Crown to do can thenceforth only be done by and under the statute, and subject to all the limitations, restrictions and conditions by it imposed, howsoever unrestricted the Royal prerogative may theretofore have been.' But the *De Keyser* principle also suggests that where a statutory provision covers the same grounds as the prerogative, the latter falls into abeyance and might be re-activated should the statute be repealed.

---

[4] A Dicey, *Introduction to the Study of the Law of the Constitution*, 10th edn (London, Macmillan, 1959) p 424.
[5] [1920] AC 508.

There may be areas where statutory powers and prerogative powers can exist in parallel without inconsistency.[6] However, the House of Lords has more recently held that it was unlawful to act using the prerogative power where Parliament has given a minister a specific statutory power. In *R v Secretary of State for the Home Department, ex parte Fire Brigades Union*[7] there was a successful challenge by the Fire Brigades Union when the minister sought to introduce a method for compensating victims under his prerogative powers. In doing so, in effect, he was by passing the scheme which had not yet been activated but had already been approved by Parliament under section 171 of the Criminal Justice Act 1988.

In a somewhat different context, the decision of the House of Lords in the *GCHQ* case[8] is of great importance. The challenge concerned a decision (under her prerogative powers) by the Prime Minister, as Minister for the Civil Service, to ban the union membership of civil servants at the government communication headquarters in Cheltenham without any prior consultation. In a famous judgment in which Lord Diplock explained the principles of judicial review (see chapter seven), it was established beyond any doubt that, in principle, the exercise of prerogative powers by ministers could be subject to judicial review. However, it was also recognised by Lord Scarman that the capacity of the courts to intervene might be qualified by other factors:

> '[T]he law relating to judicial review has now reached the stage where it can be said with confidence that, if the subject matter in respect of which prerogative power is justiciable, that is to say if it is a matter on which the court can adjudicate, the exercise of the power is subject to review in accordance with the principles developed in respect of the review of the exercise of statutory power.[9]

In other words, while in general prerogative powers can be challenged, certain types of exercise of the prerogative are non-justiciable. For example, these areas would include decisions relating to: the making of treaties, the defence of the realm, the prerogative of mercy, the grant of honours, the dissolution of Parliament and the appointment of ministers. The application for judicial review was ultimately unsuccessful in the *GCHQ* case because the Prime Minister was able to bring forward sufficient evidence to show that the failure to consult in the proper way had been made because of legitimate concerns over the risk to national security.

---

[6] *R v Secretary of State for the Home Department, ex parte Northumbria Police Authority* [1989] QB 96.
[7] [1995] 2 All ER 244.
[8] *Council of Civil Service Unions v Minister for the Civil Service* [1985] AC 374.
[9] *Ibid* at 407.

THE CONSTITUTIONAL ROLE OF THE MONARCH

The pivotal convention which applies to the monarch is that he or she is bound to act on the advice of his or her ministers. The fact that the UK constitution can be described as a constitutional monarchy rests upon this and other conventions. In other words, many things are done in the name of the monarch, and are performed under prerogative powers, but the monarch's action is frequently governed by constitutional practice or by other *political* actors. However, there are also important technical questions over whether the residue of important, but sometimes ill-defined prerogative powers left in the hands of a reigning monarch can be justified in a contemporary constitutional context. For example, given the difficulties that have arisen with the formation of a government (discussed below) it has been suggested that legislation should be passed to determine who would become Prime Minister in the event of a future hung Parliament.[10]

(1) *The formation of a government*—The basic rule is that following a general election the monarch will always call upon the leader of the majority party in the House of Commons to form a government. A majority in the House of Commons is, of course, necessary to ensure that legislation can be passed. Given that the ability of voters to elect a government is the principle at the heart of parliamentary democracy, it is extremely important that the monarch accepts the verdict of the electorate in performing this role. The electoral system usually provides a clear winner, but this is not always the case. For example, after the February 1974 election neither the Conservatives nor Labour secured an overall majority. Labour emerged from the election with 301 seats, five more than the Conservatives, but the Conservatives polled a higher aggregate total of votes. To form a government either the Labour Party or the Conservative Party required the support of a combination of Liberals, Scottish Nationalists, Welsh Nationalists, and Northern Ireland MPs. The constitutional role of the monarch in this situation is to ensure that a viable government is formed. This means she should ask the leader of the party most likely to be able to sustain a government to become Prime Minister. After the February 1974 election, Mr Heath, the incumbent Prime Minister, did not resign but was unable to reach agreement with the Liberals. In consequence, the Queen had no real alternative to sending for Harold Wilson, whose Labour Party had the largest number of seats. Mr Wilson managed to govern for six months with a minority government before calling another election. The survival of any government will depend upon its

---

[10] See, eg, D Bean, *The Future of the Monarchy* (London, The Fabian Society, 2003).

ability to maintain a majority among MPs in the House of Commons. All the main political parties (Conservative, Labour, and Liberal Democrat) now elect their leader by process involving the balloting MPs and party members, but until 1965 the Conservative Party did not have a formal method for electing its leader. As a result, when a serving Conservative Prime Minister had to leave office prematurely, the monarch performed the task of deciding who should be the successor. This occurred with the resignations of Prime Minister Eden in 1956 and Prime Minister Macmillan in 1963.

(2) *The calling of elections*—The Prime Minister can decide to call an election at any time within the five-year period specified by the Parliament Act of 1911. However, once the decision is taken, the monarch must, according to convention, dissolve Parliament on the advice of the Prime Minister. It is clear that this power to dissolve Parliament could not be exercised independently of the intervention of the Prime Minister. There have been exceptional situations. One such arose in February 1974 when no party emerged from the election with a majority in the House of Commons. It has been suggested that, had Harold Wilson been unable to win a vote in the House of Commons after being invited to form a government, the Queen might have been in a position to refuse a request for a dissolution of Parliament, at least until other party leaders had been given the opportunity to attempt to form a government that was acceptable to Parliament.

(3) *Ministerial appointments*—In regard to ministerial appointments at all levels the monarch follows the advice of the Prime Minister in approving the selections that he or she makes. There is no requirement that the monarch is consulted by the Prime Minister over the suitability of these choices, and there is no longer power to refuse any of these choices. In the eighteenth and nineteenth centuries there were some instances when the monarch was reluctant to take advice. There is nothing that formally prevents the monarch expressing his or her opinion about the suitability of the choices proposed by the Prime Minister. George VI was reported to have expressed clear reservations when Winston Churchill selected Lord Beaverbrook as Minister for Aircraft Production and member of the War Cabinet in 1940, but nevertheless the Prime Minister's choice prevailed.[11]

(4) *Appointments and honours*—There are many other official appointments which are conferred by the monarch, but these choices are nearly always made on the advice of the Prime Minister. These include the creation of peers, the appointment of archbishops and bishops, the appointment of all senior judges, and the conferment of most honours, such as knighthoods. However, the Queen is personally able to select members of the royal household,

---

[11] R Brazier, *Constitutional and Administrative Law*, 7th edn (London, Penguin, 1994) p 125.

including her Private Secretary. In addition, there are a few honours that remain in the personal gift of the Queen.

(5) *Assent to legislation*—In respect to passing of legislation, it should be remembered that, following its passage through Parliament, the royal assent is required for a Bill to become law. It is an established convention (certainly since Queen Anne's refusal in 1708 to sign the Scottish Militia Bill—and on that occasion she was acting on ministerial advice) that the monarch never refuses to give the royal assent to legislation, and that to do so would be unconstitutional. However, it might be argued that there could be extreme circumstances when refusal of the royal assent would be justified, for example, if Parliament approved legislation that sought to postpone indefinitely a general election in peacetime. The royal assent is also required for legislation passed by the Scottish Parliament and the Northern Ireland Assembly (when it is operative).

(6) *Following ministerial advice and collective responsibility*—It is a crucially important convention of the constitution that the Queen always acts on the advice of her ministers. This doctrine is demonstrated at the opening of each session of Parliament. The Queen's speech setting out her government's policy is, in practice, always written by the government. Another equally important convention, collective Cabinet responsibility, is derived from the idea that any advice to the monarch should be unambiguous. This convention requires that members of the Cabinet are bound to defend the policy agreed around the Cabinet table, or alternatively a minister should resign from the government (this convention is discussed in greater detail in chapter six). It should be stressed that there is no active involvement by the monarch in the routine business of government. She has access to classified information and has confidential weekly meetings with the Prime Minister during which she is briefed on government policy. On these occasions the Queen can express her views and provide advice. However, the Prime Minister is not under any obligation to take account of these views. It is of crucial importance that the monarch is perceived as being above politics and impartial when it comes to performing the main constitutional functions. The Queen has resisted any such involvement, but Prince Charles as heir to the throne has been criticised for making comments on issues such as the banning of fox hunting which have a political dimension.

(7) *Commander-in-chief of the armed forces*—The Queen performs an important symbolic function as the nominal head of each of the armed forces, but under the Bill of Rights 1689 the keeping of an army by the Crown is made subject to the consent of Parliament. While the forces are now largely regulated under statute, ministers act under the prerogative to direct the armed forces in their strategic operations.

(8) *Head of state*—As head of state, the Queen represents the nation on the international stage. In this capacity she hosts events at home and makes visits abroad. However, the Prime Minister, the Foreign Secretary, or other senior ministers will be entirely responsible for determining any matters of government policy or negotiating treaties that involve meetings with other heads of state or heads of government, and in this capacity ministers will be acting under their prerogative powers.

(9) *Head of the Commonwealth*—At the turn of the twentieth century the British monarch was the figurehead for the British Empire. Independence has been conferred on virtually all former colonial possessions and many (53 nations and 2 billion people) have joined the British Commonwealth, which seeks to promote co-operation between member nations. The Queen has a mainly symbolic role at its head.

DOES THE MONARCH RETAIN REAL POWER?

A famous statement of the constitutional role was provided by Bagehot in the nineteenth century when he stated 'she has the right to be consulted, the right to encourage and the right to warn,' meaning by this that the monarch had become a 'dignified' rather than an 'efficient' (ie working) element of the constitution.[12] We have already observed that in nearly every case the monarch's powers and discretions are constrained by established conventions. However, the hung Parliament after the February 1974 election illustrates that there may be occasions when a convention is not clearly defined, and where considerable discretion is left in the monarch's hands.

The present Queen has the accumulated experience of having worked with ten different Prime Ministers since she acceded to the throne in 1952. She is kept very closely in touch with the exercise of governmental power by means of a weekly audience with the Prime Minister during which she is fully briefed about the affairs of government, and she has access to all Cabinet papers. The meetings with the Prime Minister are strictly confidential, which allows her the opportunity to express views about matters of government policy. For example, it was widely reported in the press that there were misgivings expressed by the Queen over certain aspects of Margaret Thatcher's domestic policy during the late 1980s. Also, in times of crisis, such as the involvement of British troops in the war in Iraq in the Spring of 2003, the Queen is kept fully informed of the latest developments. It should be emphasised that the Prime Minister is not under any obligation to take account of

[12] W Bagehot, *The English Constitution* (London, Fontana, 1963) p 111.

any royal opinions. Indeed, if a declared position on controversial political matters were to leak out, this would undermine the reputation for impartiality which is so important to the monarch's constitutional role. Bagehot could almost be describing the present position when he summed up the powers of Queen Victoria more than 100 years ago as the rights to be consulted, to encourage and to warn ministers, but it has been suggested in light of the Queen's current role that the right to be informed and to advise could now be added to the list.[13]

WHAT IS THE 'CROWN'?

The 'Crown' is a generic term used to refer to persons or bodies exercising powers which historically were the monarch's personal powers. Now 'Crown' is applied to the executive branch of government. Ministers are servants of the Crown. But 'the concept of the Crown distorts reality in representing different elements of the executive as a unified whole, concealing their interrelationships.'[14] The concept masks the fact that there are often conflicts and tensions between central government departments. We have already noted that the political prerogative is exercised by, or on the advice of, the Crown. In consequence, the term 'Crown' as it is employed in the United Kingdom is a product of constitutional history, and it might be described as anachronistic. Comparable powers in Europe or the United States would be constitutionally exercised by, or on the advice of, what is called the state, executive, or government.

The Crown has enjoyed certain legal immunities. For example, it may be able to avoid liability under a statute that is not expressed as being applicable to it. Such immunity has allowed public bodies to remain outside the scope of statutory provisions which otherwise provide for social welfare, employment rights, and public safety. However, most contemporary legislation has tended to restrict or entirely dispense with this immunity.[15] The intention has been to ensure that government departments are not shielded from obligations that are placed upon them.

[13] R Brazier, 'The Monarchy' in V Bogdanor (ed), *The British Constitution in the Twentieth Century* (Oxford, Oxford University Press, 2003) p 78.
[14] C Turpin, *British Government and the Constitution*, 5th edn (London Butterworths, 2002) p 191.
[15] See, eg, National Health Service and Community Care Act 1990, s 60, and Environmental Protection Act 1990, s 159.

PUBLIC INTEREST IMMUNITY

The immunities enjoyed by the Crown have also been important in a judicial context. In proceedings involving the Crown (ie, the various manifestations of the government) there are occasions where the normal rules of evidence are waived to protect a wider public interest. In an adversarial system, discovery is an important part of the trial process. This rule enables the parties to the action to examine information and documents from the other side. In general, courts will order the disclosure of relevant documents that are not voluntarily produced to allow a case to be prepared thoroughly in advance. At the same time this access to evidence reduces the possibility of either side being surprised or ambushed by the production of unexpected issues. In criminal cases, there is an even stronger right to be notified in advance of the prosecution's case because of the importance of acquitting the innocent. However, it has been recognised by the courts that the Crown (and certain other public bodies, for example the police) occupied a special position. Crown privilege, now termed public interest immunity (PII), can be invoked if it is considered contrary to the public interest for the document(s) to be released on specified grounds, for example, doing harm to national security or revealing the name of a police informer. Although section 28 of the Crown Proceedings Act 1947 provides that the courts can make an order for the discovery of documents against the Crown, this right of discovery is subject to the major qualification that it does not affect the rule that evidence can still be withheld if the wider public interest so demands.

The courts in cases such as *Duncan v Cammell Laird and Co Ltd*,[16] *Conway v Rimmer*[17] and *R v Chief Constable of West Midlands Police, ex parte Wiley*[18] have been required to strike a balance between defining this public interest, on the one hand, and, on the other hand, ensuring that the power to withhold information is not abused by public authorities to shield them against legitimate claims from aggrieved members of the public or defendants. Defining the extent of such an immunity touches on some fundamental questions. For example, how far ought official bodies be allowed to cloak their activities in a veil of secrecy by preventing the release of information when matters are being disputed in open court? These issues were brought to wide public attention in the Matrix Churchill affair in 1992. The directors of the Matrix Churchill company were prosecuted for selling defence equipment (a super gun) to Iraq in contravention of an arms embargo, and they were prevented

---

[16] [1942] AC 624.
[17] [1968] AC 910.
[18] [1995] 1 AC 274.

by public interest immunity certificates signed by ministers from disclosing their association with the security services. It was argued that ministers should not have been advised by the Attorney-General that they were under a duty to sign these certificates when the guilt or innocence of these defendants was at stake. Finally on this point, the Freedom of Information Act 2000 introduces a legally enforceable right to information but in Part II it also sets out Public Interests exemptions. This area of the law may be developed further by the courts in light of the FOI 2000.

LIABILITY OF THE CROWN IN TORT AND CONTRACT

The United Kingdom lacks a well-developed theory of the state and of a state administration,[19] which means that contracts are entered into by Crown servants as agents acting on behalf of the Crown itself. It has been established that officials responsible for negotiating contracts on behalf of a government department are not personally liable under contract because it is the principal (the department) and not the agent (the official) who is responsible. A general right to sue the Crown under contract is provided by section 1 of the Crown Proceedings Act 1947, which removes the need to obtain the leave of the Attorney-General to bring an action against the Crown. Until 1947, prior to this enactment, a petition of right was required to recover damages from the Crown.

Similarly, under section 2 of the Crown Proceedings Act 1947, the Crown (as opposed to the state) is liable in tort (which covers the other civil wrongs under the common law). For example, it can sue or be sued in the courts where there is a claim for negligence. In addition, as an employer, the Crown is liable for torts committed by its employees while in the course of their employment. It is also worth pointing out that other public bodies such as local authorities are in a similar position to the Crown with regard to their general exposure to liability in tort. In most respects, the Crown is treated in the same way as any other defendant, that is, to initiate an action against the Crown a litigant sues the department concerned or the Attorney-General.

There are, however, fundamental limitations to the award of damages against the Crown and other public bodies.[20] The extent to which individuals or corporations are able to recover damages from government and governmental bodies has the potential to call into question the place of private law

[19] See further J Allison, *A Continental Distinction in the Common Law* (Oxford, Oxford University Press, 2000) p 32.

[20] See, eg, *X (Minors) v Bedfordshire County County Council* [1995] 2 AC 633, which set narrow limits on claims against local authorities working under a statutory scheme, and *Barrett v Enfield Borough Council* [2001] 2 AC 550, which recognised access to a court before a claim could be struck out.

remedies. A *general* right to recover damages against the Crown or a public body in regard to the manner in which it performs its statutory duties would indeed carry with it serious implications. More specifically, if policy matters were amenable to challenge by means of a claim for damages, this would be an indirect method of influencing the formulation and application of policy by democratically elected and publicly accountable bodies. Broadly speaking, the courts have been reluctant to grant damages for pure economic loss, except where there is a contract. As Professor Harlow puts it: 'The judges have always been concerned to maintain the "floodgates". They do not wish to contribute to the creation of a society bent on litigation, premised on the illusion that every misfortune merits compensation. Even if there is little concrete evidence to justify fear of a "compensation culture", . . . many modern cases are . . . test cases, . . . with serious implications for public funds.'[21]

EVALUATION: REFORM OR ABOLITION?

The monarchy is a costly institution to preserve and it has been the subject of considerable controversy in recent years. In fact, there has been a varying tide of media criticism which has ebbed and flowed prompted by: the failure of Royal marriages; the Queen's initially cold reaction to the death of Princess Diana (the former wife of Prince Charles and mother of his children, William and Harry); and the inappropriate comments and conduct of certain other members of the royal family. The British monarchy is an institution which retains many arcane procedures, and its members have been accommodated at taxpayers' expense in palatial finery. While the associated pomp and ceremony of trooping of the colour to celebrate the Queen's birthday and the state opening of Parliament might be an attraction for visitors from abroad, spectacles on a grand scale can be objected to as expensive and anachronistic luxuries. There have been calls to review the extent to which state funding through the 'civil list' should go beyond supporting the monarch and her immediate heirs, and to assess whether the public purse should extend to a total of seven royal palaces and to pay for transport in royal yachts, trains, and planes.[22] In other words, it might be suggested that the British monarchy could be trimmed down, assuming a lower profile and becoming more like its Scandinavian counterparts.

An equally trenchant objection is that 'The monarchy remains symbolic of privilege over people, of chance over endeavor, of being something, rather

---

[21] C Harlow, *Understanding Tort Law*, 3rd edn (London, Sweet & Maxwell, 2005) p 150.

[22] R Blackburn and R Plant, 'Monarchy and the Royal Prerogative' in *Constitutional Reform: The Labour Government's Constitutional Reform Agenda* (Longman, London, 1999) p 145.

than doing something. We elevate to the apex of our society someone selected not on the basis of talent or achievement, but because of genes.'[23] Given this type of criticism, namely of a class-based system founded on privilege by birthright, it is not surprising that republican alternatives have gained a more prominent place on the political agenda.[24] For instance, there have been proposals to replace the monarchy with a republican constitution.[25] However, in devising an alternative it would be difficult to match the range of significant constitutional functions which are exercised by the Queen to a new office without including significant changes to the role of Prime Minister, the Cabinet, and the civil service. The design of the office of President as Head of State viewed from an international perspective can have many forms. The United States (or French) variant of a directly elected President with formidable executive powers and the ability to veto legislation[26] would be much too radical a departure for the UK constitution to take on board. On the other hand, a directly elected President with a mainly ceremonial role similar to that granted to the President of the Irish Republic could serve as a possible model. Even if the type of role for a future President is defined, a further question which arises concerns reaching agreement on the type of candidates who might be suitably qualified to stand for election and hold such a high profile public office. Indeed, the difficulty in reaching sufficient consensus upon an acceptable alternative was recently demonstrated when a referendum was held in Australia in 1999. Despite misgivings over the status quo expressed in opinion surveys, the Australian electorate rejected the republican alternative to the Queen as head of state which was on offer.

CONCLUSION

Many nations throughout the world have not accepted the republican case and continue to have constitutional monarchies. Spain can be cited as an example of a European nation which has welcomed the introduction of a constitutional monarchy in recent times. After the divisive Spanish Civil War (1936–39), which was followed by a generation of fascist dictatorship, Juan Carlos was named by Franco as his successor. His accession to the throne in 1975 reinstated a recognised dynasty and provided a means of reconnecting with a legitimate tradition associated with the nation's history. However, Juan Carlos was intent on democratic reform and after elections were held a hereditary monarchy became the central feature of a new liberal democratic

23 'Time for the Monarchy to Step Aside', (2000) *The Observer*, 30 June.
24 A Gray and A Tomkins, *How we should Rule Ourselves* (Edinburgh, Canongate, 2005).
25 Commonwealth of Britain Bill 1995–96.
26 M Vile, *Politics in the USA* (London, Hutchison, 1976) p 183ff.

constitution adopted in 1978. Under the constitution the King has limited powers but he acts as a symbol of the 'unity and permanence' of the state and also stands in a position of neutrality, safeguarding the regular functions of the institutions of the state.[27] The robustness of the new constitution was tested in 1981 when decisive action by the King, at the very pinnacle of the constitution, thwarted a military coup. At the same time, this intervention arguably demonstrated the value of a constitutional monarchy which is backed by strong public support.

Turning back to the United Kingdom, there is wide acknowledgement (even by detractors) that Queen Elizabeth II has performed her constitutional functions with an unflinching dedication to duty; rather, it is the prospect of a less sure-footed successor who might lack equivalent respect for accepted constitutional practice which has raised doubts about the future of the institution. Abolition of the monarchy is not on the immediate horizon. As has been noted above, it would require a written constitution embodying the comprehensive codification of the current conventions relating to the monarch, many of which have been discussed in this chapter. Indeed, notwithstanding the criticisms set out above, it can still be argued that the institution of the monarchy in the United Kingdom is very important in constitutional terms, because the reigning King or Queen personifies the nation as head of state and confirms a link with the nation's past constitutional history. Moreover, as Bagehot stressed, the presence of an experienced and respected monarch acts as a stabilising influence, particularly during times of war or of political crisis.

FURTHER READING

Bagehot W, *The English Constitution* (London, Fontana, 1963).

Bogdanor V, *The Monarchy and the Constitution* (Oxford, Oxford University Press, 1995).

Blackburn R, 'Monarchy and Personal Prerogatives' [2004] *PL* 546.

Brazier R, 'The Monarchy' in V. Bogdanor (ed), *The British Constitution in the Twentieth Century* (Oxford, Oxford University Press, 2003).

Brazier R, *Constitutional Practice*, 3rd edn (Oxford, Oxford University Press, 1999).

Brazier R 'Constitutional reform and the Crown' in M Sunkin and S Payne (eds) *The Nature of the Crown: A Legal and Political Analysis* (Oxford, Oxford University Press, 1999).

[27] E Merino-Blanco, *Spanish Law and Legal System*, 2nd edn (London, Sweet & Maxwell, 2006) p 178.

Craig P, 'Prerogative, Precedent and Power' in C Forsyth and I Hare (eds), *The Golden Metwand and the Crooked Cord* (Oxford, Clarendon Press, 1998).

Freedland M, 'The Crown and the Changing Nature of Government' in M Sunkin and S Payne (eds), *The Nature of the Crown: A Legal and Politcal Analysis* (Oxford, Oxford University Press, 1999).

Leyland P and Anthony G, *Textbook on Administrative Law*, 5th edn (Oxford, Oxford University Press, 2005), chs 17, 20, and 21.

Loughlin M, 'The State, the Crown and the Law' in M Sunkin and S Payne (eds), *The Nature of the Crown: A Legal and Political Analysis* (Oxford, Oxford University Press, 1999).

Pimlott B, *The Queen: A Biography of Queen Elizabeth II* (London, Harper Collins, 1996).

Tomkins A, *Public Law* (Oxford, Oxford University Press, 2003), ch 3.

5

Parliament

INTRODUCTION

IN THE UNITED KINGDOM, Parliament is the body in which the legislative power is vested. It consists of an elected House of Commons and a House of Lords which is largely comprised of life peers (appointed for their lifetime) but with a residual membership of hereditary peers (whose titles are inherited), bishops and Law Lords (see later discussion on the composition of the House of Lords). In addition, in order for legislation approved by Parliament to become law, the royal assent is required. Apart from acting as the legislature for the United Kingdom, Parliament authorises the levying of taxation and controls national expenditure and it keeps a check on the executive. In this capacity it provides the main forum for providing political accountability. It also acts as a sounding board for the nation by debating issues of public concern and by giving the public and other vested interests the chance to lobby their MPs.

This chapter will consider Parliament's role as part of the contemporary constitution. However, it should be remembered that a power struggle between Parliament and the monarch was an important feature of constitutional history. Parliament's origins were merely as an advisory body to the King. It was made up of the land-owning aristocracy and the established church, who were represented in the House of Lords. The House of Commons consisted of elected representatives of the gentry on a roughly geographical basis. Parliament functioned as a kind of representative body of local interests available for consultation, but by the fifteenth century it also assumed a more prominent role in passing legislation. Under the Tudor monarchs (Henry VIII, Mary I, and Elizabeth I) it reverted to a more passive role. However, although it could be summoned and dismissed at will, Parliament was required by the King to approve requests for the raising of revenue. The constitutional clashes of the seventeenth century were a direct result of attempts by the King to rule without recourse to Parliament. This overlooked the established practice that the King could not enact statutes without the consent of the two Houses of Parliament. 'Parliamentarian theories maintained that God originally conferred the highest powers of government on the community as a whole, rather than a single person.'[1] During the seventeenth century such responses to absolute monarchy led to Parliament asserting its role. The Civil War was waged by Parliament against King Charles I, and constitutional constraints were finally placed on the monarchy towards the end of the seventeenth century by the Bill of Rights of 1689. This established that Parliament must meet on a regular basis. It also conferred special privileges on Parliament. For example, Article 9 of the Bill of Rights provides that the freedom of speech and debates and proceedings in Parliament shall not be called into question by any court.

PART I: ELECTIONS AND THE HOUSE OF COMMONS

Before we look at the way both Houses of Parliament operate, it is important to investigate the relationship between the House of Commons and representative government. In order to do this, there will be a brief discussion of the electoral system and the role of political parties.[2]

---

[1] J Goldsworthy, *The Sovereignty of Parliament: History and Philosophy* (Oxford, Oxford University Press, 1999) p 96.

[2] For an overview see: J Curtice, 'The Electoral System' in V Bogdanor (ed), *The British Constitution in the Twentieth Century* (Oxford, Oxford University Press, 2003).

THE ELECTORAL SYSTEM

The first-past-the-post method of election in the United Kingdom has contributed to the political dominance of large parties. During the eighteenth and nineteenth centuries, the Tories and Whigs were the names of the parties in the ascendancy, but both tended to represent narrow factional interests, in particular, the landed gentry and the industrial entrepreneurs. By the end of the nineteenth century the Conservatives (originating from the Tories) and Liberals (originating from the Whigs) were the main parties who alternated in power. The Labour Party as the political voice of the trade union movement was founded in the late nineteenth century. After World War I, Labour began to replace the Liberals as the main left-of-centre party. However, Labour was mostly in opposition until 1945. Since the end of the World War II, the Conservative and Labour Parties have alternated between government and opposition.

The first-past-the-post (simple plurality) system operates by dividing the nation into 645 approximately equal constituencies in terms of population, each of which sends a single member to Parliament. It produces MPs who represent clearly defined geographical areas and, as we shall see, an MP might be regarded as an 'ombudsman' for his or her own constituents. Candidates selected by the political parties, and independent persons who pay the required deposit of £500 and are able to get sufficient nominations, can stand at general elections or at by-elections. The Political Parties, Elections and Referendums Act 2000 regulates the conduct of political parties and establishes an election commission to oversee the electoral process. The Act also requires political parties to be registered and it imposes restrictions on the source of donations to prevent foreign and anonymous support for political parties. The Act further requires that any donation of over £5,000 to a political party is declared. Both the Labour and Conservative Parties have faced criticism following the 2005 election for accepting loans from donors in order to circumvent the provisions of this Act.

The electoral system is extremely straightforward to understand. A voter simply puts a cross next to the name of his or her preferred candidate. The candidate receiving the most votes wins the seat. This is whether or not he or she receives a majority of the votes cast in that constituency. Although it is not in any sense proportionate, 'first past the post' registers the relative support between the parties with the widest following in the country. The major parties nearly always win the seats in their heartlands, but the outcome of elections is decided in more marginal constituencies, where a shift in support between the main parties will lead to a change in the member elected. The system favours parties polling nationally over 30 per cent of the popular vote. Moreover, a single party receiving between 40 per cent and 45 per cent of the national vote stands a good chance of gaining an overall majority of seats in the House of Commons and therefore of forming a government. In 1997 Labour achieved an overall majority of 180 seats with just under 44 per cent of the popular vote, and their majority hardly diminished when they received 42 per cent of the popular vote in 2001.

2001 General Election Results

Labour	42% popular vote	413 seats	62.7% seats
Conservative	32.7% popular vote	166 seats	25.2% seats
Liberal Democrat	18% popular vote	52 seats	7.9% seats[3]

However, the 2001 result also shows that the system tends to favour two large parties because, to get elected, a concentration of support is required in any given constituency. Parties with national support which is distributed more thinly find it difficult to pick up seats. The Liberal Democrats with national support at around 18 per cent succeed in having candidates elected only in the parts of the United Kingdom where there are pockets of concentrated support. Equally, the Scottish and Welsh nationalist parties benefited from the intensity of support in parts of Scotland and Wales. The Greens, with less than 5 per cent nationally, were unable to get a single member elected to the Westminster Parliament. Constituencies in Northern Ireland are contested by locally based parties mainly representing the loyalist majority (Ulster Unionists and Democratic Unionists) and the republican minority (Social Democratic and Labour and Sinn Fein).

2005 General Election Results

Labour	35% popular vote	356 seats	55.19% seats
Conservative	32% popular vote	197 seats	30.54% seats
Liberal Democrat	22% popular vote	62 seats	9.06% seats[4]

Once again, in the 2005 general election, Labour achieved an overall majority of 66 seats over all other parties in the House of Commons but the party was returned with an even smaller share of the popular vote.[5] Assuming Labour MPs continue their loyalty to the party, this decisive majority will be sufficient to ensure the passage of most, if not all, of its legislative proposals.

---

[3] The remaining proportion of votes and seats went to smaller parties and independents, eg Scottish Nationalists, Welsh Nationalists, Democratic Unionists, and Sinn Fein.

[4] As for the 2001 election results above, the votes and seats of smaller parties are not set out.

[5] P Norris, 'The Third Blair Victory: How and Why?' [2005] *Parliamentary Affairs* 657.

'FIRST PAST THE POST' OR PROPORTIONAL REPRESENTATION?

In turn, the endorsement of one side in preference to the other at elections has allowed the party with most seats to claim a popular mandate for policies, and to ensure that its legislation passes through the House of Commons without much disruption. This is the case even when the government has a small overall majority in the House of Commons. The risk of defeat in the voting lobby is a strong incentive for tribal party loyalties to prevail over personal conscience on any single issue. The system generally provides decisive government, since a party with a majority can carry through its policies without having to enter into pacts and compromise, as is often the case where a system of proportional election is adopted. Advocates of 'first past the post' argue that, on most occasions, it provides a clear outcome, and that it also prevents 'extreme' minority parties from doing well. These are crucial strengths which should be retained. Opponents to the present system, particularly the Liberal Democrats, not only object because minority parties are greatly under-represented, but also because the shifts between political parties which govern has allowed lurches from the relatively extreme positions adopted by the Labour and Conservative Parties. The emergence of coalitions from the centre is regarded as preferable. There are many different systems of proportional representation which might be adopted as an alternative. All the alternatives are more difficult to understand and each system has different strengths and weaknesses. For example, party list systems, such as the one now used in the United Kingdom for European Union elections, accurately reflect the votes cast for each party, but this method of election tends to give a great deal of power to the party leadership in drawing up the lists. Where it is used for electing national Parliaments (eg Israel), minority parties often end up holding the balance of power, and this method of voting provides an opportunity to extreme minority parties.

ELECTRONIC VOTING

Electronic voting at election time by computer is on the horizon. It would cut down the expense of elections and allow results to be declared as soon as the polls close (assuming a secure system is devised). However, quite apart from the normal electoral process, more frequent consultation online from the citizen's home is in prospect. Such an innovation would amount to an entirely new form of participatory democracy by allowing dialogue between government and the wider citizenry. The prospect of broadening consultation to inform decision-making by central and local government might be welcomed. It could help deliberations on many routine matters. On the other hand, the holding of online plebiscites as indicators of the public mood would have to be rigorously controlled, as testing the water in this way could easily be abused by government. For example, in order to justify the introduction of repressive legislation following a violent crime or terrorist attack the Home Secretary might calculate on getting 'knee jerk' approval for such measures in an electronic vote.

THE HOUSE OF COMMONS AND THE FORMATION OF A GOVERNMENT

In terms of the broader constitutional context we can see that Parliament is crucial to the formation of the government. After a general election, the leader of the party with a majority in the elected House of Commons (the procedure which is followed in the event that no single party emerges from an election with a majority is discussed in chapter four) will be invited by the monarch to become Prime Minister. The first job the Prime Minister has to perform is to select a government from the MPs elected to the House of Commons and peers who are members of the House of Lords. The predominance of the House of Commons over the House of Lords has given rise to the recognition of a convention dating back to 1902, that in order to be accountable to the electorate, the Prime Minister must be a member of the House of Commons. In 1963 Lord Home and Lord Hailsham, two of the leading contenders to succeed Harold Macmillan, renounced their inherited titles in order to be viable candidates to take over as Prime Minister, and Home (Sir Alec Douglas Home) actually succeeded to the Premiership.

We have noted that one of the most important constitutional conventions requires that a government maintains its majority in the House of Commons. This convention dictates that the Prime Minister of a government that is defeated in the House of Commons on a vote of confidence must offer his or her resignation prompting an early general election. The last recent occasion when this occurred was in 1979. The Labour government of James Callaghan lost a vote of confidence by a single vote, giving rise to an early election. The requirement that a governing party sustains its majority in the House of Commons has a very important influence on the way Parliament operates. It means, for example, that, even where there are considerable factional divisions within a party in government on matters of policy, there is still a strong reason for backbench MPs on the government side to support the party line. This is because failure to do so could result in the loss of a confidence vote leading to an early general election and possible defeat at the ballot box.

PART II: THE HOUSE OF COMMONS

THE HOUSE OF COMMONS AND THE ROLE OF MPS

The House of Commons consists of 645 elected MPs, each of whom represents an individual constituency which is based on geographical area. MPs who are not members of the government or shadow government are referred to as 'backbenchers'.[6] Apart from representing their constituents, MPs participate in debates, vote on legislation, and serve on parliamentary committees. The House of Commons is presided over by the Speaker (and three deputies), who is elected by MPs. The Speaker detaches him/herself from previous party associations and has enormous authority. He or she determines who can contribute to debates and is required to rule on procedural matters as well as performing a quasi-judicial function when dealing with internal disciplinary issues concerning the conduct of MPs.

MPs are sent to Parliament to represent their constituents, but they are not delegates. They may win their seat on the basis of manifesto pledges made by a political party to the electorate. However, once elected, there is no formal mechanism available to individual electors to compel their MP to follow manifesto policies. On the other hand, the political party to which MPs belong (exceptionally there may be MPs who do not belong to a major political party) is in a position to exert pressure to encourage them to tow the party line. MPs may seem free to dissent from this position and vote with the opposition or abstain from voting. The divisions in the Conservative Party over the European Union led to a number of rebellions by eurosceptic MPs. This made it difficult for the government of Prime Minister John Major, 1990–97, to introduce legislation incorporating the Treaty of Maastricht (which extended the role of Europe with the formation of the European Union). The matter was subject to a vote of confidence, but the government narrowly prevailed. In 1995 the same divisions in the Conservative Party in the House of Commons prompted Major to trigger a leadership election which he was able to win against his eurosceptic opponent. Prime Minister Tony Blair, who has enjoyed a much larger majority, has lost the support of a significant minority of backbench MPs over some issues (eg the introduction of foundation hospitals and the war against Iraq). Behind the scenes, the party machine (whips) exerts strong pressure on individual members. In consequence, MPs who persistently vote with the opposition may lose the endorsement of their party (have the whip withdrawn). This punishment can be imposed on a temporary or on a permanent basis.

---

[6] R Brazier, *Constitutional Practice*, 3rd edn (Oxford, Oxford University Press, 1999) ch 10.

Also, there is a geographical and local dimension to the role of MPs. They seek to represent the interests of their constituents and promote what they regard as their constituency interests. There are many examples of MPs articulating local views on contentious matters. One such issue concerned opposition voiced in Parliament to proposals to build a fifth terminal at London's Heathrow Airport (which went ahead anyway despite a public inquiry). Local opposition is spearheaded in Parliament by local members. MPs will take up grievances on behalf of their constituents. But there may be limits to such support. MPs may be reluctant to back a local cause when this conflicts with the official party line.

The adversarial character of parliamentary politics has exerted an enormous influence on the procedures that have developed. A two-party system derived from having rival factions outbidding each other to act as advisers to the monarch (one in government; the other in opposition). In order to succeed in an adversarial system political parties have tended to be made up of broad coalitions of individuals with diverse shades of opinion. The factions need to keep together for a government to maintain its majority in Parliament. Nevertheless, if the policies of a party change too much, or if the leadership loses touch with the grass roots, the tension caused may result in rebellions inside the party and defections to other parties. One of the most dominant Prime Ministers of recent times, Margaret Thatcher, faced a leadership contest and was forced to step down because of divisions in her own parliamentary party.[7]

Parliamentary questions provide an important opportunity for individual members to raise matters on behalf of constituents and of general concern. MPs are expected to represent the interests of constituents whether or not they are political supporters. 'Question time' is the highlight of the parliamentary day, and it brings matters to the attention of the wider public. It will be pointed out below that 'question time' is also a procedure that permits MPs to call the executive to account for its actions. Early-day motions are another method for drawing attention to a matter of concern. There are limited opportunities for backbench MPs to initiate debates on subjects that they feel are important. Adjournment debates are available for raising issues and are held at the end of parliamentary business. These may be matters that cause embarrassment to the government, but emergency debates are granted only occasionally by the Speaker.

The question of representation in Parliament, and particularly in the House of Commons, should also be considered in terms of the extent to which it achieves a gender and ethnic balance[8]. The Parliamentary Labour

---

[7] J Cole, *As It Seemed to Me* (London, Phoenix, 1996) p 375.

[8] See, eg, R Campbell and J Lovenduski, 'Winning Women's Votes? The Incremental Track to Equality' [2005] *Parliamentary Affairs* 837–53.

Party has very many more women than the Conservatives and the Liberal Democrats. This is because of a deliberate policy before the 1997 election that favoured the selection of female candidates. Ethnic minorities are unevenly represented with only a handful of MPs. The Scottish Parliament (40 per cent) and the Welsh Assembly (50 per cent) have among the highest concentrations of female representation in Europe.

The so-called 'West Lothian question' has once again arisen as an issue since devolution. The problem is that, since Scotland acquired its own Parliament and executive with powers over devolved matters, Scottish MPs at Westminster can vote on matters affecting England, while English MPs no longer have voting rights over devolved matters. There is a similar situation in respect to Northern Ireland, which also has a law-making assembly of its own. The point is that devolution has modified the role of Westminster MPs for constituencies in Scotland, Wales, and Northern Ireland because local constituents are more likely to turn to members of the devolved bodies to deal with problems concerning devolved matters coming under the devolved executives—for example, agriculture, education, environment, housing, and health. A Scottish constituent is therefore much more likely to go through a Member of the Scottish Parliament if he or she needs help with resolving a devolved matter. Thus the workload of Scottish MPs to Westminster has been much reduced. Further, there is an obvious iniquity, because Scottish MPs at Westminster are still allowed to vote on English legislation, but English MPs no longer have the right to vote on the majority of Scottish matters. This is because these policy areas have been handed over to the devolved Scottish executive and Parliament, which not only has law-making powers but also has an executive oversight function (The impact of devolution is discussed further in chapter eight.)

THE SPEAKER

The Speaker of the House of Commons was the elected official who spoke for his or her fellow members by communicating requests to the King or Queen. In the present set-up, the Speaker (and the deputy speakers), apart from presiding over debates and determining the order in which members speak, performs an important quasi-judicial function in giving rulings on procedural points of order that arise. Unlike the Lord Chancellor who presides over debates in the House of Lords the Speaker is disqualified from direct participation. The Speaker retains a historic role in formally representing the views of the House of Commons to the monarch.

GOVERNMENT AND OPPOSITION

The official opposition has a vital part to play in the parliamentary system.[9] It will be obvious that the role of the opposition is to oppose the government of the day, both by raising reasoned objections to its legislative proposals, and by criticising its performance as a government. The opposition also has to present itself as a government-in-waiting. As well as having a distinct set of policies, it has an alternative leader and government team in what is termed a 'Shadow Cabinet'. On top of any earnings as MPs, the Leader of Her Majesty's Opposition and the opposition Chief Whip are paid salaries, which is further acknowledgement of their formal status. In order to perform its function, the official opposition and other opposition parties are granted parliamentary time, and they are represented on all parliamentary committees. The opposition has a particularly important role in relation to public expenditure. A certain amount of time, called supply days (now opposition days), is set aside to debate in detail the estimates for public expenditure, but these opposition days can be used to discuss other policy issues.

The opposition will often chose a sensitive topic which is likely to cause embarrassment to the government in anticipation that the debate will attract adverse publicity and a modification of policy. But the outcome of debates and votes in the House of Commons are usually a foregone conclusion. This is because the government whips are nearly always able to ensure a government majority for the ruling party (see references to 'elective dictatorship'[10]). However, an effective opposition may be able to cause long-term political damage to the government. For example, although the administration of Prime Minister John Major survived for several more years, the government's credibility was seriously damaged by criticisms of economic mismanagement levelled at it by the opposition following the United Kingdom's forced withdrawal from the European Exchange Rate mechanism on 16 September 1992. A degree of co-operation between government and opposition is required to allow many parliamentary procedures to operate and to facilitate the passage of legislation. For example, there will usually be agreement over the amount of time to be devoted to clauses of a government Bill. Finally, as a potential leader, the Prime Minister may confide in the Leader of the Opposition on matters of national importance or crisis, for example, where UK forces are engaged in action overseas.

---

[9] G Ganz, *Understanding Public Law*, 3rd edn (London, Fontana, 2001) p 30.
[10] From Lord Hailsham's phrase: *Elective Dictatorship* (London, British Broadcasting Corporation, 1976).

PARLIAMENTARY PRIVILEGE

Parliament has been given a number of important legal privileges which allows it to conduct its constitutional role without interference from the Crown or from the courts, and these amount to a source of constitutional law in their own right.[11] The grant of these special privileges by the sovereign must be related to the struggle between the King and Parliament which came to a head in the seventeenth century with the English Civil War of 1642–49 and the 'Glorious Revolution' of 1688. The English Bill of Rights of 1689 provided under Article 9 that the freedom of speech and debates or proceedings in Parliament ought not to be impeached or questioned in any court or place outside Parliament. The special privileges afforded to Parliament have been unchallenged by the Crown since 1688. In the absence of a codified constitution as a form of guarantee, these privileges are demanded from the monarch by the Speaker of the House of Commons and confirmed (as a symbolic gesture) at the beginning of each parliamentary session. In effect, this acknowledges the independence of Parliament, and Parliament is granted special rights to do certain things without having its legitimacy or its authority challenged by the sovereign, the government, or the courts. This means that, for example, in theory, MPs have an unqualified freedom of speech. In practice, this means that what is said in Parliament cannot be the subject of defamation actions or prosecution in the courts. However, if this privilege is abused MPs may be disciplined by Parliament itself. The absolute freedom of speech can be regarded as the most significant of the privileges enjoyed today. This immunity has the potential to enable MPs to voice concern about matters of public concern in Parliament in circumstances where they would otherwise be forced to remain silent. It permits accusations in Parliament which, if repeated outside, would result in legal proceedings. For example, in 1955 at the height of the so-called 'Cold War' Kim Philby was exposed in Parliament as a spy. This revelation was the prelude to uncovering of the biggest security scandal in British history.

The case of *Bradlaugh v Gossett*[12] confirmed that the courts have no power to intervene in relation to the internal management and procedures of the House of Commons. It also confirmed that Parliament is able to determine the nature and limits of parliamentary privilege. The recognition of parliamentary privilege has meant that Parliament has the right to control its own internal proceedings without question. Moreover, Parliament is a court

---

[11] C Munro, *Studies in Constitutional Law*, 2nd edn (London, Butterworths, 1999) ch 7.
[12] (1884) 12 QBD 271.

which can discipline and, if necessary, imprison its own members for mis-behaviour. In recent years further steps have been taken to oversee the activ-ities and behaviour of MPs.

PARLIAMENTARY STANDARDS AND CONDUCT OF MPS

The conduct of some MPs became a particular cause of concern during the 1990s and Lord Nolan, a senior judge from the judicial panel in the House of Lords, was given the task of reformulating guidelines in respect to regulating the conduct of MPs and setting up the Committee on Standards in Public Life. Lord Nolan identified public duty, selflessness, integrity, objectivity, accountability and openness, honesty and leadership as forming the prin-ciples which should underpin the codes of practice that should be applied to MPs. Members of Parliament are required not to bring the office of Member of Parliament into disrepute. One issue which brought this matter to the attention of the public was the revelation that some Conservative MPs (eg Tim Smith and Neil Hamilton) had received cash for asking questions in Parliament on behalf of private individuals, including Mohammed Al Fayed, the owner of Harrods. The disquiet was not because of the link with outside interests. It has already been pointed out that significant number of Conservative MPs, and some Labour and Liberal Democrat members, have links with business. Equally, the parliamentary Labour Party was formed to further the aims of the trade union movement and other affiliated bodies on the left of politics. The problem was that a number of MPs were presenting themselves as consultants and were acting through agents without declaring this role. In return for cash they promised to raise issues in Parliament. The concern was not only that there had been no declaration of interest, but also that this had the potential to interfere with an MP's main job, namely, to rep-resent the interests of their constituents. It has been established as a matter of principle that MPs should declare any personal interest in a matter brought before Parliament. For this purpose a Register of Members' Interests is pub-lished and there are strict rules governing the financial interests that have to be declared. Failure fully to disclose such interests is regarded as a serious matter, which will lead to disciplinary action.[13]

The Parliamentary Commissioner for Standards has an investigatory role and MPs are required to co-operate with any investigation that is under-taken.[14] The Standards Commissioner performs the functions previously

---

[13] See *First Report of the Committee on Standards in Public Life*, Cm 2850, 1995.
[14] See P Leopold, 'Standards of Conduct in Public Life' in J Jowell and D Oliver (eds), *The Changing Constitution*, 5th edn (Oxford, Oxford University Press, 2004), at p 423ff.

carried out by separate Select Committees on Members' Interests and on Privileges. These committees were combined in 1995, with the formation of a new House of Commons Select Committee on Standards and Privileges. It is chaired by a respected member of the opposition, has 11 members, and a quorum of 5, with the power to appoint sub-committees. This Committee oversees the work of a new officer of the House of Commons, the Parliamentary Commissioner for Standards, Sir Philip Mawer. He is responsible for the maintenance of the Register of Members' Interests and advises MPs on the registration requirements, but he also has the task of investigating specific complaints about the conduct of MPs. The Committee on Standards considers matters relating to privileges referred to it by the House, and matters relating to the conduct of MPs, including specific complaints about MPs' conduct which have been made to the Commissioner and referred by him to the committee. In particular, the committee has power to order the attendance of any MP before the committee, and to require that specific documents or records in the possession of an MP relating to its inquiries, or to the inquiries of the Commissioner, be laid before the committee. In July 1996 the House adopted the committee's proposals for a Code of Conduct for Members, which was accompanied by a Guide to the Rules relating to the Conduct of Members. In recent years under Labour a steady stream of cases have been referred for investigation. For example, in 2006 the failure of Deputy Prime Minister, John Prescott, to declare a stay on the ranch of an American tycoon (who had previously expressed a business interest in a government-sponsored project) attracted much attention in the press. The investigation and report by the Commissioner demonstrate that these procedures are strictly enforced, but also reveals the complexity and ambiguity of some of the rules governing what MPs and ministers are expected to enter on the register.[15]

PART III: THE HOUSE OF LORDS

INTRODUCTION AND HISTORY

Although members of the House of Lords are not elected, the so-called Upper House has broadly similar functions to the House of Commons. It scrutinises legislation as it passes through Parliament, and it requires the government to account for its policies. The House of Lords operates as a revising chamber with more time available and, in many cases, more expertise to

---

[15] Select Committee on Standards and Privileges, *Thirteenth report*, 20 July 2006.

perform this task. The House of Lords, which serves as the second chamber in the United Kingdom, is a very unusual body. In common with the Canadian Senate, it is entirely unelected and, as well as having a legislative role, it has performed the crucial judicial function of being the highest domestic appellate court, although it was announced in June 2003 that a Supreme Court would be established to perform this judicial appellate function. The House of Lords has been the subject of reform on several occasions, the most recent and far reaching, certainly in terms of composition, was in 1999, when the hereditary element was heavily pruned. This was to be the prelude to further reform, but, to date, there has been a lack of consensus as to what should happen next. While most commentators and politicians recognise that a second chamber should continue to have a role as a body which revises legislation and helps to scrutinise the executive, there has been much disagreement over the composition of the House of Lords or any such body that might replace it.

The prospect of conflict between the two Houses resulting in gridlock has generally been avoided because there is an important convention (known as the 'Salisbury' convention) that establishes that the government's manifesto commitments, in the form of Government Bills, are not voted down by the House of Lords at second reading stage.

The legitimacy of the Lords had been called into question with the extension of voting rights during the course of the nineteenth century. As a hereditary body the House of Lords largely represented the landed aristocracy, but the social and economic changes resulting from the Industrial Revolution, including the growth of towns and cities, the emergence of powerful industrial interests, and the activities of protest movements and organised labour had an important bearing on politics. The response of the House of Lords to electoral reform is particularly relevant to this discussion. When the first Reform Bill of 1832 proposed a limited extension of voting rights and a fairer distribution of seats, the landed aristocracy in the House of Lords attempted to prevent the Bill's passage through Parliament. It resisted again at the beginning of the twentieth century when a Liberal government was elected on a radical manifesto. The tactics of the Conservative opposition in the House of Lords, which thwarted the government's attempts to introduce many of its policies by voting them down, triggered a constitutional crisis. The clash between the two Houses culminated in the rejection by the House of Lords of the Finance Bill (Budget) of 1909. This intervention departed from what was believed to be a convention that prevented the Lords from blocking money Bills. To overcome the stalemate, the Liberal government was required to contest two elections in 1910. The first was on the budget, and the second on the government's proposals to curtail the powers of the

Lords permanently. The prospect that the King would create sufficient Liberal peers to vote in favour of the Parliament Bill and thereby overwhelm the opposition prompted sufficient Conservatives in the House of Lords to back down and vote in favour of reform.

The Parliament Act, which became law in 1911, clipped the wings of the House of Lords by replacing its capacity to veto legislation with a delaying power of two years (this was later reduced to one year by the Parliament Act 1949). The delaying power has been used on only a handful of occasions since 1949. The reluctance to invoke this power confirms the subordinate role of the House of Lords.[16] It is mainly a revising chamber. In addition, the Parliament Act 1911 entirely removed any rights to delay financial Bills. Nevertheless, in order to provide some balance between the two Houses the 1911 Act left the House of Lords with an absolute power to reject any legislation which sought to prolong the lifetime of a Parliament and, at the same time, it reduced the maximum period between parliamentary elections from seven to five years. The present House of Lords is left with the power to delay legislation for up to a year. It can also amend legislation emanating from the Commons, but any such amendments may not be accepted by the Commons.

COMPOSITION OF THE HOUSE OF LORDS

The House is composed of a number of different categories of peers. Viewed from a historical standpoint the Upper House of peers represented the families who had been elevated to the nobility by the King (dukes, marquises, earls, viscounts, and barons). It contained peers whose ancestry dated back to the medieval period. They also represented the interests of the established church. The power to appoint peers, which originally lay with the sovereign, has effectively since the eighteenth century been in the hands of the Prime Minister, whose nominees are rubber-stamped by the sovereign. An appointments commission, which is meant to be independent, is expected to take over the role of making recommendations for life peerages.

By the time the Parliament Act 1911 reformed the House of Lords, it was already evident to many that birthright was not a legitimate qualification for service in a modern legislature. Moreover, the predominance of hereditaries was iniquitous because the Conservatives were able to muster a majority by summoning their supporters amongst the hereditaries to vote. This built-in

---

[16] As was pointed out in ch 3, the constitutional status of the Parliament Acts was recently considered by the House of Lords in *Jackson v Attorney-General* [2005] UKHL 56.

Conservative majority presented a particular problem for Liberal and later for Labour governments. Nevertheless, until 1999 hereditary peers, numbering over 758 out of 1,325, remained the largest single group. The House of Lords Act 1999 removed the voting rights of all but 92. A ballot was held among the hereditary peers to establish which of their number were to remain as a residue of working hereditary peers. It was argued that the 92 were necessary to provide continuity until the next phase in the process of reform was completed.

The Lords Spiritual, representing the Church of England, also have a traditional right to sit in the House of Lords. The Archbishops of Canterbury and York and 22 other bishops are entitled to participate in the affairs of Parliament. Although the leaders of other denominations may be given life peerages, there is no guarantee of equivalent representation. The Royal Commission sought to address this anomaly by suggesting that all the major religions should be represented in a reformed second chamber.

By far the largest category of members is that of the (around) 620 life peers. The Life Peerage Act 1958 allowed the appointment of a new category of barons serving for their lifetime only. In addition, the 1958 Act removed the sex discrimination barrier that had prevented women from sitting in the House of Lords. Although life peerages were available as an alternative to the hereditary principle from 1958, it was not until the election of Labour in 1964 that it became accepted practice to appoint exclusively life peers (there were a handful of hereditary peerages awarded as an exception during Margaret Thatcher's term as Prime Minister, eg to Viscount Whitelaw and Viscount Tonypandy). It is worth noting that nominees for life peerages have fallen into two main categories. A certain number have been created on a regular basis as the political nominees of the main political parties. It has been a convention that, in order to perform the role of opposition effectively, opposition parties should be entitled to make recommendations to the serving Prime Minister. A substantial proportion of these political appointments is made up of politicians with experience in the House of Commons or at European, devolved, or local level. The second category of nominees comprises those appointed in recognition of exceptional contributions to the wider community. Included under this head are captains of industry, retired leaders of trade unions, distinguished academics, former senior civil servants, retired generals, admirals, and air marshals, leading figures from the professions, arts, and sciences, and so on. The intellectual distinction and specialist knowledge of many life peers contributes to the high quality of debate in the House of Lords and to the contribution it makes as a body which revises legislation. With the exception of ministers and shadow ministers, peers are not paid, but are entitled to claim back expenses for travel, subsistence, and secretarial costs.

The last distinct category is that of the Law Lords, created under the Appellate Jurisdiction Act 1876, who are appointed to serve on the highest domestic appellate court and are made life peers. The judicial committee has 12 working Law Lords, but there are a further 15 retired Law Lords, who have the right to sit and vote for the remainder of their lifetime. There was a convention that serving Law Lords do not routinely participate in political debate. However, the Constitutional Reform Act 2005 provides that the judicial committee of the House of Lords is to be replaced by a Supreme Court, and this change will mean the end of the anomalous situation which allowed the Lord Chancellor, and the most senior serving judges, also to be members of the legislature.

On 1st December 2006 the party strengths in the House of Lords based on declared allegiances were: 212 Labour; 207 Conservative; 201 cross-benchers; and 78 Liberal Democrats. Of a total of 750 eligible to sit in the House, 142 were women. Daily attendance averages between 350 and 450 peers.

HOUSE OF LORDS: WHAT NEXT?

As has already been observed, the House of Lords Act of 1999 partially tackled the anomaly of hereditary peers, but this was intended only as a temporary measure until such time as the composition of a second chamber could be agreed.[17] Each of the various options for reform has far wider constitutional implications. If the United Kingdom was to follow most other nations and introduce an elected second chamber, this would provide an important element of democratic legitimacy. The method of election and gap between elections could be chosen on a different basis from the House of Commons; also the terms of office of members could be for a different period. In addition, the constituencies could be drawn so as to introduce a significant regional dimension. However, there are reasons for objecting to an elected, or mainly elected, second chamber. If it is accepted that the House of Commons should continue to have a predominant role, the democratic legitimacy of a reformed second chamber arising through election could be problematic. It might lead to the second chamber asserting its authority, and thereby acting as a competitor to the House of Commons. It could, for example, delay legislation more regularly, disrupting the process of government. Another potential drawback is the danger that an elected second chamber might duplicate the political tribalism of the House of Commons, with members dragooned by the party machine. Politicians mindful of having to

---

[17] For an evaluation of reform so far, see G Phillipson, '"The Greatest Quango of them all", "a rival chamber" or "a hybrid nonsense"? Solving the Second Chamber Paradox' [2004] *PL* 352–80.

face the voters at some future date would be less likely to display the relative independence compared to the Commons demonstrated by many members of the House of Lords in recent years. Moreover, there is evidence to suggest from a comparative study of the situation in Ireland, Spain, and Italy that the contribution of a second chamber as an effective legislative body tends to be undermined where the government enjoys a majority in both Houses.[18]

The recommendations of the Royal Commission under the chairmanship of Lord Wakeham,[19] which was set up to address the fundamental problem of the composition of a reformed body, in fact demonstrates the difficulty of reaching consensus on the next stage of reform. The Royal Commission considered that there should be an elected element of between 65 and 195 members (up to about 20 per cent) serving for between 12 and 15 years, elected at different times. Second, it recommended that the remaining members should be appointed by an independent statutory appointments commission. The independent commission would operate under statutory guidelines designed to correct the under-representation of groups such as ethnic minorities, women, minority religions, and so on.

The government later published a White Paper, *The House of Lords— Completing the Reform*.[20] This was strongly criticised as it failed to satisfy either those favouring a predominantly elected second chamber or those preferring a nominated body. This also opted for a very limited elected element of 20 per cent of the 600 members, an insufficient proportion to satisfy the pro-election lobby. However, it also proposed that 330 would be nominated by the main political parties and that only 120 members would be appointed by the independent election commission. The continued influence of the main political parties and reduced role of an independent appointments commission was unacceptable to many otherwise more predisposed to a substantial appointed component. No viable model emerged from a series of votes that were held in the House of Commons in February 2003 to consider a number of alternative solutions, and the matter appeared to have been put to one side by the government. House of Lords reform was mentioned, once again, in the Queen's Speech in 2005 and 2006, indicating that further legislation was about to return to the government's agenda.

In September 2003 the government announced plans to introduce a Bill abolishing the 92 remaining hereditary peers (which was dropped in the face of opposition) and setting in place a new independent appointments com-

[18] M Russell, *Reforming the Lords: Lessons from Overseas* (Oxford, Oxford University Press, 2000), pp 150–2 and 226–7.

[19] The Royal Commission on the Reform of the House of Lords, *A House for the Future*, Cm 4534, 2000.

[20] Cm 5291, 2001.

mission. The commission would have responsibility for the appointment of all life peers and for determining the size of the second chamber. These are powers which have, until recently, rested with the Prime Minister. This stop-gap solution remains controversial, given the support among individual MPs and peers for a second chamber which is either entirely elected or predominantly elected. The most likely result is some kind compromise between an elected and an appointed second chamber. Finally, by international standards the membership of the House of Lords remains very large (750), and only a limited proportion of peers attend on a regular basis. In consequence, there appears to be a compelling case for reducing the number entitled to participate in the business of the House.

PART IV: PARLIAMENT AS LEGISLATOR

We will now consider the legislative process in more detail. In looking at this question the focus will be on considering how effective Parliament is as a legislative body and to what extent it is able to deliver high quality legislation.

In the simplest terms, according to the doctrine of the mandate, Parliament has legitimacy because the most important part of it, namely, the House of Commons, is elected. The party with the strongest support in the Commons (usually a majority over other parties) is in a position to form a government. In turn, the government will introduce the policies that have been approved by the electorate. However, this only roughly describes the relationship between Parliament and law-making. To some extent it is possible to see a correspondence between declared political aims at election times, and the legislation that is introduced by government.[21] However, apart from legislation to put into effect manifesto pledges in the main policy areas, governments will also needs to introduce laws in response to pressing matters of topical concern which range from management of the economy and regulation of industry to measures in response to the threat of terrorism. Legislation also originates from a variety of other sources, some of which are outside Parliament. Some government Bills arise from the routine work of the Law Commission, which reports on the state of various aspects of civil and criminal law. Another increasingly important reason for the introducing legislation is to meet the requirements of EU law. Directives may need to be implemented by means of primary legisla-tion.[22] The introduction of devolution with a separate law-making apparatus

---

[21] J Bara, 'A Question of Trust: Implementing Party Manifestos' [2005] *Parliamentary Affairs* 585–99.

[22] The European Scrutiny Committee of the House of Commons assesses the implications of laws coming from Brussels and decides which ones are debated at Westminster.

has meant that now just over half of all legislation from Westminster applies only to certain parts of the United Kingdom.[23]

PUBLIC BILLS

A process of consultation may precede the introduction of government legislation. In order to facilitate this, a Green Paper or White Paper (government publication setting out intentions) will be issued to elicit responses from individuals and organisations likely to be affected by the proposed legislation. An important innovation in recent years has been the publication of some legislation as draft Bills well in advance of their passage through Parliament in order to give more opportunities for consultation. In line with the practice in the Scottish Parliament, this process of pre-legislative scrutiny has allowed departmental select committees to take evidence, report, and make recommendations on proposals before the legislation goes through its formal parliamentary stages, and there is evidence to suggest that a signifcant proportion of recommendations have an impact on the final form of the legislation.[24] Parliament is the focus for the activity of pressure groups. The central lobby of the House of Commons is where members of the public can meet their MPs to make representations. The modern trend has been to cultivate contacts with MPs and for MPs to take consultancies with commercial organisations. Labour MPs are frequently sponsored by trade unions, and some MPs, mainly Conservative, are associated with business interests, either as directors or as consultants. An intervention from the MP will be expected when the subject of discussion concerns areas where the pressure or interest group has a direct interest. As mentioned earlier, members are required to declare any such connections on a Register of Members' Interests.

As we review the parliamentary stages of government legislation, it is worth noting that Bills can be introduced in either the House of Commons or the House of Lords. The initial stage for legislation is called the first reading. This simply marks the announcement of the publication of the Bill. The principles contained in the Bill will be debated by the assembled House at the next stage, which is referred to as the second reading. The second reading is the main opportunity for MPs to debate the issues of principle contained in the proposal. If there is disagreement on the principles of the Bill, amendments

---

[23]   R Hazell, 'Westminster as a "Three-in-One" Legislature' in R Hazell and R Rawlings (eds), *Devolution, Law Making and the Constitution* (Exeter, Imprint, 2005) p 228.

[24]   J Smookler, 'Making a Difference? The Effectiveness of Pre-Legislative Scrutiny' [2006] *Parliamentary Affairs* 522–35; *The Briefing Paper Issues in Law Making, Number 5: Pre-Legislative Scrutiny* (Hansard Society, 2004).

may be put forward and a vote will take place at the end of the debate. While MPs have an opportunity during the debate to criticise the Bill, it should be recognised that it is extremely unusual for a government with a majority in the House of Commons to lose a vote on a division following the second reading. Defeat on a major platform of a government's legislative programme might result in a vote of confidence. If the government were to lose such a vote, the Prime Minister would be under a constitutional obligation to ask the sovereign for a dissolution of Parliament, prompting an immediate election. The government side will be made aware by the party whips at the time of the vote of the consequences. As we saw earlier over the passing of the Bill incorporating the Maastricht Treaty, the prospect of defeat almost invariably leads to a win for the government side.

After a Bill has surmounted the hurdle of being approved by a vote of the whole House, it moves on to the committee stage. This is when the Bill is normally considered by a standing committee, although Bills of major constitutional importance (eg European Committees Bill 1972) are considered by a committee of the whole House. There is a different emphasis at this point, as the standing committee concentrates on examining the provisions in much greater detail, clause by clause. A standing committee comprises between 16 and 50 members, and the parties are represented on the committee according to their strength in the House of Commons. As a result, the government (assuming it has a majority in the Commons) is guaranteed a majority on the committee. It is also relevant to mention that the whips (who are the party managers) decide on the MPs that will serve on these committees. Members who tow the party line will be favoured, and those who tend to be independently minded will be kept off these committees. This has a significant impact on the approach of standing committees, as the whips are prepared to use their influence to keep the proposals of the government intact in situations where there is opposition to a Bill, and where amendments are likely to be suggested by the committee but resisted by the government. There are occasions when committees may be able to persuade a minister to change or reconsider parts of a Bill, but it is clear that standing committees have limited success in securing modifications from the government. Of course, the opposition may simply use the committee as a platform to present its alternative view and to inconvenience ministers.

The effectiveness of standing committees has been criticised for reasons other than the tendency towards partisanship just alluded to. Unlike the 'subject' committees that perform this function in the Scottish Parliament, standing committees are non-specialist, in the sense that MPs assigned to standing committees are not required to have any special interest or expert knowledge of the subject matter of the legislation. Moreover, standing committees are not equipped with support staff able to undertake research or to provide the committee with advice. These are serious deficiencies, if it is accepted that the prime role of such committees is to improve the quality of the measure in question. This can be done only by drawing attention to potential weaknesses and by making carefully considered alternative suggestions. Under present procedures many clauses of proposed legislation may not be scrutinised at all by standing committees.[25] With reference to the successful operation of Australian and New Zealand models, it has been suggested that the quality of legislative scrutiny could be improved by the systematic application of check-lists and standards, which would flag up issues such as: sub-delegation, Henry VIII clauses, retrospective effect, human rights implications, and so on.[26]

The report stage follows the committee stage and this is when the amended Bill is brought before the whole House. It is still possible for addi-tional amendments to be made by ministers and for the opposition to suggest amendments. After the completion of the report stage, the Bill receives its third reading. At this point it is still possible to make verbal amendments. There can be short debates at the third reading stage, and the opposition can oppose the Bill by forcing a vote.

After a Bill has successfully negotiated its passage through one House, it is sent to the other where it passes through the same stages. The procedures for the consideration of Bills in the House of Lords are broadly similar to those in the Commons. The committee stage of legislation is different, as in the Lords it will be considered by the whole House. One of the main arguments for retaining a second chamber has been because of the performance of the House of Lords as a revising body for legislation. There are several reasons for this. The life peers, who are, in the main, the working members of the House of Lords, include leading members of the community and politicians. Although many may be past the peak of their careers, these peers will have specialist expertise and, in the case of politicians, useful experience of Parliament and government gained prior to their 'elevation' to the House of Lords. In addition, the House of Lords has more time to devote to detailed consideration of legislation. This element is especially important, as the pro-cedural devices to curtail discussion and debate do not apply in the same way in the Upper House. Perhaps the biggest advantage over the Commons is that the party machine, operating through the whips, is much less effective in the Lords. Peers are more independently minded because failure to support the party line will not effect career prospects. The members are appointed for life, and thus have no election looming over the horizon, and the composi-

[25] D Oliver, *Constitutional Reform in the United Kingdom* (Oxford, Oxford University Press, 2003) p 177.

[26] D Oliver, 'Improving the Scrutiny of Bills: The Case for Standards and Checklists' [2006] *PL* 219–47 at 241.

tion of the Lords is no longer skewed towards one party, as it used to be. The upshot is that since the abolition of most hereditary peers in 1999 the government suffers defeats in the House of Lords with increasing regularity (300 plus times since 1999), and legislation will frequently be amended during its passage through the House of Lords.[27] If this occurs, the amended Bill returns to the Commons, where the Bill may be accepted by the Commons in its amended form. At this point negotiation is possible between the two Houses over the final form of the Bill. The Commons may simply reject the amendments and return the Bill to the House of Lords for approval. If the House of Lords is unwilling to accept the Bill, it has the option of invoking its powers under the Parliament Acts 1911 and 1949 which will delay the legislation for one year. The power is hardly ever used.[28] The rarity of the application of the Parliament Act is mainly because of a convention ('the Salisbury Convention') that the House of Lords will not block legislation that is introduced as part of an election manifesto commitment. However, there are occasions when government Bills are substantially amended through the intervention of the House of Lords.[29]

It will be apparent that sufficient time needs to be allocated to legislation for Parliament to adequately perform its function as a revising body. For instance, standing committees should be given an opportunity to turn their attention to all the important clauses of a Bill. There is an obvious tension which arises. This is because the government will be keen to expedite its legislative programme in order to ensure that as many of its Bills as possible are fitted into the parliamentary session, while the opposition, which will often be resistant to the character of the changes proposed in a government Bill, could use the revising process as a means of blocking its progress. A number of procedural rules are available to facilitate the passage of legislation and these tend to operate in favour of the government. The *closure* shortens debate by allowing a vote to be taken but this requires the support of 100 members to apply. The *guillotine* involves the allocation of a strict timetable for the debate of each part of the Bill. This agreement may mean that some clauses are not discussed at all. The *kangaroo* at report stage enables only specified clauses to be selected for discussion. The application of these procedures depends on co-operation between government and opposition.

The requirement of maintaining a majority in Parliament is a feature of the parliamentary system which the United Kingdom shares with Italy but, of

---

[27] R Whitaker, 'Ping Pong and Policy Influence: Relations Between the Lords and Commons, 2005–6' [2006] *Parliamentary Affairs* 536–45.
[28] The last occasion was in regard to the Hunting Act 2004. See the discussion in ch 3 of *Jackson v A-G* [2005] UKHL 56.
[29] For example, the Identity Cards Act 2006. See Whitaker, above n 27, at 540.

course, the United States has an altogether different system. A President can and often does have a hostile majority in Congress (eg the Democrats were in control of both Houses following the mid-term elections in November 2006). The struggle by a President to get legislation through Congress may result in gridlock but, although this might have a bearing on the effectiveness of the Federal government, it does not threaten the continuance of the government in office.

PRIVATE MEMBERS' BILLS AND PRIVATE BILLS

Backbench MPs have limited opportunities to introduce legislation on their own initiative. There is an annual ballot for gaining a place high up in the queue. These Bills (private Members' Bills) undergo a similar procedure to government legislation but any such proposals depend upon first having 100 sympathetic members to get through the second reading stage and the government allocating sufficient time for the Bill to pass through Parliament. This is the case even when the measure has considerable support, for example banning foxhunting; without time from the government, the measure will be likely to fail.

Unlike public Bills and private Members' Bills, private Bills are introduced to grant benefits or impose obligations on a specifically defined class of persons or to a particular private company or public body. Equally, private Bills may be used to authorise specific works or activities in a particular area. For example, the Channel Tunnel rail link between the Kent coast and central London was made possible by virtue of a private Bill. These measures are subject to a somewhat different procedure in Parliament to enable objections to be heard, but they must pass through both Houses and receive the royal assent.

PARLIAMENTARY SCRUTINY OF DELEGATED LEGISLATION

The pressure on parliamentary time has given rise to an increasing trend towards the delegation of power to the executive. The use of skeleton legislation which allows ministers and their officials to draw up sub-rules has become widespread as a means of dealing with technical detail. The cumulative effect has been to give more broad-based powers to ministers and to officials. One example that illustrated the trend towards giving very widely drawn powers, so-called 'Henry VIII clauses', can be found in the Deregulation and Contracting Out Act 1994, which allows the minister responsible to: 'repeal or amend any Act which authorises or requires the imposition of a burden on any trade, business or profession.' Even more extreme, the Legislative and Regulatory Reform Bill which went before Parliament 2005/06 proposed in its original form to give ministers powers to alter *any* law passed by Parliament (This clause was modified following strong objections). The volume of delegated legislation, and the powers conferred as a consequence, has contributed to a discernible shift in the balance of power from the legislature to the executive. The procedures in Parliament for scrutiny are inadequate.[30] Delegated legislation is published and laid before Parliament before it is introduced, but most of these measures will automatically come into effect after 40 days, unless a challenge is made. The parliamentary Joint Committee on Statutory Instruments can bring to the attention of Parliament measures over which it has concern but it does not have any power to challenge such measures. The ease with which delegated rules can be introduced further illustrates the degree of executive dominance over Parliament.

PART V: PARLIAMENT AS WATCHDOG

In this section of the chapter we will evaluate the oversight function of Parliament. At this point we will discuss the mechanisms and procedures that have been formulated to undertake this crucial task and assess their effectiveness. It is worth considering as the discussion proceeds whether Parliament's main function is really as a legislative body or as a body which effectively scrutinises the government.

PARLIAMENTARY QUESTIONS

It has already been mentioned that parliamentary questions provide an important opportunity for individual members to raise matters on behalf of constituents. Backbenchers have a chance to interrogate the executive by framing oral questions that are directed at ministers. Ministers take turns in providing answers on most weekdays, as does the Prime Minister on Wednesdays for half an hour. Such probing can potentially be a source of deep embarrassment to the government. For example, the questioning of Margaret Thatcher by a Labour MP over the sinking of the Argentinian warship, the *General Belgrano*, during the Falklands conflict, revealed that the vessel was in fact heading away from the British forces, not towards them, as Parliament had previously been led to believe. There are important limitations, however, that reduce the ability of

---

[30] G Ganz, 'Delegated Legislation: A Necessary Evil or A Constitutional Outrage' in P Leyland and T Woods (eds), *Administrative Law Facing the Future: Old Constraints and New Horizons* (London, Blackstone, 1997) p 80ff.

MPs adequately to fulfil their ostensible function of holding the executive to account at question time. First, the balloting procedure which determines whether a question is chosen for oral reply is determined by luck and not according to the gravity or relevance of the matter raised. Second, only limited time is available, with ministers answering questions for around 60 minutes each day except Fridays. Third, questions are limited to a narrow departmental remit. Fourth, compared to MPs who may rely on government sources for information related to questions, ministers are at an advantage in they are supported by civil servants and may be able to choose whether to release sensitive information into the public domain.

DEPARTMENTAL SELECT COMMITTEES

Departmental select committees were established in 1979 to oversee the work of the major government departments. There were originally 14 of these committees but there are now 18. The committees consist of between 11 and 17 MPs, with the parties represented according to their relative strength in the House of Commons, which means that the governing party will have a majority on the committee. In fact, select committees should be regarded as an important extension of ministerial responsibility, helping to keep track of what ministers do with their responsibility for their departments and other agencies. Unlike the courts, which deal with *ultra vires* executive action or the abuse of power, the committees are at an advantage in that they can have an informal influence on the formative stage of policy-making, examining at their discretion political, social, and economic issues as they arise.

The departmental select committees have been compared to those within the US system. However, there are substantial differences in their structure and effectiveness. With regard to structure, a central characteristic of the separation of powers under the US constitution is the way the legislature keeps check on the executive by means of Congressional committees. Although their wider reputation has been based on a number of scandals that have been revealed by special investigations (the most notable of all being Watergate in 1973/4), the committees undertake, on a day-to-day basis, the more routine tasks of initiating policy and scrutinising the executive, with their specific terms of reference being administration, policy, and expenditure. In fact, the Congressional committees are powerful bodies which are generously funded and equipped with full-time staff. They have formidable powers to summon before them papers or persons, including Secretaries of State (ministers) and top civil service officials and advisers. The Scottish Parliament and Welsh Assembly have introduced subject committees which combine the role of standing and select committees. The declared objective is for specialisation to achieve a degree of expertise in a particular area. This also addresses a criticism of the departmental committees working outside the parliamentary legislative process.

In the UK system, Parliament (within the existing framework of the Westminster model) has always assumed the crucial role of acting as a formal check on the executive It became apparent to many MPs in the 1970s that to perform this task more effectively the place of select committees had to be revised and their inquisitorial powers needed to be strengthened. The new departmental committees were to have a clear function, that being to shadow all the main departments of state, with the aim of examining 'expenditure, administration, and policy. To assist in their investigative role these committees have limited capacity to employ a staff of expert advisers, mainly on a part-time basis. Serving on these committees provides backbench MPs with an opportunity to be involved in the policy process. These committees also promote a degree of co-operation between MPs of all parties who may identify with the broad objectives of executive accountability. On the other hand, it might be argued that a more adversarial approach would provide greater accountability.

Departmental Select Committees, July 2006

Name of committee	*Government department*	*Maximum no of MPs*	*Quorum*
Communities and Local Government	Dept for Communities and Local Government	11	3
Constitutional Affairs	Dept of Constitutional Affairs	11	3
Culture, Media & Sport	Dept for Culture, Media and Sport	11	3
Defence	Ministry of Defence	11	3
Education and Skills	Dept for Education and Skills	11	3
Environment, Food and Rural Affairs	Dept of the Environment, Food and Rural Affairs	17	5
Foreign Affairs	Foreign and Commonwealth Office	12	3
Health	Dept of Health	11	3
Home Affairs	Home Office; Lord Chancellor's Dept	11	3
International Development	Dept for International Development	11	3
Northern Ireland Affairs,	Northern Ireland Office;	13	4
Science and Technology	Office of Science and Technology	11	3
Scottish Affairs	Scottish Office	11	3
Trade and Industry	Dept of Trade and Industry	11	3
Transport	Department of Transport	11	3
Treasury	Treasury, Board of Inland Revenue, Customs & Excise	11	3
Welsh Affairs	Welsh Office	11	3
Work and Pensions	Dept for Work and Pensions	11	3

Since 1979, with each new Parliament following a general election, the departmental select committees have been reconstituted. Each is chaired by a member from one of the two largest parties, usually the government party. The committee then decides on appropriate subjects for scrutiny, although it should be noted that this very selectivity can be a source of weakness as well as strength. These subjects will include major matters of policy as well as more detailed administrative questions. It will be immediately apparent that the departmental select committees have a crucial advantage in comparison to standing committees, in that they have the means to conduct more in-depth inquisitorial investigations which can give them considerable information not available to the mass of individual MPs, rather than being dependent, as these are, on asking particular questions and relying on the co-operation and goodwill of ministers and officials. This information will include not simply evidence before the committee, but also written submissions, departmental (official) briefs, visits (at home and abroad), informal meetings with non-parliamentarians, etc. The published reports of the departmental select committees, and their accompanying volumes of memoranda, provide MPs with a countervailing source of information to that of ministers and the executive departments, and in that sense the committees are of growing importance in holding ministers to account and in questioning civil servants.

Ministers and senior civil servants appear regularly before the department select committees. However, ministers (and MPs and peers) can refuse to attend (unless charged with contempt of Parliament and required by a vote of the House of Commons to do so). For example, the junior minister for agriculture, refused at first to appear before an inquiry into salmonella in eggs by the Agriculture Select Committee in 1988. Under previous practice ministers were able to refuse to allow officials to appear before the committees. This issue arose in 1992, when the Select Committee on Trade and Industry wished to question two retired named officials in the Ministry of Defence regarding matters arising from the Scott Inquiry concerning information they had about aspects of the controversy surrounding Matrix Churchill and the supergun affair. The Cabinet Office guidance to civil servants who are summoned to appear before these committees was revised following the Scott Report (for further discussion, see chapter six). These guidelines encourage officials to be helpful but specifically rule out: disclosing advice given to ministers or inter-departmental exchanges on policy issues; disclosing the level at which decisions were taken; and discussing the work of Cabinet committees or their decisions. Furthermore, civil servants are not permitted to express their own views on matters of policy. This supports the view that policy emanates from the politicians and not from civil servants. To some extent limitations as to time and resources result in a restricted focus of attention and, in consequence, an invariably selective impact on the issues of the day. Another shortcoming is that the reports of the departmental committees are not debated by the House of Commons as a matter of course.

It is important to recognise that the government is in a powerful position in regard to departmental select committees. This is mainly because it exercises control over the information that is made available. The debate surrounding a freedom of information Act was partly concerned with the test which would be used to determine whether information is released into the public domain. The original 'substantial harm' test that appeared in the 'Right to Know' White Paper[31] was diluted to a simple harm test included in the Freedom of Information Act 2000. The Information Commissioner now has an important role in deciding how the guidelines are applied.

Departmental select committees were intended to be more independent than standing committees. This position was to be achieved by establishing a committee of selection to nominate members thus minimising the influence of the party whips. However, this situation did not long survive the partisanship that dominates the way Parliament operates, and the whips have been regularly consulted on the membership of these committees. Indeed, government whips sought to remove the chairs of the Transport Committee and the Foreign Affairs Committee after the 2001 general election. Both of these chairs had earned a reputation for independence and presided over committees that had made reports that were critical of aspects of government policy. However, the failure to renominate these widely respected MPs caused a minor rebellion on the backbenches and their re-appointment was eventually confirmed. More recently, however, following the recommendations of the Modernisation Committee in its second report 2001/02, the House of Commons rejected the proposal to remove the appointments to committees from the control of the whips. In 2003 the House of Commons decided that the chairs of the departmental select committees should receive an additional salary of £12,500 pa in recognition of the additional workload the job entails. It was envisaged that chairing these important committees could provide an alternative career structure for MPs not reaching the front ranks of government or opposition.

The Modernisation Committee of the House of Commons has recommended that departmental select committees should have a much extended role and perform all of the following tasks. consider major policy initiatives; consider government responses to major emerging issues; propose changes where evidence persuades the committee that recent policy requires amendment; conduct pre-legislative scrutiny of Bills; examine and report on main

---

[31] *Your Right to Know*, Cm 3818, 1997.

estimates, annual expenditure plans, and annual resource accounts; monitor performance against targets in the public service agreements; take evidence from each responsible departmental minister at least annually; take evidence from independent regulators and inspectorates; consider the reports of Executive Agencies; consider major appointments made by a Secretary of State; examine treaties within their subject areas.[32]

These committees tend to work more effectively at times when there is a narrow government majority, as this encourages a greater degree of inter-party co-operation. For example, in 1993 at a time when the Conservative government of John Major had a majority of only 21 seats the Trade and Industry Select Committee issued a critical report on the government's policy in relation to the closure of coal mines, and in 1995 the Defence Select Committee reported unfavourably on the government's handling of the effects of 'Gulf War syndrome' in 1995. On other occasions the committees have been criticised for tending to divide along party lines over controversial matters which involve direct criticism of the government and which might attract adverse publicity. For example, the Select Committee for Culture, Media and Sport repeatedly investigated plans for the Millennium Dome and the Millennium celebrations which involved the abuse of large amounts of public funds and inefficient management of the project, but, after intervention from the party whips, the censure of the government was toned down, so that the published reports referred to 'constructive' criticism of the government's scheme.[33]

PUBLIC ACCOUNTS COMMITTEE AND NATIONAL AUDIT OFFICE

The Public Accounts Committee (PAC) is one of the oldest and most prestigious parliamentary committees. Despite the fact that the scope of government was then much more limited than is now the case, WE Gladstone, as Chancellor of the Exchequer, recognised the need to provide a mechanism of accountability for public expenditure. The PAC was first created in 1861, while the office of Comptroller and Auditor General (described below) followed in 1866. In essence, this framework has survived to the present day.[34] The House of Commons exercises some degree of control over government

---

[32] Modernisation Committee, *First Report, Select Committees,* HC 224–1, 2001/02.

[33] For example, see Select Committee for Culture, Media and Sport, *Back to the Dome, Third Report,* HC 21–1, 1998/99.

[34] See J McEldowney, 'The Control of Public Expenditure' in J Jowell and D Oliver (eds), *The Changing Constitution,* 5th edn (Oxford, Oxford University Press, 2004) p 393ff.

finance through the PAC. The amount of government spending is over £350 billion per annum. The PAC, more than most other parliamentary committees, operates in a less-partisan, non party-political way and consists of 15 MPs, the chair being a senior member of the opposition, usually with experience as a Treasury minister. The PAC's remit is limited to the audited accounts of government departments. Ministers and departmental accounting officers (usually the senior civil servant, called a permanent secretary) appear before the PAC to be questioned, even interrogated, on issues arising from the annual audit of departmental accounts. Further, the introduction of television cameras in the House of Commons has brought these proceedings, and the important issues examined, to the wider public. Reports prepared by the PAC each year (30–40 in number) are always debated annually by the House of Commons. The government will be expected to respond to any criticisms made by taking any necessary remedial action.

The PAC is the only parliamentary committee which has comprehensive administrative support in the form of the National Audit Office (NAO), which is headed by the Comptroller and Auditor General (C & AG) (Sir John Bourn at the time of writing).[35] The Comptroller used to be appointed by the government of the day, but the National Audit Act 1983 modified his or her status and that of the staff (around 750), establishing the post as an officer of the House of Commons. The method of appointment now is by means of a commission, of which the Prime Minister and the chair of the PAC are both members. This reinforces the element of independence in the system of accountability. The point to note is that the Comptroller and Auditor General and the National Audit Office are independent of government, and certify the accounts of all government departments and a wide range of other public sector bodies. Most of the PAC's work consists in examining the value for money (VFM) reports undertaken by the NAO, which are intended to measure economy, efficiency and effectiveness of departments and other bodies in the way they have used their resources. The NAO works closely with the PAC, examining the effectiveness with which governmental bodies implement their assigned policy goals. Reports are based on the annual audit of all government departments. They are passed to the PAC where the evidence contained therein can be used effectively as a tool with which to probe into the details of expenditure, and this gives the reports of the PAC added authority.

---

[35] The National Audit Office has a website which publishes its reports: http://www.open. gov. uk/nao/pn.htm.

PAC and NAO: Investigations and Reports

A widely publicised example concerned serious delays that occurred in issuing passports in 1999. This problem was caused by the introduction of a new computer system. The backlog led to much anxiety and inconvenience for members of the public who had booked their summer holidays abroad. By June, the Passport Agency had around 565,000 applications awaiting processing and applications were taking on average 50 days. The NAO immediately reported to Parliament, and the Committee of Public Accounts took evidence on its report in November 1999. The report points out that the Agency's financial objectives were to recover, via the passport fee, the full cost of passport services and it recorded that the unit cost to the taxpayer of producing a passport would rise, in the absence of other changes. The NAO went on to estimate the cost of the additional measures taken by the Passport Agency to deal with the failures to be around £12.6 million. The figure included £6 million for additional staffing. In addition, at the time of the report £161,000 in compensation had already been paid to members of the public for missed travel and other expenses (including the purchase of umbrellas for members of the public waiting in the queue for emergency passports). The report has a strongly practical application and identifies key lessons that should be learned from such an episode. In particular, it identifies a need: (i) for proper testing of new systems before committing to live operation, in particular for staff to learn and work the system; (ii) to have realistic contingency plans in place; and (iii) when service delivery is threatened, to have the capability to keep the public well informed.[36] There have been numerous instances of strongly critical investigations both by the NAO and the PAC. To take a recent example, in 2005 the PAC investigated the Department for Work and Pensions, concentrating on fraud and error in the benefits system amounting to £3 billion. The PAC recommended simplification of the benefits system, introduction of benchmarking, and measuring performance against other comparable organisations.[37]

Although the PAC and the NAO have a crucial part to play in the process of scrutiny, they are concerned only with past expenditure, that is, on funds that have already been allocated. Essentially, this auditing work, although very important, is Parliament looking over its shoulder at items of expendi-

[36] National Audit Office, *United Kingdom Passport Agency: The Passport Delays of Summer 1999*, HC 812, 1998/99.

[37] Public Accounts Committee, *Fourth Report: Fraud and Error in Benefit Expenditure*, HC 411, 2005/06.

ture with a paramount concern for the efficient and economical use of public money. However, the auditing process is relatively rigorous when compared with the well-known deficiencies in Parliament's general control of proposed expenditure.[38]

THE PARLIAMENTARY OMBUDSMAN

The Parliamentary Ombudsman (PO) was introduced by the Parliamentary Commissioner Act of 1967 to plug a manifest gap in dealing with grievances against officialdom. The main function of the PO is to investigate cases of maladministration (not actually defined in the Act) referred to him or her by MPs, but no actual power to grant a remedy is given to the PO. Nevertheless, in most cases the recommendations of the PO are followed by the department or public body concerned. The PO has formidable investigatory powers and a staff to assist with inquiries. The remit of the PO, first set out in Schedules 1 and 2 to the 1967 Act (later extended by the Parliamentary and Health Services Commissioners Act 1987), applies to most government and quasi-governmental bodies. The filtering of complaints through MPs was insisted upon during the passage of the original bill in order that the role of backbench MPs would not be usurped, and it is certainly true that MPs continue to pursue matters against government departments on behalf of their constituents and often proceed more quickly than the formal approach of the PO. Moreover, this lack of direct access has been seen by many critics as a weakness. There have been high profile investigations by the PO which have resulted in awards of compensation in line with the PO's recommendations, for example in regard to losses suffered by householders through the building of the Channel Tunnel rail link. The reports of the PO are submitted to the Public Administration Select Committee of the House of Commons and are also laid before the House.[39]

CONCLUSION

The central question for us has been to consider how far Parliament contributes to a system of 'representative and responsible' government. The

---

[38] See, eg, J McEldowney, above n 34, at p 381ff, who illustrates this point with reference to the lack of control over the contingencies fund.

[39] 'The Ombudsman in Question: the Ombudsman's report on pensions and its constitutional implications', HC 1081, 2006.

executive dominance of Parliament remains the most conspicuous feature of the legislative process. According to Bagehot this was the 'efficient secret' of the constitution.[40] Even when there is determined opposition, as was the case with a recent Social Security Act, it is very unusual for the government not to get a measure passed by Parliament. The dominance of the government is a particular cause of concern when the opposition within Parliament is weak. In fact an important reason for having a reformed second chamber with some legitimacy is to provide some counter to the dominant position of a government with a substantial majority in the House of Commons.

On the positive side, the PAC and NAO have improved their performance as examiners of government expenditure. We have seen in this chapter that departmental select committees perform an important role, but they do so unsystematically and not entirely adequately. Professor Tomkins has sought to argue that 'we should abandon the notion that Parliament is principally a legislator. We should instead see Parliament as a scrutineer, or as a regulator, of government.'[41] It is difficult to sustain such a view for as long as Parliament continues to function in its law-making capacity by approving a high volume of legislation each year. Indeed, Parliament should be criticised for neglecting to update its procedures sufficiently in order to secure improvements in the methods it employs for scrutinising legislation.[42] More response is needed to the common complaint from individuals and organisations that it is difficult to inform and influence the policy-making process. To date, there have only been experiments with a two-year legislative programme to allow publication, and pre-legislative scrutiny of draft Bills. Furthermore, departmental select committees still do not routinely engage in post-legislative scrutiny by monitoring legislation after it comes into force.[43] Finally, it will be apparent from chapter nine that devolution has introduced some improved methods for delivering accountability within Scotland, Wales, and Northern Ireland (eg subject committees), which might be transferable to the Westminster Parliament.

---

[40] W Bagehot, *The English Constitution* (London, Fontana, 1963) p 65.

[41] See A Tomkins, 'What is Parliament For?' in N Bamforth and P Leyland, *Public Law in a Multi-Layered Constitution* (Oxford, Hart Publishing, 2003) p 55.

[42] M Ryle, 'House of Commons Procedures' in R Blackburn and R Plant (eds), *Constitutional Reform* (London, Longman, 1999) p 110.

[43] *First Report of the Select Committee on the Modernisation of the House of Commons*

FURTHER READING

Brazier R, *Constitutional Practice*, 3rd edn (Oxford, Oxford University Press, 1999), chs 10 and 11.

Kennon A and Blackburn R, *Griffith and Ryle on Parliament: Functions, Practice, and Procedures*, 2nd edn (London, Sweet and Maxwell, 2003).

Leopold P, 'Free Speech in Parliament and the Courts' (1995) 15 *Legal Studies* 204.

Leopold P, 'Standards of Conduct in Public Life' in J Jowell and D Oliver (eds), *The Changing Constitution*, 5th edn (Oxford, Oxford University Press, 2004).

McEldowney J, 'The Control of Public Expenditure' in J Jowell and D Oliver (eds), *The Changing Constitution,* 5th edn (Oxford, Oxford University Press, 2004).

Munro C, *Studies in Constitutional Law*, 2nd edn (London, Butterworths, 1999).

Oliver D, 'The Modernization of the United Kingdom Parliament' in J Jowell and Oliver D (eds), *The Changing Constitution*, 5th edn (Oxford, Oxford University Press, 2004).

Oliver D, *Constitutional Reform in the UK* (Oxford, Oxford University Press, 2003).

Oliver D, 'Improving the Scrutiny of Bills: The Case for Standards and Checklists' [2006] *PL* 219.

Russell M, *Reforming the House of Lords, Lessons from Overseas* (Oxford, Oxford University Press, 2000).

Ryle M, 'House of Commons Procedures' in R Blackburn and R Plant (eds), *Constitutional Reform* (London, Longman, 1999).

Tomkins A, *The Constitution after Scott: Government Unwrapped* (Oxford, Oxford University Press, 1998).

Tomkins A, 'What is Parliament for?' in N Bamforth and P Leyland, *Public Law in a Multi-Layered Constitution* (Oxford, Hart Publishing, 2003).

Walters R, 'The House of Lords' in V Bogdanor (ed) *The British Constitution in the Twentieth Century* (Oxford, Oxford University Press, 2003).

Modernising Parliament: Reforming the House of Lords, Cm 4184, 1999).

Report of the Jenkins Commission on the Voting System, Cm 4090, 1998).

6

Government and Executive

Introduction – The Prime Minister – The Prime Minister and the Cabinet – The Prime Minister: Policy Formation and Implementation – Prime Minister's Press Office and Government 'Spin' –Shaping Government Departments – Political Accountability and Individual Ministerial Responsibility – Ministerial Responsibility: Answerability or Resignation – The Scott Report – Ministerial Responsibility and the Press – The Civil Service – New Public Management and Executive Accountability – A Civil Service Act for the UK – Government Openness and the Freedom of Information Act 2000 – E-government Revolution – Conclusion

INTRODUCTION

THIS CHAPTER FOCUSES on the constitution in respect to the conduct of central government in the United Kingdom. It starts at the pinnacle of government by looking at the role of the Prime Minister and the Cabinet, before going on to consider the governmental mechanisms for the implementation of policy in the form of the civil service, and the constitutional significance of the Freedom of Information Act 2000. As we proceed with this discussion, and observe the way in which power is exercised, it is worth remembering the term 'elective dictatorship': this is because the principle concern is to assess what constitutional limits, safeguards, and democratic controls are placed on the Prime Minister, Cabinet, and civil service in the way they perform their functions. In terms of the exercise of constitutional power, it is helpful to view the UK political system as hierarchical, with the Prime Minister, and the Office at 10 Downing Street, at the apex of a triangle. At the next level we find the Cabinet Office, the departments of state, and then junior ministers responsible for particular policy domains. In turn, the entire machinery of government relies on a permanent civil service, which is, itself, hierarchical in structure.

THE PRIME MINISTER

Not only does the holder of prime ministerial office head the government, represent the nation, and lead the largest political party, but the Prime Minister is responsible for taking many decisions that determine domestic policy and the conduct of foreign affairs and for making an enormous range of appointments (in many cases these are rubber-stamped by the monarch). The Prime Minister is able to determine the date of a general election within the five-year time frame set out by the Parliament Act 1911.

While it is widely recognised that a UK Prime Minister[1] has wide-ranging powers at his or her disposal, it is also clear that there is considerable scope to pursue a personal style of leadership. Some Prime Ministers, for example, John Major, favoured a more collegiate approach (a style referred to as *primus inter pares*) while others such as Margaret Thatcher and Tony Blair mould the office around their own personality, and they have become known for a more presidential style of leadership (virtually an *elected monarch*). If we look back to trace the constitutional derivation of the post it will be apparent that the office of Prime Minister is not defined under the constitution or any Act of Parliament, and, in fact, it originates from the early eighteenth century, when the sovereign found it convenient to rely on a small coterie of ministers. Authority from among them was assumed by a leading political figure. Sir Robert Walpole, generally acknowledged as the first Prime Minister, held the office of First Lord of the Treasury. Here was a politician who could be entrusted with the monopolisation of power and patronage, but to hold the position of head of government, the incumbent needed to have the confidence of the sovereign, and also to have the full support of Parliament.[2] In the contemporary constitution it is the support of Parliament, or more precisely the elected House of Commons, that is crucial. After a general election the leader of the political party with a majority in the House of Commons will be called upon by the sovereign to form a government, and he or she will automatically become Prime Minister. (The procedure if no party has a majority is more complicated. It involves the intervention of the Queen and is briefly discussed in chapter four.)

---

[1] P Hennessey, *The Prime Minister: The Office and its Holders since 1945* (London, Penguin, 2001).
[2] R Crossman, 'Introduction' in W Bagehot, *The English Constitution* (London, Fontana, 1963) pp 20–22.

Once confirmed in office by the monarch, a Prime Minister is responsible for forming the government. The only limits on the selections dictated by convention are that all ministers must be members of Parliament and that the Prime Minister and the Chancellor of the Exchequer must be members of the House of Commons. In practice, however, there may be strong political constraints that limit the scope of a Prime Minister's choices. For example, Prime Minister Tony Blair could not easily have denied Gordon Brown a major government post, given his prominent position in the parliamentary Labour party. A Prime Minister can also dismiss ministers and reconstitute the government at any time by reshuffling the pack. On one famous occasion, referred to as the 'night of the long knives', Harold Macmillan dispensed with seven cabinet ministers at one stroke.[3] The Home Secretary was sacked in an extensive re-allocation of senior ministerial positions by Tony Blair following the poor performance of the Labour Party in local government elections in May 2006.

Many of the powers that the Prime Minister now enjoys are prerogative powers which were formerly the personal prerogatives of the Sovereign. For example, this includes extensive powers of patronage and the right to negotiate treaties with other nations. Some appointments, such as appointments to the government, archbishops and bishops, and other honours, are entirely in the gift of the Prime Minister, while others are merely confirmed by the Prime Minister. These include life peerages,[4] appointments of the most senior civil servants, and the highest judicial appointments (see chapter four).

As head of the government, the Prime Minister represents the nation on the international stage and at EU summits. In this capacity the UK Prime Minister often takes a leading role, together with the Foreign Office, when entering into treaty negotiations with other nations.

THE PRIME MINISTER AND THE CABINET

The Cabinet might appear to be the focal point of government decision-making. It comprises the group of senior ministers appointed by the Prime Minister to head the main government department and has between 22 and 24 members. According to Bagehot, it was a combining committee: 'a hyphen which joins, a buckle which fosters, the legislative part of the State to the executive part of the State. In its origins it belongs to the one, in its

---

[3] A Sampson, *Macmillan: A Study in Ambiguity* (London, Penguin, 1967) ch 13, 'The Purge'.

[4] Recommendations for life peerages are now first made by the House of Lords Appointments Commission and approved by the Prime Minister.

functions it belongs to the other.'[5] Major policy issues are often discussed at Cabinet, and conflicts between departments may be finally resolved over the Cabinet table, but key decisions may be taken in one of the many Cabinet committees which specialise in the various policy areas. It is generally recognised that there is a growing degree of dominance over the Cabinet by the Prime Minister. He or she is able to determine the composition and who chairs these committees.[6] The Prime Minister will preside over the most important committees and is able to set the agenda for Cabinet meetings. This means that decisions of great importance may be reached by Cabinet committee and effectively kept within the Prime Minister's inner circle of associates and advisers without providing an opportunity for discussion by the Cabinet. Examples of this have included the decision by the Attlee government (1945–51) to test Britain's atomic bomb, and, much more recently, in 1997, the decision to change the management of financial policy by granting the Bank of England the power to set interest rates independently of government.

The Prime Minister has a predominant role over the conduct of government, and this tended to increase during the course of the twentieth century. The fact that a Prime Minister has sole charge over appointing and dismissing ministers obviously means that he or she wields enormous power over the Cabinet and other ministers. A minister who fails to perform as expected, or who falls out of line, can be summarily dispensed with. For instance, Harriet Harman experienced difficulties with welfare reform and was replaced as Secretary of State for Social Security in the first reshuffle of the Labour government in June 1998. The Prime Minister has the capacity not only to change the complexion of the government by means of appointments that are made but also to remould the institutional structures of government departments to suit the direction of policy. Only the Prime Minister can call a Cabinet meeting.[7]

Collective Cabinet responsibility further contributes to this authority. This constitutional convention originates from the need for a Prime Minister to present the sovereign with unified advice from the government on matters of policy. The convention allows for the fact that the decision-making process will be controversial, with ministers frequently expressing divergent views on any issue brought to Cabinet for final decision. The convention demands confidentiality as any dissenting opinions are expressed privately. At the end of the discussion, after a free and frank exchange has taken place, the Prime

---

[5] W Bagehot, *The English Constitution* (London, Fontana, 1963) p 68.
[6] For a full list of Cabinet committtees, see: http://www.cabinetoffice.gov.uk/secretariats/ committees /index.asp.
[7] P Hennessey, *Whitehall*, 2nd edn (London, Pimlico, 2001) p 306ff.

Minister, who chairs the meeting, is responsible for identifying the feeling of the meeting and noting an agreed position. The convention of collective responsibility dictates that a member of the Cabinet who during the discussion voiced opposition to the view which is finally adopted must accept the decision. This requires him or her to vote and speak actively for the policy, or alternatively that minister should resign. As Secretary of State for Defence in 1986, Michael Heseltine was so annoyed, both by the decision not to support Westland, a British helicopter manufacturer, and by the way the decision was forced through Cabinet, that he resigned from Margaret Thatcher's government by walking out of Cabinet to brief waiting journalists.

The source of the Prime Minister's political authority derives from his or her place as party leader. All major political parties elect a leader with the assumption that, should the party be victorious at a general election by emerging with a majority of seats in the House of Commons, the leader will become the next Prime Minister. Once in office, the Prime Minister is in a position of enormous authority but the fall of Margaret Thatcher demonstrated that it is possible for even the most powerful of Prime Ministers to lose the support of the parliamentary party and be forced from office. A number of issues contributed to Margaret Thatcher's downfall after more than 11 years in Downing Street. For example, she had insisted upon the introduction of a new and highly unpopular local government tax, called the community charge or poll tax, against the advice of senior ministers. She was unable to reconcile the differences within her own party over Europe, and because of her own euroscepticism inflamed her critics. Most tellingly, her abrasive style of leadership led to numerous sackings and resignations, culminating in the unexpected departure of her deputy, Sir Geoffrey Howe. The political enemies on her own side, now on the backbenches, were eventually prepared to mount a challenge. Once it was clear from the result of an election among Conservative MPs for the party leadership, which had been forced by Michael Heseltine, that support from the parliamentary Conservative party was haemorrhaging, the huge authority and power that she had exercised for so long appeared to evaporate. This failure to win decisively on the first ballot made her resignation inevitable. In effect, the 'emperor' had been deposed without ever suffering defeat at a general election.[8]

The Prime Minister has a special position in relation to the operation of the intelligence services.[9] The Prime Minister is head of the intelligence and security services, with overall responsibility for security matters. In this sphere it is the Intelligence and Security Committee, established by the Intelligence

[8]   Hennessey, above n 1, p 432ff.
[9]   http://www.intelligence.gov.uk/.

Services Act 1994, which provides some parliamentary oversight over the three main organisations responsible for national security, namely: MI6, officially the Secret Intelligence Service (SIS); Government Communication Headquarters (GCHQ); and MI5, officially the Security Service.[10] The committee examines expenditure, administration, and policy within what has been termed the 'ring of secrecy'. The committee is appointed by the Prime Minister, after consultation with the Leader of the Opposition, is comprised of a cross-party membership of nine, taken from both the House of Commons and the House of Lords, and is required to report annually to the Prime Minister on its work. The introduction of some oversight mechanisms is a useful development, but it is difficult to assess accurately how effectively the committee, tribunal, and Security Services Commissioner perform their respective roles as their most valuable work relates to classified material, which is deliberately placed beyond the public gaze and, as we shall see later, such information is designated as an excluded category under the Freedom of Information Act 2000.[11]

THE PRIME MINISTER: POLICY FORMATION AND IMPLEMENTATION

The growth of the Prime Minister's Office at 10 Downing Street, with its own staff and with an increasingly high profile in co-ordinating the activities of government, has meant that a structure now exists for policy co-ordination. The capacity of a Prime Minister to drive the complex machinery of modern government from the top has increasingly depended on having in place an apparatus of administrative back-up. In the first place, the Cabinet Office emerged as the department with overall responsibility for supporting the work of the Cabinet. Its primary function was (and is) to provide secretarial support to the Cabinet, and to the network of Cabinet committees where much of the detailed work of the Cabinet is carried out across departments on key issues. In charge of the Cabinet Office, which is at the same time the civil service department, is the Cabinet Secretary. As head of the home civil service, he or she also has the task of working as a conduit between the government and the civil service more generally. For example, he or she must guarantee the impartiality of a permanent civil service. In another capacity, the Cabinet Office deals with public sector appointments and promotions

---

[10] http://www.mi5.gov.uk/output/Page7.html; http://www.mi6.gov.uk/output/Page79.html.

[11] See P Birkinshaw, *Freedom of Information: The Law, the Practice and the Ideal*, 3rd edn (London, Butterworths, 2001) chs 1, 3, and 6,

within the civil service. The Cabinet Office has overseen many of the public sector reforms which have been introduced in recent years. The Cabinet Secretary, as head of the civil service, presides over the Cabinet Office and from this position is responsible for upholding the integrity of the civil service. This includes overseeing the conduct of the civil service, civil service promotion, and public sector appointments.

During the course of the twentieth century the importance of the Cabinet Office and the Prime Minister's personal office in Downing Street greatly increased. In particular, the co-ordination of the activities of government was essential in both world wars (1914–18 and 1939–45). It should be remembered that in wartime the government comprised a national coalition made up of the most talented individuals from all parties, but the Prime Minister, assisted by a very small War Cabinet, was able to run the government.[12] Since the 1960s the staffing levels have expanded, and there have been repeated attempts to improve the structure and organisation to meet challenges as they have arisen. For example, inside Downing Street itself, the Central Policy Review Staff (CPRS) was introduced by Prime Minister Heath in 1971 under the direction of Lord Rothschild to provide advice from outside the civil service. Subsequently, Prime Ministers have stamped their mark on the way the Cabinet Office and 10 Downing Street are organised. For example, the CPRS was dispensed with by Margaret Thatcher, who decided to build up her own Policy Unit into what Hennessey describes as 'what has in effect [become] a proper Downing Street version of a French Prime Ministerial cabinet.'[13] This presented the opportunity for Margaret Thatcher to introduce her own gurus into Whitehall, including for example, the chief executive of Marks and Spencer, a merchant banker, and two professors of economics. The Policy Unit was formed into a group of experts that took a keen interest in many of the key policy areas of government, and it assumed a position to promote the main principles of Thatcherism throughout the government. This included the introduction of market principles and privatisation. (In a later section of this chapter we will discuss the impact of the 'Next Steps' initiative on the structure of the civil service.) Despite recognising the extensive powers apparently placed in the hands of the office holder, Mount rejects what he calls 'the alternative theory of prime-ministerial government' expounded by commentators such as Mackintosh and Crossman. For example, one barrier to be surmounted by the Prime Minister in exercising this power is a fiercely independent civil service which often provides incomplete briefing and

---

[12] See, eg, A Calder, *The People's War* (London, Panther, 1969) ch 3.
[13] Hennessey, above n 1, p 424.

advice, and then there are problems of communication and implementation which still have to be overcome before any policy is put into effect.[14]

The Prime Minister's Office, based at 10 Downing Street, is relatively small in terms of numbers, certainly when measured against the size of the Cabinet Office and the wider civil service, but it has assumed growing importance in the conduct of government.[15] In the main this has been in respect to giving advice on policy formation, in respect to overseeing the co-ordination and effective delivery of policy, and in respect to the communication of the government message through the Prime Minister's press office. The Prime Minister is assisted by a Chief of Staff. But Prime Ministers have tended to surround themselves with a select group of policy advisers reflecting their own ideological viewpoint. In turn, this trend has confirmed the growing importance of the organisation based at 10 Downing Street. There were 36 special advisers under the Conservative government of John Major, and this figure has escalated to 77 under the Labour government which first came to office in 1997.

Moreover, Tony Blair as Prime Minister has placed a strong emphasis on the effective delivery of policies in the public sector. To this end, the Strategy Unit was set up in 2002, bringing together the Performance and Innovation Unit (PIU), the Prime Minister's Forward Strategy Unit (FSU), and parts of the Centre for Management and Policy Studies (CMPS). The Strategy Unit is responsible for doing long-term strategic reviews of major areas of policy, and it helps to co-ordinate the activities of government by undertaking studies of cross-cutting policy issues, and by working with departments to promote strategic thinking and improve policy-making across Whitehall. The Unit undertakes investigations and issues regular reports which make practical recommendations. These are designed: to encourage stronger leadership from ministers and senior civil servants; to improve policy formulation and implementation; and to enhance the capacity for co-ordination across government.

The PIU, which was responsible for overseeing and facilitating the reform of public services, was renamed the Office of Public Service Reform (OPSR). In order to place this initiative under the direct supervision of the Prime Minister, the unit was moved from the Cabinet Office to 10 Downing Street after the 2001 general election. The OPSR disseminates a reform agenda based on best practice to all government departments. This is an approach tailored around the needs of the citizen, who is to be regarded as a customer,

---

[14] F Mount, *The British Constitution Now* (London, Mandarin, 1992) p 136ff.
[15] See A Seldon, 'The Cabinet System' in V Bogdanor (ed), *The British Constitution in the Twentieth Century* (Oxford, Oxford University Press, 2003).

and Charter Marks are awarded in recognition of excellent service delivery measured according to criteria set out by this unit.

The use of the internet to promote the government's message represents an important innovation. The citizen is drawn into a new style of participatory democracy based on a transformed relationship between the individual and the information superhighway, which also embraces government and local government. The Strategy Unit seeks to make government more open and accessible through its e-government strategy and UK online campaign, aiming to improve the online information provided by government.[16] The Strategy Unit, based in 10 Downing Street, has a leading role on issues which cut across government departments, including promoting information technology, which do not sit clearly in a single government department.

PRIME MINISTER'S PRESS OFFICE AND GOVERNMENT 'SPIN'

In order to present the government's position effectively the need for a press office has been recognised for many generations, but in recent years the role of the opinion-formers has changed and become much more important. In part, this can be seen as a response to the fact that information is now constantly circulated 24 hours a day, and is available from foreign sources, through the internet, and by satellite. It has become increasingly clear that policy initiatives can be seriously compromised by facing sustained adverse comment on television and radio, and in the press. Ultimately, the public perception of the government through the coverage it receives in the mass media has a major impact on the electoral fortunes of a political party. The role of the media in opinion-forming has transformed the way the business of government is conducted. The Prime Minister, as leader of the party, needs to keep in touch with the public mood and has a press office to assist with this task. Press secretaries are appointed to champion the cause of the government, and they have always been political appointments, introduced from outside government and civil service, to work in harmony with the serving Prime Minister. However, the pejorative term 'spin doctor' has been applied by critics to suggest that in recent years the function of the press secretary and the press office has gone beyond assisting the Prime Minister (and other ministers) with media management and opinion-forming. The task has in fact changed from putting the best possible interpretation on issues that

---

[16] J Morison, 'Modernising Government and the E-Government Revolution: Technologies of Government and Technologies of Democracy' in N Bamforth and P Leyland (eds), *Public Law in a Multi-Layered Constitution* (Oxford, Hart Publishing 2003); S Ward and T Vedel, 'The Potential of the Internet Revisited' (2006) 59(2) *Parliamentary Affairs* 210–25.

come up, to actually taking the initiative in setting a political agenda for a particular area of government policy. Alistair Campbell, as press secretary and later director of communications at 10 Downing Street (until 2003) was widely criticised in the media for wielding a great deal of power behind the scenes, but without being subject to any direct control. Furthermore, Tony Blair decided when he became Prime Minister that any policy announcement across the entire government had to be cleared through the Downing Street press office. This practice was introduced to avoid an impression of disunity conveyed by the previous government led by John Major which resulted from inconsistent and contradictory messages being released by individual departments. However, the requirement that policy announcements have to be approved at the centre has meant that Downing Street and the press office have been able to control the political agenda across the entire spectrum of government activity.[17] As a result, enormous power has been placed in the hands of appointed officials who are not directly accountable under the constitution for their activities.

In response to some of these criticisms, the independent Phillis report in 2004 attempted to delineate the political and civil service roles more clearly.[18] In line with the recommendations contained in the report, a new Permanent Secretary, Government Communications has been appointed (2004) whose remit is to focus on a strategic approach to communications across government to better inform and respond to the requirements of citizens and people who use and work in public services. In a complementary role, on the political side of the communications machine, the Prime Minister's Director of Communication has responsibility for the day-to-day media activity at 10 Downing Street. He or she also assists Cabinet ministers and their special advisers with the political context for departmental communications, but does not directly exercise any executive power over the civil service.[19]

SHAPING GOVERNMENT DEPARTMENTS

The Prime Minister is not only able to reshuffle the team of ministers serving in the government, but he or she also has an apparently unlimited capacity to create and to reshape government departments. In another context the

---

[17] See T Daintith, 'Spin: a Constitutional and Legal Analysis' (2001) 7(4) *European Public Law* 593–625, at 606.

[18] http://archive.cabinetoffice.gov.uk/gcreview/News/index.htm.

[19] Howell James, 'What future for Government Communications?', Speech at the CPPS Seminar, 20 January 2005, available at http://www.cabinetoffice.gov.uk/about_the_cabinet_office/speeches/james/html.

accountability issue within departments, between government departments, and between departments, agencies and other public bodies is determined by the distribution of competencies for distinct policy areas. The exercise of this kind of control has the advantage of allowing a Prime Minister who has received a mandate from the electorate to fashion the administrative organs of the state to facilitate the policy objectives that are regarded as a priority. A good example, dating from the 1960s, was when Prime Minister Wilson created the Department of Economic Affairs to manage economic planning and, then as its contribution to policy diminished, dispensed with the department in 1969.[20] The Ministers of the Crown Act 1975 allows departmental re-organisation to be made by Order in Council, which is a form of delegated legislation. This provides scope for both transfers of functions and dissolutions of departments.

More recently, Tony Blair, since becoming Prime Minister in 1997, has on a number of occasions recrafted major departments. After his first election victory he was able to combine the parts of the former Department of the Environment responsible for local and regional government with the Department of Transport to form a mega-department, the Department of Transport, Local Government, and the Regions (DTLR). This was a portfolio created for his deputy, John Prescott. The problems in adequately delivering policy initiatives in the often distinct fields of transport and local government could to some extent be attributed to the unwieldy departmental structure in Whitehall. The lack of focus on issues relating to local government became more pronounced following the May 2001 general election. For example, attention was diverted by the rail crisis and the collapse of Railtrack, in particular. The resignation of the Secretary of State for Transport resulted in the Prime Minister deciding to introduce a significant departmental re-organisation which involved scrapping the DTLR. Responsibility for local government and the planning inspectorate was moved to a newly formed Office of the Deputy Prime Minister, while Transport became a separate department in its right. The Deputy Prime Minister's department (in effect, a relaunched Department of the Environment) brought together regional and local government (including the regional government offices), housing, planning, and regeneration, and it also included the social exclusion unit and neighbourhood renewal. As part of this structure, the Regional Co-ordination Unit was responsible for the co-ordination of regional and local government. In the May 2006 reshuffle, the Office of the Deputy Prime Minister was again reconstituted, this time as the Department for Communities and Local Government.

---

[20] S Sked and C Cook, *Post-War Britain: A Political History* (London, Penguin, 1979) p 230.

The break-up of the DTLR might have removed an unmanageable con-glomeration but, in itself, such action does not resolve the problem of policy co-ordination. In what has been termed an age of multi-layered governance, the present government has sought to deliver what it has called 'joined up' government. Co-ordination and control was proving particularly difficult to achieve in this policy domain. For instance, the policy networks that cut across local government are complex and involve a multiplicity of over-lapping strands. These include housing, planning, environmental protection, and waste management, over which local authorities tend to have direct con-trol, and education, transport, and regulation, where responsibility is split not only between central and local government but also with other bodies such as statutory regulators.[21] Further powers have been conferred on London's Mayor and Assembly (see chapter eight). Despite repeated attempts to redraw departmental boundaries on an ad hoc basis, many inconsistencies remain in the allocation of responsibilities between policy areas. In most other nations, departmental re-organisation can be undertaken only by a more formal legal process. For example, in Italy a statute was passed in 1997 to allow a re-allocation of functions at the highest level of government between ministries, which has resulted in the compression of 20 ministries into 12.[22]

POLITICAL ACCOUNTABILITY AND INDIVIDUAL MINISTERIAL RESPONSIBILITY

Individual ministerial responsibility is the constitutional convention which is concerned with the accountability between Parliament, the political decision-makers, and professional civil servants and the administrators responsible for implementing policy in the United Kingdom. In essence, a model of the constitution was conceived which sought to accommodate the existence of discretionary public power by the device of ministerial responsibility. The rule of law, as explained by Dicey,[23] works on the basis that the courts police the boundaries of excessive ministerial power under the ultra vires principle, while Parliament oversees the actions of ministers within the boundaries of these powers. What does this add up to in practice? In a formal and proce-dural sense, ministers are responsible: this responsibility is in the sense that

---

[21] P Leyland, 'UK Utility Regulation in the Age of Governance' in N Bamforth and P Leyland (eds), *Public Law in a Multi-Layered Constitution* (Oxford, Hart Publishing 2003).

[22] See Italy: Law 59/97.

[23] A Dicey, *An Introduction to the Study of the Law of the Constitution*, 10th edn (Basingstoke, Macmillan, 1959) p 188ff.

they are answerable to Parliament for their departments. In this way individual ministerial responsibility describes a 'chain of accountability'. Officials answer to ministers, who answer to Parliament, which, in turn, answers to the electorate. This demonstrates how individual ministerial responsibility emerged as the convention which described constitutional accountability for policy matters, but, as we shall see from the examples cited below, the problem is that accountability is often no more than a requirement to give reasons and explanations for actions or decisions as part of the process of government.

For the convention to operate, the basic requirement is that ministers are members of Parliament. As was recognised in the previous chapter, the answerability of ministers to Parliament is acted out in a number of ways. In particular, the relevant minister in the House of Commons or House of Lords introduces a public Bill concerning his or her department in Parliament; backbench MPs are able to table questions to ministers on a regular basis; ministers are called to account for their policies before departmental select committees (of which there are 18); and the Public Accounts Committee in harness with the National Audit Office investigates past government expenditure by undertaking value for money (VFM) audits (see chapter five, 'Parliament').

MINISTERIAL RESPONSIBILITY: ANSWERABILITY OR RESIGNATION

Ministers, then, are made accountable or answerable to Parliament by these routine procedures. In terms of general principle, individual ministerial responsibility recognises that the continuation in office of ministers depends upon them enjoying the confidence and support of MPs or peers. In practice, however, attempts to challenge the credibility of a minister are seldom successful when the government in power enjoys a substantial majority in the House of Commons. In 1954 Sir Thomas Dugdale resigned over the famous Crichel Down affair, where blame for departmental incompetence was clearly attributable to officials. Furthermore, the blameworthy action mostly occurred well before this minister took up office. In fact, this sacrifice was prompted by political reasons, and the resignation should be regarded as an exception to general practice. Unless the matter is taken up as a crusade by the press, what Richard Crossman explained, writing half a century earlier, still applies: ' [since] the Government party controls Parliament, both resignations and dismissals for incompetence have become rare. Indeed, the incompetent minister with a departmental muddle to cover up may be kept in office for years . . . more votes will be lost by admitting the incompetence than by concealing it.'[24] The government can nearly always rely upon the support of its backbench MPs to sustain its majority and therefore there will be no need for a minister to fall on his or her sword and resign. Apart from Crichel Down, there have been examples of ministers accepting responsibility for policy and resigning, but this is rare. One such was the resignation of Lord Carrington as Foreign Secretary following the invasion of South Georgia by the Argentinians prior to the Falklands War in 1982. Lord Carrington accepted the blame for not responding to intelligence reports warning about the impending invasion. On the other hand, blame can be deflected for political mistakes by a sacrificial resignation, which identifies an individual minister rather than the Prime Minister or the government as a whole as being responsible for a policy oversight. For example, the Secretary of State for Trade and Industry took full responsibility for a departmental leak relating to the Westland affair, and his resignation in 1986 shielded the Prime Minister and the government from intensifying criticism at a time of crisis.[25]

Assuming the minister is the architect of the policy, it would appear to follow that, should the policy design prove to be fundamentally flawed, the minister should be held responsible. For example, in the previous chapter attention was drawn to critical reports from the departmental select committee in respect to the running of the Millennium Dome project.[26] Project directors came and went, but there were no ministerial resignations. Ministerial responsibility has always been an imprecise convention, which delivers partial accountability. At best, it will normally require ministers to provide Parliament with information and also an explanation. The evidence demonstrates that resignations are unusual, and supports the view that political considerations nearly always predominate.

THE SCOTT REPORT

The reluctance of ministers to resign was further illustrated following publication of the Scott Report.[27] A public inquiry chaired by a senior judge was set up to look into the processes of government after it emerged that arms had been supplied to Iraq with the covert support of government during the

---

[24] R Crossman (ed), 'Introduction' in W Bagehot, *The English Constitution* (London, Fontana, 1963) pp 43 and 45.
[25] See Hennessey, above n 6, p 307.
[26] See, eg, Select Committee on Culture, Media and Sport, *Back to the Dome, Third Report*, 1998–99 HC 21–1.
[27] *Report of the Inquiry into the Export of Defence Equipment and Dual-Use Goods to Iraq and Related Prosecutions*, 1995–96 HC 115.

Gulf War between Iran and Iraq during the 1980s. This action was clearly in contravention of published government policy at the time. The issue came to public attention following the collapse of a prosecution against two directors of the Matrix Churchill company, which had been contracted to supply a supergun to Iraq. Although government ministers had used public interest immunity to prevent the disclosure of information in court on grounds of national security, the fact that these directors were working in collusion with the secret intelligence services came to light. It appeared that the government had been prepared to suppress this information in order to prevent embarrassment for having misled Parliament over its involvement, even if this meant imprisonment for these directors of Matrix Churchill. Many of Lord Justice Scott's criticisms in the report related to the conduct of ministers, including the suggestion that the House of Commons had been misled by one minister, and that guidelines for the signing of public interest immunity certificates had been wrongly interpreted by the Attorney-General, but, despite criticism appearing in the report, neither minister resigned.[28] The Scott Report also exposed a lack of candour, which amounted to a failure by ministers to meet the obligations of ministerial accountability by providing adequate information about the activities of their departments, and it was recognised that this failure tended to undermine the democratic process. In response, a revised code of practice was introduced for civil servants and ministers which has made it more difficult to mislead Parliament.[29]

MINISTERIAL RESPONSIBILITY AND THE PRESS

In recent times, with the greater proliferation of information, the power of the media in attaching blame to ministers has been very much in evidence. For example, Stephen Byers resigned in May 2002 as Secretary of State for Transport. The trigger for his departure was not that his department had to manage the crisis on the railways following the collapse of Railtrack, or dealing with the unpopular policy of part-privatisation of the London Underground, but, rather, his credibility had been fatally undermined by the intense controversy surrounding his press secretary, who attempted to use the distraction of the events in the United States on 11 September 2001 to release bad news. Failure to dismiss this appointed official led to a campaign in the press, which uncovered further dissent within the department and ultimately exposed the weakness of the minister.

---

[28] A Tomkins, *The Constitution After Scott: Government Unwrapped* (Oxford, Oxford University Press, 1998) provides a detailed discussion of the report and its implications.

[29] *Ibid,* p 51.

Once again, in October 2002, the Secretary of State for Education and Employment resigned at least partly because of the level of media criticism over education policy in general, and in particular over criticism concerning her handling of the crisis regarding the grading of A-level examinations. This prompted a personal loss of confidence by the minister over the general strategic management of the department. However, these departures are unusual, for it appears that ministers very rarely sacrifice themselves as a result of policy failure or departmental shortcomings.[30]

Other examples of ministerial incompetence can be cited, however, where the minister survived. In 1992 the value of the pound collapsed, forcing the United Kingdom to withdraw from the exchange rate mechanism (ERM), but not before the Chancellor of the Exchequer on 'Black Wednesday' had used up £11 billion, virtually half the nation's currency reserves, in a futile attempt to support the value of the currency. On this occasion it would appear that Chancellor of the Exchequer's failure to resign immediately had the effect of substantially weakening the government of Prime Minister John Major.

Professor Woodhouse has summed up the position as follows:

> Moving into the twenty-first century, the convention of ministerial responsibility can be defined loosely, as requiring, first, information rather than resignation; secondly, ministerial 'accountability' for everything but 'responsibility' for only some things; thirdly, civil service 'responsibility' for some things but 'accountability' only when this suits ministerial interests.[31]

A reformulation of ministerial responsibility has been called for which recognises the integral responsibilities of ministers for supervision of their department or agency. In particular, this would require that ministers make sure that adequate resources are available for the effective implementation of policies and that they assume direct control at times when things go wrong as part of explanatory and amendatory responsibility.[32]

THE CIVIL SERVICE

In order to consider the issues of accountability in respect to the operation of government itself, we need to explore in more detail the relationship between

---

[30] D Woodhouse, 'UK Ministerial Responsibility in 2002: The Tale of Two Resignations' (2004) 82(1) *Public Administration* 1–19.

[31] D Woodhouse, 'Ministerial Responsibility: Something Old, Something New' [1997] *PL* 280.

[32] D Woodhouse, 'The Reconstruction of Constitutional Accountability' [2002] *PL* 262, p 86.

ministers and civil servants, and the re-organisation of the institutions of central government.[33] In the first place, it is worth noting that there has never been a single statute or a set of delegated rules that regulates the conduct of civil servants or which establishes their constitutional position (as is mentioned below, Parliament may soon pass such a statute). For example, civil servants have a special position in law as servants of the Crown, but on matters of employment law, the Equal Pay Act 1970, the Employment Protection Consolidation Act 1978, the Sex Discrimination Act 1975, and the Race Relations Act 1976 all apply to the civil service. Civil servants are bound by the Official Secrets Acts 1911 and 1989 and by the Freedom of Information Act 2000 (subject to statutory exceptions discussed below). Civil servants are also regulated by an assortment of codes of conduct and disciplinary codes. As we have already observed in our discussion of ministerial responsibility, some of these codes have an important bearing on the relationship of civil servants with ministers and with Parliament.

For many generations, ministers have been in a position to rely upon a permanent and professional civil service, which, in most cases, has been led by an elite class of Oxford- and Cambridge-educated officials, with a reputation for neutrality. The foundations of the modern service were laid following the Northcote-Trevelyan Report of 1854.[34] This ground-breaking report, among other things, established the idea of appointment on merit and led to the division of the civil service into two classes comprising, on the one hand, policy-makers, and, on the other, more routine workers. The civil service remains a system of centralised hierarchical administration comprised of trained professionals, who operate according to prescribed and objective rules. The structure is designed to enable those at the base of the pyramid of administration to carry out the commands of those at the pinnacle. The role of the civil service is to implement policy, often by putting into effect detailed legislative provisions, and it establishes a system which limits the arbitrary exercise of power by officials. Nevertheless, in the United Kingdom, as in other comparable nations (eg France, Italy, and Germany), the legal framework of legislation will inevitably leave scope for the exercise of discretionary power, with the traditional model regarding ministers and civil servants as partners. This means that officials have been allowed some discretion to act, but this discretion is set within strict limits. It will be apparent from our discussion of political accountability below that the courts can be called upon to intervene to ensure that the exercise of any such discretion remains lawful.

[33] See generally G Drewry, 'The Executive: Towards Accountable Government and Effective Governance' in J Jowell and D Oliver (eds), *The Changing Constitution*, 5th edn (Oxford, Oxford University Press, 2004).

[34] Northcote-Trevelyan Report on the Organisation of a Permanent Civil Service 1854.

The UK civil service serves whichever government is in power and, unlike in the United States, there is no 'spoils system' allowing politicians to change the most senior officials with a change of government. The service has a high reputation for intellectual excellence and integrity. It is considered to be neutral, with a capacity to give impartial advice to ministers. However, it has also attracted criticism for lack of managerial competence and efficiency, and for a failure to attract the specialist expertise needed in many areas of government (see, for example, the Fulton Report 1968,[35] which made more than 100 recommendations).

The situation in regard to the structure and organisation of the civil service has changed significantly in recent years. The Conservative governments between 1979 and 1997 were critical of the traditional approach of many civil servants to questions of policy implementation which, it was argued, resulted in ineffective government. In order to pursue the radical Thatcherite agenda, which departed from the consensual policies of post-war generations, the association between the civil service and established interests in both business and the public and voluntary sector was revised. Since the 1980s there have been radical managerial innovations to help overcome resistance to reform by senior officials. Another manifestation of this change of approach, already alluded to, is that there has been an increase in the appointment by ministers of political advisers and special advisers, who exercise a growing influence on policy-making, and these advisers can also be involved lower down the administrative hierarchy to monitor progress with policy initiatives.

NEW PUBLIC MANAGEMENT AND
EXECUTIVE ACCOUNTABILITY

The New Public Management (NPM) initiative and the Next Steps re-organisation have been inspired by an ideological commitment to introduce the disciplines of the free market to the processes of government. A series of changes were introduced under the Conservative governments between 1987 and 1997 (and continued under Labour) which were designed to transform the performance of central government. In the interests of economy, the size of the civil service was reduced. Also, large proportions of what remained were called 'Next Steps Agencies'. Indeed, the idea of running a public enterprise on a similar basis to a private business became a prevalent theme in publicly funded bodies throughout Europe and beyond. It depended upon the introduction of a new kind of contracting between the

---

[35] *The Report of the Committee on the Civil Service* (Fulton), Cmnd 3638, 1966–68.

various levels of government and between government and the private sector. However, these administrative changes, which began in late 1980s, had serious implications for the political accountability of the civil service.

The Conservative government, when it took office in 1979, inherited a central government bureaucracy of nearly 750,000 civil servants. The bare statistics demonstrate the impact of these reforms. By the time the Conservative left office in 1997 there were less than 500,000 remaining. The structure and organisation had also changed: 362,000 were assigned to 138 Next Steps Agencies (explained below), accounting for approximately 75 per cent of the service. This re-organisation resulted in the disappearance of a relatively uniform and monolithic structure, and its replacement by a much looser federation of many smaller units.[36] In many cases, the initiative relieved departmental overload by handing over responsibility for budget and staffing to the agencies. These agencies, dealing with anything from the allocation of passports (part of the Home Office) to child support (Works and Pensions), continue to be run by civil servants who remain under the same conditions of employment, and staff continued to be bound by the Civil Service Management Code. Another aspect of this reform was the exposure of the service to business models. For example, it provided the opportunity to recruit private sector managers as agency chiefs, who could be 'incentivised' by high salaries. Such re-organisation, however, provided scope for internal restructuring.

This reform enabled the role of ministers and senior civil servants engaged in the task of policy formulation to carry on more or less as before, as part of a main department under which the newly formed agency functioned. The new structures required the operational tasks to be placed in the hands of the agency by a form of non-legally binding contract, and this division conveyed an impression of agency autonomy based on an apparent separation between policy decisions and operational decisions. The entire scheme was deceptive. In practice, the agency was not a separate legal entity, and a dependency existed between the sponsoring department and the agency. For example, an agency would be granted fixed budgetary allocations, which arguably imposed even more rigid control over the policy process. A contradiction was thereby created between apparent independence of an agency and the control imposed from above. An equally worrying development which emerged following the introduction of Next Steps programme has been the deployment of a policy/operations dichotomy between the minister and the agency chief to shield the minister from blame before Parliament under

---

[36] R Rhodes, P Carmichael, J McMillan, and A Massey, *Decentralising the Civil Service: From Unitary State to Differentiated Polity in the United Kingdom* (Buckingham, Open University Press, 2003) ch 2.

the doctrine of ministerial responsibility for serious shortcomings within the departmental sphere. For example, in 1995, faced with criticism from an official inquiry following the escape of IRA prisoners from the Isle of Wight, the Home Secretary dismissed the head of the prison service for what he claimed was an 'operational matter' rather than personally accepting responsibility for any shortcomings.[37]

From the outset, NPM has been centrally concerned with the three 'Es', namely, 'economy, efficiency and effectiveness'. Public services are forced to confront market-related disciplines.[38] There is a presumption that the state (that is, central and local government) can function more effectively and efficiently while at the same time costing the taxpayer less. Central government agencies are expected to undertake market testing to ascertain whether service delivery can be achieved more efficiently. As part of the NPM process, internal performance is systematically monitored and assessed. Staff members have their performance annually reviewed, with pay levels often related to results achieved. This style of managerialism to improve outputs and introduce public sector 'benchmarking' has continued in phases, the latest of which is called 'Capability Review', focusing on leadership, strategy, and delivery.[39] However, it is much more difficult to assess efficiency and effectiveness that reaches beyond simple measures of cost-effectiveness. In the sphere of government, measuring performance simply in terms of increased throughput on a 'cost per unit' basis is often misleading, particularly when dealing with services that involve the provision of care.

Another important way in which market solutions have been introduced is through privatisation. Many functions, ranging from prisoner escort services to the cleaning of government offices, that were formerly carried out by staff employed by the department are now performed by independent, privately owned, companies. The services are provided under a formal private law contractual obligation which has been negotiated between the department and the company, and the enforcement of the contract will generally be a matter of private law. But this calls into question any meaningful accountability in a public law sense for policy issues that might arise in relation to operational matters. The terms of the contract define all the parameters of the service provision, and there is no going back on such terms until such time as there is an opportunity to renegotiate the contract. In this sense, the same applies to public–private partnerships (PPPs) and Private Finance

[37] A Barker, 'Political Responsibility for UK Prison Security—Ministers Escape Again' (1998) 76 (Spring) *Public Administration* 1–23 at 11ff.

[38] See C Harlow and R Rawlings, *Law and Administration* (London, Butterworths, 1997) ch 5, 'Blue Rinse'.

[39] http://www.civilservice.gov.uk/reform/capability_reviews/news/index.asp.

Initiatives (PFIs), which have been used to attract private finance into the public sector.

The revised ministerial code recognises that 'ministers have a duty to Parliament to account, and be held to account, for the policies, decisions and actions of their departments and agencies.'[40] It is apparent that in some respects this re-organisation has led to a significant redefinition of the doctrine of ministerial responsibility. Less emphasis is placed upon detailed day-to-day supervision of the entire department. Accountability between the department and the agency tends to be mainly in respect of overall finance and budgeting matters. Great emphasis is placed on measurable criteria of financial efficiency. In consequence, greater autonomy brought about by agency status has promoted a divergence of interests between the agency and the department. It has resulted in a division into two distinct accountabilities, but no revised mechanism to address the problem.[41] For example, ministerial responses to parliamentary questions on matters of detailed financial policy might fall under the remit of the agency chief executive, and in some cases the answers to questions provided by the chief executive may be considered inadequate.

Although the precise criteria and terminology are modified to reflect local conditions, aspects of the NPM model have been manifest in much of Europe. This idea is not fundamentally concerned with democratic control and accountability, but rather with control through forms of contractual relationship.

A CIVIL SERVICE ACT FOR THE UNITED KINGDOM

It has been argued in some quarters that codification is required as an antidote to the creeping politicisation of the civil service. In preference to the use of Orders in Council under prerogative powers, which are not open to parliamentary scrutiny, there have been published proposals to put the regulation of the civil service under parliamentary legislation through the introduction of a Civil Service Act.[42] The case was recently examined by the Parliamentary Committee on Standards in Public Life, and the committee recommended that the civil service should be placed on a statutory footing.[43]

[40] Civil Service Code, 2006.
[41] P Barberis, 'The New Public Management and A New Accountability' (1998) 76 (Autumn) *Public Administration* 45–70.
[42] N Lewis, 'A Civil Service Act for the United Kingdom' [1998] *PL* 463; D Oliver, *Constitutional Reform in the UK* (Oxford, Oxford University Press, 2003) ch 3.
[43] See Parliamentary Committee on Standards in Public Life, *Ninth Report: Defining the Boundaries within the Executive: Ministers, special advisors and the permanent civil service*, 2003.

A new Civil Service Act would set out the relationship between ministers and civil servants, and would result in the codes of practice for ministers and civil servants being reconstituted and supported by law. In addition, the constitutional position of the Civil Service Commission and special advisers would be defined in a wider constitutional context, and the Civil Service Commissioners would be made responsible under the Act for upholding the core values of the service. Advocates of a Civil Service Act believe that such a measure would make it much more difficult than is currently the case under prerogative powers for any government to politicise the civil service or erode its core principles. On the other hand, critics argue that: 'The quest for defined boundaries and roles at the top of government, where politics and administration intertwine, is misguided. Ambiguity, fuzziness, and grey areas are assets since they enable flexibility, and practical responses to unexpected happenings.'[44]

GOVERNMENT OPENNESS AND THE FREEDOM OF INFORMATION ACT 2000

The Freedom of Information (FOI) Act 2000 requires the disclosure of information by the government and other public bodies and, as a result, it is having an important impact in delivering accountability in many areas.[45] It will already be apparent that the convention of individual ministerial responsibility, which is central to executive accountability, hinges on an obligation to provide information. Until quite recently, the corridors of Whitehall and public authorities in general were shrouded in a cloak of secrecy. The blanket protection that public bodies had enjoyed under the 'catch-all' section 2 of the Official Secrets Acts 1911 was relaxed to some extent by the Official Secrets Act 1989. The failure of the government in the 1980s to prevent the circulation of the *Spycatcher* book,[46] which had been written by an ex-spy in breach of the Official Secrets Act 1911 was a foretaste of difficulties to come in controlling the currency of information.[47] The book had been published abroad, but it was imported and became available in the United Kingdom despite injunctions issued by the courts.

---

[44] G Jones, 'Against a Civil Service Act' (2002) October–December *Public Money and Management,* 6.
[45] See R Austin, 'The Freedom of Information Act 2000—A Sheep in Wolf's Clothing' in J Jowell and D Oliver (eds), *The Changing Constitution,* 5th edn (Oxford, Oxford University Press, 2004).
[46] P Wright, *Spycatcher* (New York, Viking, 1987).
[47] See *Attorney-General v Guardian Newspapers Ltd (No 2)* [1990] 1 AC 109.

In a different context, the trenchant criticism contained in the Scott Report (see above), which looked into the collapse of the Matrix Churchill case, signalled a change of approach in regard to Parliament. The previous assumption that information in the possession of public bodies could be routinely held back was fundamentally questioned in this report, and the codes of practice which applied to ministers and civil servants were modified subsequently.[48] Latterly, information placed in the public domain has proliferated exponentially through the internet, and this has, of course, transformed public expectations over the level of disclosure which is expected from public bodies.

On its return to power in 1997 after 18 years in opposition, the Labour Party was committed to introducing a Freedom of Information Act. Despite its shortcomings touched on below, the FOI Act 2000 is a ground-breaking constitutional measure. The Act, which came fully into force on 1 January 2005, provides under section 1 a general right of access to information held by public authorities, including government departments. It imposes an obligation to provide information within a limited time frame. As well as meeting the requirement under the Act to provide publication schemes, government, local government, and public authorities have responded to the new situation by making vast amounts of information available to the public, often on their websites.

Information which is exempt from disclosure is set out in Part II of the FOI Act 2000. The exempt categories fall into two classes, as the effect of the provisions differs depending on whether the sections confer absolute exemption, or qualified exemption subject to a prejudice test.[49] In essence, the areas which have an 'absolute exemption' are those where the need to balance the public interest in disclosure against the public interest in maintaining the exemption does not arise. This covers information relating to secret intelligence services, criminal intelligence matters, and national security.[50] For these categories, a certificate signed by a Cabinet minister, the Attorney-General, the Attorney-General for Northern Ireland, or the Advocate General for Scotland certifying that the exemption is necessary is regarded as conclusive evidence. There is limited scope for challenge before the Information Tribunal, but the grounds are very narrow.

For the second category of (qualified) exemptions, the application for information has to be balanced against the public interest in refusing disclosure. A test of *prejudice* has to be satisfied to justify non-disclosure. The areas that may be exempted are very wide ranging, as the following list illustrates:

---

[48] See Sked and Cook, above n 20.
[49] Section 26 deals with the effect of the exemptions in Part II.
[50] Sections 23 and 24.

defence; communications with the royal family; all political advice; international relations; relations between the parliaments and assemblies of the United Kingdom, Scotland, Wales, and Northern Ireland; the economy; investigations by the police and customs and excise; court records; commercial information; health and safety; and all personal information and information provided to government in confidence. It will be apparent that this list includes any information relating to the formulation of government policy and investigations and proceedings carried out by a public authority. This exemption has been made subject to a test in order to deter public authorities from routinely suppressing such information. It was argued that a higher threshold of *substantial prejudice* (as applies in Scotland) would have been more effective in encouraging disclosure.

Under the FOI Act 2000, the Information Commissioner performs an important function in overseeing the application of the Act. Should a matter be contested, the Commissioner is empowered to rule that material should be made available in the public interest, and an enforcement notice can be issued, but the minister retains an ultimate veto over any such decision.[51]

An important test case concerned the freedom of information requests which were made to force the disclosure of the advice given to the Prime Minister by the Attorney-General in March 2003 on the controversial matter of the legality of the second war against Iraq. Despite its initial argument that the advice from the Attorney-General was protected by client privilege, the opinion was released by the government in May 2005. The Commissioner later served a single enforcement notice in May 2006 requiring the disclosure of some, but not all, of the information relating to the advice that had been requested under the Act. He also ruled, after balancing the issues by applying the prejudice test, that sufficient information had been disclosed by the government.[52]

E-GOVERNMENT REVOLUTION

From cradle to grave, the encounter with information communication technology (ICT) and, in particular, the internet has become a significant and an increasing part of everyday experience. The new regime of openness under the FOI Act 2000, the introduction of publication schemes, and the sheer quantity of official information available on the internet have trans-

---

[51] Section 53.
[52] See ICO press release at: http://www.ico.gov.uk/sendICONewletters/newsletters/english.html#story15.

formed public access to information, but equally these developments have implications for the accountability and accessibility of public bodies.[53]

Computers are used universally to store, process, and communicate large amounts of data, and this technology is well suited to delivering many government services. The Cabinet Office launched a large-scale consultation on a policy for electronic democracy based on the premise that ICT can 'facilitate, broaden and deepen' participation.[54] As a result, computer technology is changing the ways in which services are delivered. For example, websites have been constructed allowing direct access to many services. The government gateway already allows many public services to be available online. It has been envisaged that the staged introduction of such technology as part of an evolutionary process might ultimately result in fully integrated online government, which, in turn, would require the radical modification of the structure and culture of administration to facilitate the introduction of this technology in the home. 'From the point of view of the citizen he or she would not be interacting with individual government departments any longer but with "Government" as a single entity.'[55]

A practical issue which is crucial to the general application of ICT concerns the extent of internet access. Before government bodies at central and local level can depend upon the internet, an even playing field is needed in the form of universal access to computers and a general capacity for citizens to connect online. It is estimated that 24 million UK households have access to the internet,[56] but the challenge is to overcome the difficulty of extending internet usage without introducing a form of social exclusion affecting disadvantaged groups (the poor, the elderly, individuals with limited literacy), who may well be particularly reliant on government and local government services. As Morison states:

> Ideas of separation of powers, rule of law and basic principles of legality do not seem to have troubled the information systems engineers. From the standpoint of formal constitutional theory, not only are there issues over the penetration of the voluntary and private sector into government but also there should be concerns over the deployment of information gathered in one (public) context within another (private) one and vice versa . . . [giving] rise to a whole host of other issues about privacy, data protection and confidentiality and human rights.[57]

---

[53] S Ward and T Vedel, 'Introduction: The Potential of the Internet Revisited' (2006) 59(2) *Parliamentary Affairs* 212–25.

[54] *In Service of Democracy: A Consultation Paper for Electronic Democracy* (2002)

[55] J Morison, 'Modernising Government and the E-government Revolution: Technologies of Government and Technologies of Democracy' in N Bamforth and P Leyland (eds), *Public Law in a Multi-Layered Constitution* (Oxford, Hart Publishing, 2003) p 177.

[56] http://www.statistics.gov.uk/downloads/theme_social/Social_Trends35/Social_Trends_35.pdf.

[57] Morison, above n 55, p 179.

The internet has impacted on public engagement with political protest and debate through weblogs. It presents the possibility of flash mobilisation of opinion, but equally this technology is capable of being subverted by organised crime, extremist parties, and terrorist organisations. Although the handling of personal data is controlled under the Data Protection Act 1998, the internet itself is largely self-regulated. Ofcom has a role in regulating competition but the internet is placed beyond the reach of the Communications Act 2003. Internet regulation consists mainly of a series of regimes of self-regulation, which have been developed to apply to the different technical layers of delivery.[58]

CONCLUSION

Enormous power is focused on the office of Prime Minister. The most important political decisions are generally taken not by the full Cabinet, but through Cabinet committees, many of which are chaired by the Prime Minister, and the policy which goes before these committees is frequently drawn up by advisers in the Prime Minister's office at 10 Downing Street, together with inputs from close political allies inside and outside of government. Indeed, 'elective dictatorship' is useful shorthand for the executive dominance which is a central characteristic of the UK constitution. It refers to the ease with which the government is able to secure a majority in Parliament for nearly all legislative proposals. The Prime Minister can control the parliamentary party through the power exercised by the party whips. The ascendancy of the Prime Minister over domestic politics is further boosted by extensive powers of patronage, including the uncontested right to appoint and dismiss ministers.

Constitutional safeguards exist, but they are of limited effect. For example, the convention of individual ministerial responsibility requires the Prime Minister, ministers, and civil servants to appear before Parliament and before parliamentary committees to be interrogated on matters of policy. Members of Parliament may be constrained from asking searching questions by narrow guidelines, which inhibit officials in their responses. Official secrets legislation can be invoked when treading on the most sensitive and controversial aspects of the policy process. Also, the inquisitors on a parliamentary committee may be following an agenda dictated not by the qualitative aspects of the matter before them, but by political considerations identified by government or opposition whips. The FOI Act 2000 extends access to information and provides a mechanism, under the supervision of the

---

[58] R Collins, 'Networks Markets Hierarchies: Governance and Regulation of the Internet' (2006) 59(2) *Parliamentary Affairs* 325.

Information Commissioner, to obtain the release of documents, but many legitimate areas of scrutiny are placed beyond its scope. Finally, a high-quality permanent civil service may be counted as one of the nation's supreme constitutional assets. The attempts by successive governments to modernise the service by the imposition of free market disciplines associated with NPM and e-government has also had the effect of redefining, and, at the same time, attenuating, traditional channels of constitutional accountability.

FURTHER READING

Austin R, 'The Freedom of Information Act 2000—A Sheep in Wolf's Clothing' in J Jowell and D Oliver (eds, *The Changing Constitution*, 5th edn (Oxford, Oxford University Press, 2004).

Daintith T, 'Spin: a Constitutional and Legal Analysis' (2001) 7(4) *European Public Law* 593.

Drewry G, 'The Ombudsman: Parochial Stopgap or Global Panacea?' in Leyland P and Woods T (eds), *Administrative Law Facing the Future: Old Constraints, New Horizons* (London, Blackstone, 1997).

Lord Hailsham, *The Dilemma of Democracy* (London, Fontana, 1978).

Harlow C and Rawlings R, *Law and Administration*, 2nd edn (London, Butterworths, 1997).

Hennessey P, *The Prime Minister: The Office and its holders since 1945* (London, Penguin, 2001).

Hennessey P, *Whitehall*, 2nd edn (London, Pimlico, 2001).

Lewis N, 'A Civil Service Act for the United Kingdom' [1998] *PL* 463.

Leyland P and Donati D, 'Executive Accountability and the Changing Face of Government: UK and Italy Compared' (2001) 7(2) (June) *European Public Law* 217.

Marshall G, *Constitutional Conventions: The Rules and Forms of Political Accountability* (Oxford, Oxford University Press, 1984) ch 4.

Oliver D, *Constitutional Reform in the UK* (Oxford, Oxford University Press, 2003) ch 3.

Palmer S, 'Freedom of Information: A New Constitutional Landscape?' in Bamforth N and Leyland P (eds), *Public Law in a Multi-Layered Constitution* (Oxford, Hart Publishing, 2003).

Smith M, 'Reconceptualising the British State' (1998) *Public Administration* 48.

Tomkins A, *The Constitution after Scott: Government Unwrapped* (Oxford, Oxford University Press, 1998).

Tomkins A, *Public Law* (Oxford, Oxford University Press, 2003) ch 3.

Woodhouse D, ''Ministerial Responsibility' in V Bogdanor (ed), *The British Constitution in the Twentieth Century* (Oxford, Oxford University Press, 2003).

WEBSITES

http://www.number-10.gov.uk/output/Page249.asp
http://www.direct.gov.uk/QuickFind/SubjectDirectory/
  GovernmentPoliticsAndPublicAdministration/fs/en
http://www.pm.gov.uk/output/Page1.asp
http://www.cabinet-office.gov.uk/
http://www.odpm.gov.uk/

7

The Constitutional Role of the Courts

PART I: SURVEYING THE CONSTITUTIONAL ROLE OF THE COURTS

INTRODUCTION

THIS CHAPTER BEGINS by discussing the contribution of the common law and statutory interpretation in a constitutional context. The following section examines the historic office of the Lord Chancellor who has occupied a multi-faceted constitutional position which was in defiance of any formal conception of separation of powers. The UK constitution has lacked any clear separation of powers, but the extent to which Parliament, executive, and judiciary are in an ordered relationship with one another is of central importance to any constitutional concept of checks and balances. We will see that the redesignation of the ministerial position from Lord Chancellor's Department to Secretary of State for Constituional Affairs in 2003 has been much more than a nominal change. In fact, the constitutional role of the Lord Chancellor has been transformed, both in regard to parliamentary and judicial functions. Moreover, the provisions of the Constitutional Reform Act 2005 are already having significant impact in two key areas. Close attention is devoted to assessing the implications for judicial independence of the revised procedures for judicial appointments and the arrangements for a Supreme Court for the United Kingdom to replace the appellate panel of the House of Lords.

COMMON LAW AND STATUTORY INTERPRETATION

It was pointed out in chapters one and two that the common law is an important source of the constitution. Judges have the capacity to develop the law by setting precedents in the cases they decide. Some important areas of law, for example the law of contract and tort, have been largely created by judicial decisions. According to Chief Justice Coke writing in the seventeenth century: '[Cases] are not to be decided by natural reason, but by the artificial reason and judgment of law which requires long study and experience before that a man can attain cognizance of it.'[1] This principle recognises the collective wisdom of the judges refined over long periods and organised through precedents. An alternative, more critical, view would be to question any mystical notion of judicial omnipotence and would prefer to regard the common law as the creation of a professional elite of lawyers. The laws emanating from the courts have tended to reflect many assumptions and prejudices of judges drawn from a narrow class.[2]

According to the doctrine of binding precedent, a decision made by a court in one case is binding on other courts in subsequent cases involving similar facts. This rule is meant to ensure that similar cases will be decided in a similar manner. It relies on a system with a hierarchical appellate structure, and the principle depends on courts following the decisions of the courts above them. The appellate committee of the House of Lords (which will be formed into a Supreme Court from 2009) is the highest domestic appellate court and it is not bound by its previous decisions, which allows the highest court to make changes to the law when it considers them necessary.[3] This

---

[1] Coke, *Reports*, xii, 65, quoted from F Maitland *The Constitutional History of England*, 10th edn (Cambridge, Cambridge University Press, 1946) pp 268–9.
[2] See J Griffith, *The Politics of the Judiciary*, 5th edn (London, Fontana, 1997) p xv.
[3] *Lord Chancellor's Practice Direction* [1966] 1 WLR 1234.

relaxation of the rules of precedent provides scope at the highest domestic level to modify the law to bring it in line with changing circumstances and to avoid injustice. However, the need to weigh any considerations in favour of judicial innovation against the need for certainty and the danger of retro-spectivity has meant that departures from precedent are rarely in evidence.

It has been generally acknowledged that the courts will not ignore or dis-apply statutes, and the courts cannot review the legality of an Act of Parliament in matters of non-European Community law. However, the courts are responsible for the interpretation of statute law in cases that are brought before them. It is necessary for judges to perform this interpretative function when hearing cases at first instance or when deciding contested points of law on appeal. In other words, Parliament is supreme in passing laws, while judges have to decide what Parliament intended when it approved a particular piece of legislation. In situations where there is ambiguity the Interpretation Act 1978 and the common law rules of statutory interpreta-tion (the literal rule, golden rule, and mischief rule) are employed to assist the courts in performing this task. A comparatively recent innovation following the judgment of the House of Lords in *Pepper v Hart*[4] has been to allow the use by the courts of the reports in *Hansard* of debates in Parliament to clarify the intentions of Parliament in situations where legislation appears ambigu-ous or obscure.

Parliamentary sovereignty is, according to Dicey and other influential commentators, the fundamental rule of the constitution, which recognises that Parliament has the power to pass or repeal any law, including 'constitu-tional laws'.[5] This doctrine, as was noted in chapter three, not only makes the entrenchment of principles or law difficult but also means that the will of Parliament predominates over that of the courts. The position in the United Kingdom has often been contrasted with codified constitutions. In the United States, the Federal Supreme Court has a constitutional review func-tion. The decision in *Marbury v Madison*[6] in 1803 established the convention that the US Supreme Court could declare null and void as unconstitutional any statute or action of the federal or state governments which it considered conflicted with the supreme law of the constitution. This convention had the effect of establishing a principle of judicial sovereignty, giving the Court power to declare actions of other branches of government unconstitutional. Any such decision by the Supreme Court will be binding on federal and state institutions. In exercising this function, there have been many occasions

---

[4] [1993] 1 All ER 42.
[5] See J Goldsworthy, *The Sovereignty of Parliament: History and Philosophy* (Oxford, Oxford University Press, 1999) ch 1.
[6] 5 US 137 (1803).

when the Court has been called upon to adjudicate at the centre of the political process. The US Supreme Court has to decide finally the legality of contentious political issues ranging from racial segregation in schools[7] to the legitimacy of the presidential election process.[8]

It has been suggested by some academic commentators and judges that there might be limits to Parliament's legal sovereignty:

> [I]t is not unthinkable that circumstances could arise where the courts may have to qualify a principle established on a different hypothesis of constitutionalism. In exceptional circumstances involving an attempt to abolish judicial review or the ordinary role of the courts, the Appellate Committee of the House of Lords or a new Supreme Court may have to consider whether this is a constitutional fundamental which even a sovereign Parliament acting at the behest of a complaisant House of Commons cannot abolish.[9]

In the 2005–06 parliamentary session the prospect of judicial intervention was mentioned as a way of checking a trend by which Parliament grants ministers sweeping delegated powers by the use of what are called 'Henry VIII clauses'.[10] The Legislative and Regulatory Reform Bill was the focus of particular concern, because in its original form this measure proposed that ministers would have the power to alter any law passed by Parliament (thus going far beyond the Deregulation and Contracting Out Act 1994, which also give quite wide discretionary powers to ministers in a particular area). But should the judges depart from the sovereignty of Parliament established under the 1689 Bill of Rights? Any refusal by the courts to apply valid legislation would be a radical departure from constitutional principle and it would amount to a highly controversial development. This would mark a shift in the current balance of the constitution away from the executive, which is notionally accountable to an elected Parliament. Further, the danger is that a government with a majority in Parliament might respond by seeking to curb judicial authority.

The United Kingdom still lacks a codified constitution but, with the introduction of so much legislation with constitutional implications, the position has changed in recent years. The European Communities Act 1972 under sections 2 and 3 qualified the doctrine of sovereignty by recognising that a competing source of law was judicially enforceable in the courts. The English

---

    [7] *Brown v Board of Education of Topeka* 347 US 483 (1954).

    [8] *Bush v Gore* 531 US 98 (2000).

    [9] Lord Steyn, in *Jackson v A-G* [2005] UKHL 56 at 102; see also, Lord Woolf, 'Droit Public—English Style' [1995] *PL* 57–72 at 68; T Allan, *Law, Liberty and Justice: The Legal Foundations of British Constitutionalism* (Oxford, Clarendon, 1993) p 286.

    [10] D Howard, 'Who wants the abolition of Parliament Bill?' (2006) *The Times*, 21 February.

courts must put into effect laws passed by European Union institutions[11] even to the extent of invalidating provisions contained in domestic legislation. Moreover, the interpretative powers of the courts have been extended by the adoption of a rule of construction approach, which holds that words in a statute should be read to have a meaning which is consistent with Community law, even if this involves a departure from the language used in the statute.[12]

The Human Rights Act (HRA) 1998 has modified the position of the courts by incorporating the European Convention on Human Rights (ECHR) into domestic law. Parliamentary sovereignty is not directly compromised by the HRA 1998, but the ECHR may be regarded as equivalent to a domestic Bill of Rights because, in effect, Convention rights become part of domestic law by requiring public bodies to have regard to Convention rights in their dealings with members of the public. In yet another context, devolution has introduced a new kind of constitutional jurisdiction by requiring the courts to oversee the limits of the powers conferred as part of the devolution arrangements. There is further discussion of the impact of the HRA 1998 and the courts and devolution in the sections below.

REFORMING THE OFFICE OF LORD CHANCELLOR

The ancient office of Lord Chancellor, which can be traced back to the time of the Norman Conquest, exercised a combination of judicial, executive, and parliamentary functions.[13] Until recently, the office was evidence of a conflict with the idea of separation of powers. At one and the same time, the incumbent wore three hats. He was head of the judiciary, with a right to sit on the highest domestic appellate courts. He was not only a member of the House of Lords, but performed the function of Speaker. Finally, he was a prominent member of the Cabinet, as head of the executive department formerly known as the Lord Chancellor's Department, which was responsible for making judicial appointments and for the running of the courts.

In 2003, when Lord Irvine was replaced by Lord Falconer as Lord Chancellor, it was announced by the government that the Lord Chancellor's position and the judicial panel of the House of Lords would be modified to address the anomalies relating to the overlapping of powers just alluded to. The impact of other constitutional reforms, particularly conflicts between this anachronistic office and the need to conform with ECHR principles

---

[11] See *R v Secretary of State for Transport, ex parte Factortame (No 2)* [1991] 1 AC 603, discussed in ch 3.

[12] See Lord Diplock in *Garland v British Rail Engineering Ltd* [1983] 2 AC 751.

[13] D Woodhouse, *The Office of Lord Chancellor* (Oxford, Hart Publishing, 2001).

introduced into domestic law by the HRA 1998, was another underlying reason for making these changes. While recognising that the Lord Chancellor's position conflicted with any notion of separation of powers, it is important to remember that conventions operated which determined the previous boundaries of conduct in constitutional matters, and these rules prevented the Lord Chancellor from having an entirely political role. For example, although the Lord Chancellor was a senior Cabinet member, it was established that in his former capacity as a judge, he would not sit as a member of the judicial panel of the House of Lords in cases involving political controversy.

Further, as the minister responsible for courts and judges, a legal background was considered essential for a Lord Chancellor. This special nexus with the legal profession was encouraged so that the views of judges and lawyers could be voiced with some authority at the Cabinet table. In theory, the Lord Chancellor was capable of protecting the judicial branch from executive interference, particularly when it came to resource allocation (the degree to which this was true depended to a considerable degree on the personal authority of the office-holder). After the recent reforms it is unclear how far a specifically legal background will be needed in future. The Constitutional Reform Act 2005 now provides that any candidate for the office of Lord Chancellor must be 'qualified by experience'. As well as a professional legal background, parliamentary, ministerial, and academic legal experience can be taken into account by the Prime Minister in making an appointment to this office. Under the revised arrangements, the Lord Chief Justice is given the title President of the Courts of England and Wales. He or she is head of the judiciary, with the authority that comes from being appointed as chief judge. In this new capacity, he or she will be responsible for ensuring that the views of the judiciary are effectively represented.

Certain traditional aspects of the position have been retained, including the title Lord Chancellor, but at the same time obvious anomalies which conflicted with separation of powers have been removed. The position can now be summarised as follows:

(1) The Lord Chancellor/Secretary of State for Constitutional Affairs is the Cabinet minister at the head of the Department for Constitutional Affairs (the former Lord Chancellor's Department), which has responsibility for the appointment of judges, the administration of the courts, and the provision of legal aid. The Lord Chancellor is directly accountable to Parliament for the efficiency and effectiveness of the court system. In common with all other ministers, the Lord Chancellor must be a Member of Parliament, but there is no longer a requirement to be a member of the House of Lords.

(2) The Constitutional Reform Act 2005 has established a principle of judicial independence. The new legislation requires the Secretary of State and all those involved in the administration of justice, including in the appointment of judges, to be under a duty to respect and maintain judicial independence.[14]

(3) The conflict of roles in Parliament between acting as a minister and presiding over the Upper House has been eliminated.[15] The House of Lords is now presided over by 'the Lord Speaker'. Baroness Hayman, the first office-holder, was elected by members in July 2006 for an initial term of five years. She will receive a salary of £102,000.

(4) The Lord Chancellor/Secretary of State for Constitutional Affairs is no longer eligible to sit as a judge on the judicial panels of the House of Lords and Privy Council, and future holders of the office will not have any judicial role in relation to the Supreme Court when it begins to operate in late 2009.

APPOINTING AND DISMISSING JUDGES

Perhaps the most crucial area that has been transformed by these changes concerns the role of the Lord Chancellor/Secretary of State for Constitutional Affairs in relation to judicial appointments. The traditional system for judicial appointments lacked transparency. Although it involved a covert system of informal recommendations, it was accepted that the recommendations made by the Lord Chancellor for senior judicial appointments (or recommendations by the Prime Minister for Court of Appeal and House of Lords) went to the best qualified individuals rather than on the basis of any declared political affiliation.[16]

It is quite common under codified constitutions for the executive to propose and the legislature to approve appointments to the higher judiciary.[17] There are very good reasons for not imitating the procedure in the United States and involving Parliament actively in the appointment process. The Constitution of the United States was drafted to incorporate separation of powers as a core doctrine. In regard to the appointment of the most senior judges who sit on the Supreme Court, the power to nominate candidates is given to the executive in the form of the President. On the other hand, the

---

[14] Constitutional Reform Act 2005, s 3.
[15] Constitutional Reform Act 2005, s 18.
[16] Nevertheless, it has been argued that political bias is discernible in significant judicial decisions. See, eg, J Griffith, *Judicial Politics since 1920* (Oxford, Blackwell, 1993).
[17] Article 104 of the Italian Constitution is one such example.

Senate, as part of the legislature, has the duty of confirming presidential nominations.[18] However, even though justices of the Supreme Court once confirmed remain in place for their lifetime, this procedure has not been a
guarantee of independence and political neutrality. The position has been
exactly the reverse. The Supreme Court exercises a constitutional review
function and, unlike the UK courts, it has the power to police the constitution and to declare legislation invalid. This has projected the court into the
forefront of political controversy on many occasions.[19] Most obviously in
recent times it was the US Supreme Court that finally had to decide the validity of the contested presidential election result in the year 2000 in the case of
Bush v Gore.[20] The political dimension of the Supreme Court's role has
resulted in deliberate attempts by US Presidents to select judicial candidates
with views that appear to correspond to their own.[21] An obvious danger in
making any such reform in the United Kingdom to the system of judicial
appointments was introducing any form of political interference into the
process.

The central objection made by Professor Griffith to the types of appointments to the judicial bench during the 1970s and 1980s concerned the elevation to the judiciary of a public school Oxbridge-educated elite section of
society, nearly all of whom experienced a similar legal training.[22] More recent
critics, for example Lady Justice Hale, no longer view the problem mainly in
terms of social class, but rather identify the need to appoint judges who are
more representative of society as a whole.[23] Recent Lord Chancellors have
recognised the importance of placing increasing emphasis on equality and
diversity as well as the accepted qualities of integrity and judicial quality
understood in terms of intellectual ability.[24]

The task of selecting judges is now mainly in the hands of a Judicial
Appointments Commission (JAC) for England and Wales, which has been
established under the Constitutional Reform Act 2005 as an independent
non-departmental body. This body is itself largely appointed by open com-

---

[18]   Article II, Section 2. The Senate will hold hearings to examine the suitability of candidates
but presidential nominations are ratified unless there are blemishes to personal reputation:
S Finer, *Five Constitutions* (London, Penguin, 1979).

[19]   M Vile, *Politics in the USA* (London, Hutchinson, 1976) p 242; R Denenberg, *Understanding
American Politics*, 3rd edn (London, Fontana, 1992). See ch 6.

[20]   531 US 98 (2000).

[21]   C Turpin, *British Government and the Constitution: Text, Cases and Materials*, 5th edn (London,
Butterworths, 2002) p 663.

[22]   J Griffith, *The Politics of the Judiciary*, 5th edn (London, Fontana, 1997) p 18ff.

[23]   (2003) *The Guardian*, October 30, reporting a speech delivered to the Plymouth Law
Society.

[24]   See, eg, Lord Falconer, Lord Chancellor, Constitutional Reform Speech, University
College London, 8 December 2003.

petition and it is responsible for selecting judges up to and including High Court judges. It comprises 15 commissioners in total. There are five lay members, five judges (three from the Court of Appeal or High Court, one circuit judge and one district judge), two professional members (one barrister and one solicitor), one lay magistrate, and one tribunal member. The chair must be one of the lay members. Commissioners serve for between three and five years. The initial appointments to the Commission include seven women and two from ethnic minorities, one of whom chairs the Commission.

The weight attached to recommendations by the JAC for England and Wales is of central importance, especially for appointments to the higher judiciary. This issue comes down to whether the power to select which is given to the JAC can be undermined by the ratification process. For appointments up to and including those to the High Court, the Secretary of State will inform the JAC when a vacancy arises. After the selection and interviewing process has been carried out by the JAC, a single name for each vacancy, together with reasons for the selection, will be forwarded to the Lord Chancellor. The Lord Chancellor can accept the recommendation and, indeed, in the vast majority of cases selections will be approved. However, the Lord Chancellor can ask the JAC to reconsider, if it appears that the evidence submitted does not demonstrate suitability. The Lord Chancellor can reject a candidate or require reconsideration if there is some evidence that the nominated candidate cannot be considered for judicial appointment, or if he or she considers that the competition has not been conducted properly. In situations where the initial choice is not accepted the matter goes back to the JAC. The original candidate can be confirmed, or an alternative candidate can be selected with reasons. The recommended candidate goes back to the Secretary of State who can only reject a candidate if there is some evidence making the candidate unsuitable for consideration. Any such reasons must be set out in writing. If a candidate is rejected the Lord Chancellor is obliged to accept the next recommended candidate.

It will be remembered that the Act of Settlement 1700 is regarded as a significant step in securing judicial independence, as it introduced security of tenure for judges who have been appointed 'during good behaviour' ever since. In modern times judges have a retirement age (currently 70 for High Court, Appeal Court, and House of Lords judges) but parliamentary action is necessary to remove senior judges, and none have been dismissed in recent times. In addition, the Constitutional Reform Act 2005 sets out procedures for exercising disciplinary powers over judges and for removing judges. At the same time as establishing a system of appointments and discipline, the 2005 Act introduces complaints procedures overseen by a judicial appointments ombudsman who must be a non-lawyer.

A SUPREME COURT FOR THE UNITED KINGDOM

The Judicial Committee of the House of Lords will be replaced by a Supreme Court with a broadly similar appellate jurisdiction in October 2009.[25] The Supreme Court will not be established as a constitutional court although, of course, it will have to preside over cases that raise constitutional issues, and it will take over from the Judicial Committee of the Privy Council jurisdiction over 'devolution issues' arising from the Scotland Act 1998, Government of Wales Act 1998, and Northern Ireland Act 1998. While the courts frequently make judgments which develop the principles of the common law, the courts do not have a general power of constitutional review. The new Supreme Court will not have such powers. It has been confirmed that the panel of judges assigned initially to the court will include any serving Lords of Appeal in Ordinary (Law Lords), but any new Justices of the Supreme Court will not be able to sit or vote in the House of Lords. At its head the new court will have a President and a Deputy President.

For the appointment of judges to the new Supreme Court a selection commission will be specially convened for the purpose which must include the President and Deputy President of the Supreme Court and members of the JACs for England, Scotland, and Northern Ireland.[26] To ensure that all parts of the United Kingdom have appropriate representation on the Supreme Court in terms of expertise concerning their jurisdictions, the Commission must consult the First Minister in Scotland, the Welsh Assembly, and the Secretary of State for Northern Ireland before making a recommendation of a suitably qualified person to the Lord Chancellor. The Lord Chancellor has then to consult further with senior judges and representatives from the devolved parts of the United Kingdom before reaching a decision on the Commission's recommendation. If the Lord Chancellor approves of the Commission's choice he can approve ('notify') the selection, which then goes on to be finally approved by the Prime Minister. At this point the Lord Chancellor also has the option, if certain specified grounds are satisfied, of rejecting the selection or requiring a reconsideration, but he or she has no power to choose an alternative candidate. For the appointment of Heads of Division of courts and Appeal Court judges, the JAC must set up a selection panel which reports its selection to the Lord Chancellor who has broadly similar options regarding acceptance, rejection, or asking for reconsideration.

---

[25] Constitutional Reform Act 2005, Part 3.
[26] Constitutional Reform Act 2005, ss 26 and 27.

To briefly summarise the position following the implementation of the Constitutional Reform Act 2005: the Lord Chancellor has shed many of the traditional powers associated with the office, and the relationship between the Lord Chancellor, the judiciary, and the legal profession has been radically transformed. The most senior judge of the Supreme Court will preside as President of a new Supreme Court, while the Lord Chief Justice will occupy a special role as head of the judiciary and legal profession. A new Judicial Appointments Commission has been established to play a predominant role in the selection of judges. Taken together, these are far-reaching reforms of great constitutional importance. In consequence, it will be crucial that, in practice, the safeguards set out in the Constitutional Reform Act 2005 are effective in underlining a necessary separation of powers and functions between the executive branch and the judicial branch.

We have seen in this section that the role of the courts has been transformed in recent years. The government has responded with important reforms. It has decided to introduce a much stricter separation of powers, but to keep sovereignty in the hands of Parliament. The ancient office of Lord Chancellor has been reformed. The Constitutional Reform Act 2005 introduces a new system of judicial appointments, placing the main responsibility for appointments with an independent appointments commission. Serving judges will soon lose the right to be sitting members of the House of Lords in its legislative capacity. The Judicial Committee of the House of Lords is being replaced by a Supreme Court, but one with similar composition and powers to its predecessor.

PART II: ADMINISTRATIVE LAW AND JUDICIAL REVIEW

INTRODUCTION TO ADMINISTRATIVE LAW

At a time when the executive has become extremely powerful through what in this book we have called 'elective dictatorship', many commentators believe that judicial review has come to assume particular importance as a counterbalance to executive power. In particular, it performs a crucial constitutional role in the absence of any other mechanism for legislative review (eg a constitutional court). While some kind of oversight function is desirable, the extent to which the courts are able to intervene in the routine processes of government is highly controversial. We will see that the courts have come to exercise what is termed a supervisory jurisdiction, but we shall also see that administrative law needs to be understood more broadly in terms of the processes of policy implementation.

In recent years one highly nuanced academic debate has focused upon the constitutional basis of judicial review. In brief, the so called 'ultra vires' view argued that the ultra vires doctrine forms the basis for judicial review; in other words, if a decision-maker acts beyond the powers conferred by legislation the courts simply exercise a supervisory jurisdiction by interpreting the law so as to set limits on statutory authority.[27] On the other hand, the common law view has regarded this account as inadequate, and rather it maintains that judicial review needs to be explained beyond looking at legislative intent. It recognises that wide-ranging principles of judicial review have been developed by the courts under the common law. This constitutes a sophisticated body of law which has come into existence independent of the legislature, and these principle are used to control the actions of administrative bodies.[28] Leaving aside which of these views more accurately describes the position, administrative law in the United Kingdom is normally conceived around the control function of the courts described by Dicey under the rule of law. However, in terms of actual practice the implementation of administrative law is carried out by central and local government officials, and by private organisations under contract, with reference to relevant statutory powers contained in primary and secondary legislation. A network of administrative tribunals deals with disputes and appeals against decisions taken by officials. In contrast, continental systems of administrative law, such as those in France, Italy, Germany, or Spain tend to place much less emphasis on the role of courts (apart from administrative courts); rather, attention is concentrated on the nature of an administative code which provides the structure and functions of the public administration.[29] This part of the chapter will be in three sections. The first section sets out the well-known 'red light and green light theory' of administrative law, which helps to explain the historical context. The second section provides an account of the current law of judicial review. The third section discusses the impact of the Human Rights Act 1998 on the regime of public law with particular reference to some important cases.

---

[27] See, eg, C Forsyth, 'Of Fig Leaves and Fairy Tales: The Ultra Vires Doctrine, the Sovereignty of Parliament and Judicial Review' [1996] *CLJ* 122–40.

[28] P Craig, 'Ultra Vires and the Foundations of Judicial Review' [1998] *CLJ* 63.

[29] See HWR Wade and C Forsyth, *Administrative Law*, 9th edn (Oxford, Oxford University Press, 2004) as an exemplar of the UK court-centred approach, eg p 5: 'The primary purpose of administrative law . . . is to keep the powers of the government within their legal bounds. . .'

RED LIGHT AND GREEN LIGHT THEORY

In their influential study which begins by tracing the main trends in administrative law Harlow and Rawlings identify two contrasting models which are termed 'red light' and 'green light'.[30] The former is more conservative and directed at control; the latter is more liberal/socialist in orientation and facilitative in nature. The two models developed in tandem with the emergence of the modern state and serve broadly to characterise competing approaches to administrative law from the late nineteenth century until the latter part of the twentieth century. In the current situation these polarities have been largely replaced by a continuum of overlapping assumptions, combining elements from red light at one end of the spectrum to green light at the other. It might be more accurate to claim that the lights now converge at amber.

The 'Red Light' View

The 'red light' view is traced back to Professor Dicey and a political tradition of nineteenth-century *laissez-faire* (minimal state) theory which embodied a strong suspicion of governmental power exercised by emerging state bureaucracy at central or local government level. Standing behind such a view was a desire to minimise the encroachment of the state on the rights (especially property rights) of individuals. Dicey maintained that the concept of *legal* sovereignty (we have already observed that this concept was regarded by him as *the* fundamental principle of the constitution) favours the supremacy of law. Parliament establishes a framework of general rules in society. Dicey's second principle, the rule of law, was of equal importance to his account of the constitution. For it was this concept that ensured that all public and private bodies, as well as individuals, would only act according to the law. The executive should govern strictly according to the rules set out by Parliament. The rule of law proposes that the law will operate to contain illegality and abuse, but without necessarily having, or needing, an explicit moral and political foundation. Dicey did not elaborate any special guiding principles for law in general (or administrative law in particular). The philosophy underpinning the common law was entirely one of pragmatism, that is, of adjustment to changing circumstances. At its most basic level in the context of judicial review, intervention by the courts is justified when public bodies (or any other body or individual) exceed their legal powers (that is, act ultra vires or

---

[30] C Harlow and R Rawlings, *Law and Administration*, 2nd edn (London, Butterworths, 1997).

abuse their powers) when exercising a public function. If unchecked, the bureaucratic and executive power of state institutions or mechanisms will threaten the liberty of us all. Such a view is closely allied to the idea of a 'self-correcting democracy', explained by Craig, in which law performs an important control function.[31] The courts come to be regarded as part of the constitutional system of 'checks and balances'. The grounds of judicial review which have been developed by the courts might be viewed as the response of the common law.

The modern state, and its attendant baggage of administrative procedures, guidance, and discretion, was established at the same time as the emergence of party government. From the outset there have been pronounced differences in ideological perspective between the main political parties as the state has evolved. For advocates of the 'red light' view, the judiciary was regarded as being autonomous and impartial and the common law was imbued with its own standards of independence and fairness. This meant that the courts could be relied upon as a kind of referee to adjudicate, not on the political or even the practical validity of any decision, but simply on the legality of executive action. Over time, judges have developed principles which have served to keep law at a step removed from politics; in other words, the courts should not be usurping the functions of public authorities on matters of fact, judgment, or policy.[32] For example, we will soon see that *Wednesbury* unreasonableness (also known as irrationality) establishes a high hurdle to overcome in judicial review cases, which are often challenging decisions of public bodies.[33]

The main function of the judiciary according to the 'red light' view is perceived as interpreting and applying the strict letter of the law. This conceptualisation of the role of the courts serves the needs of the legal profession well by perpetuating a separation of law from policy issues, with the emphasis being placed on the strict construction of statutes or rules in isolation from their broader contextual framework. The problem is that the proposal that law *can* stand aside from politics and morality is strongly contested. Indeed, opponents of this view maintain that the ideological position of the judiciary is widely demonstrated by analysing crucial cases.[34]

The danger is now more accurately perceived as being that ministers and officials might tend to shelter behind a body of rules and delegated powers

---

[31] P Craig, 'Dicey: Unitary, Self-Correcting Democracy and Public Law' (1991) 106 *Law Quarterly Review* 105.

[32] J Jowell and A Lester, 'Beyond *Wednesbury*: Substantive Principles of Administrative Law' [1987] *PL* 369–82 at 382.

[33] *Associated Provincial Picture Houses Ltd v Wednesbury Corporation* [1948] 1 KB 223. See below under 'Grounds of Review'.

[34] J Griffith, *The Politics of the Judiciary*, 5th edn (London, Fontana, 1997).

which have been created to facilitate the tasks of administration. Thus it is that, in a negative sense, judicial intervention becomes possible as a kind of safety-net, by taking up the democratic slack in those areas where parliamentary control is manifestly found wanting. Or by being activated during those periods when parliamentary opposition is regarded as being weak and ineffective.

The 'Green Light' View

The 'green light' perspective is based on an acceptance of a social democratic view of the state and regards law as an essential tool for the delivery of communitarian policy objectives. It originates from the utilitarian tradition of egalitarian and ameliorative social reform.[35] The introduction of policies extending public service provision was supported by green light theorists. For example, this approach is typified in the writings of Laski, Jennings, Robson, and Griffiths from the London School of Economics and Political Science.[36] Statute law emanating from Parliament and resulting from the democratic process is regarded as *the* method for enabling the implementation of such policies. A statute is something concrete and can provide, in principle at least, the proper authority and framework with which to govern consensually. This position recognises that it is very much more difficult to achieve an adequate and sustainable provision of services without having the law on the side of the administration. Law comes to embody, in equal measure, both political legitimacy and moral persuasiveness. The contribution of the state is encouraged as the state bureaucracy is regarded as an effective means of facilitating the delivery of communitarian goals. It does this by assuming responsibility for at least basic minimum standards of provision, including housing, education, health, social security, and local services.

The emergence of a modern conception of administrative law not only coincides with the political and economic changes that have witnessed the development of the modern state, but it is inseparably linked to these changes. The expansion of the state has given rise to the centralisation of powers in some areas, for example, central government, the civil service, agencies (such as the Prisons Agency or the Benefits Agency), and quasi-government bodies;

---

[35] For example, see S Webb and B Webb, *A Constitution for the Socialist Commonwealth of Great Britain* (London, Longmans, 1920).

[36] R Rawlings, 'Distinction and Diversity: Law and the LSE' in R Rawlings (ed), *Law, Society and Economy: Centenary Essays for the London School of Economics and Political Science 1895–1995* (Oxford, Oxford University Press, 1997) p 5ff; W Robson, *Justice and Administrative Law*, 3rd edn (London, Stevens, 1951).

and the broad territorial diffusion of power in others, for example, the emergence of local government as an important focus of decision-taking and spending in the nineteenth and twentieth centuries (most recently marked by the emergence of a Parliament in Scotland and a National Assembly in Wales). In sum, power that is exercised by public bodies has greatly expanded; accordingly, the mechanisms for accountability have assumed a new importance, particularly since the 1960s.

It has been an equally important objective for advocates of what is termed the 'green light' view to establish organised institutions which are properly accountable, and at the same time capable of delivering these services effectively. The growth of bureaucracy in the public domain has meant a proliferation of delegated legislation, administrative rules, codes, and circulars. Some critics have argued that the emergence of strong party government (or 'elective dictatorship') has meant that Parliament no longer operates as anything like an adequate forum of accountability.[37] This is largely because it has generally failed to provide effective mechanisms for scrutiny of the executive. The question is whether citizens have sufficient rights in the face of omnipresent central and local government powers or, indeed, those powers exercised by bodies now in the private sector, for example, the privatised utilities.

The response from 'green lighters' to accountability issues has not been to rely primarily on the courts for redress but to build into the decision-making process certain rights, and a degree of participation by the citizen. We can see a reflection of this view in the growth of administrative tribunals and, perhaps to a lesser extent, in proposals centring around freedom of information, Citizen's Charter/'Service First', and the public sector benchmarking mechanism. The central concern has been to confer, for example, social welfare rights and a general empowerment of individuals in regard to the exercise of powers by public bodies. Equally, 'green light' advocates might wish to see the grounds of review in the courts developed to be more precisely focused on the detailed workings of particular administrative structures, for example, in the areas of social security or immigration control. Additional rights and powers to work through tribunals might be advocated, as these bodies can act as decision-makers/facilitators, as well as encouraging internal dispute resolution. We can see that this view implicitly challenges and corrects some of the misconceptions that may arise from the 'red light' view. It does this not by relying on the pragmatism which characterises the common law, but by adopting an instrumental approach (that is, it concentrates on the effectiveness of the measures in question). Administrative law becomes accepted as part of the

---

[37] For example, see *Report on Ministers' Powers*, Cmnd 4060 (London, HMSO, 1932); *Report of the Hansard Society Commission on Parliamentary Scrutiny, The Challenge for Parliament: Making Government Accountable* (London, Hansard Society, 2001).

total apparatus of government, not something largely distinct from it. It can be made to act as a regulator and facilitator to enable social policy to be implemented effectively and fairly. The 'green light' approach continues to be manifested in the contribution of administrative tribunals and statutory regimes of regulation (eg applying to public utilities and railways).

In recent decades there has been a fundamental change affecting the nature of government, with a widespread tendency towards marketisation through the privatisation of many services that were once in the public sector and the development of public–private partnerships, and so on. Harlow and Rawlings recognised that by the 1980s in an era of reinvented government it was no longer accurate to see things in terms of a polarisation of 'red light' and 'green light' views. In the contemporary arena the clear ideological divide of right and left between the main political parties has virtually disappeared. All major parties support market capitalism to various degrees. Despite the fact that the higher judiciary still tend to be drawn from an Oxbridge elite, it is no longer clear that the affiliations of judges can still be measured in terms of support for one political standpoint to the detriment of others, or one view of the constitution. Indeed, during the 1980s and 1990s under the Conservative governments of Margaret Thatcher and John Major, the courts entered the political fray as a counterweight to government. They did so with a number of decisions that had the effect of challenging controversial policies (illustrated in the section on judicial review cases below). In following a more interventionist course of action the courts have projected themselves as a separate branch of government.

THE IMPACT OF JUDICIAL REVIEW

By requiring public bodies to act lawfully, judicial review imposes legal limits to decision-making in the public domain. The grant of judicial review is discretionary in the sense that claims (formerly called applications) for judicial review are assessed by a judge who will consider whether they are sufficiently well founded to proceed. This remedy is available only to a claimant who has exhausted all other avenues of redress such as informal complaints procedures, ombudsmen, statutory rights of appeal, and so on. And it must normally be sought within the strict time limit of three months from the time the decision was taken.

The growing importance of judicial review would appear to be reflected in a spectacular increase in the number of cases coming before the courts. For example, between 1982 and 2005 the number of claims for judicial review increased from 685 to over 5,000. There are approximately the same numbers of claims concerning local government as central government. In the 1980s to reduce susceptibility to review civil servants were sent a circular entitled 'The Judge over your Shoulder', which contained advice on how to avoid obvious pitfalls when making decisions in the context of statutory powers. However, although the numbers of applications have steadily risen these statistics are, in themselves, somewhat misleading. First, this is because in order to filter out unmeritorious cases judicial review is a two-stage process, and only a small proportion of claims reach the final determination stage in the form of a full court hearing. (For example, a public authority may prefer to settle and reconsider its decision or a claimant may withdraw if faced with the prospect of losing at the hearing.) Second, rather than showing an even distribution across the entire spectrum of government activity, the statistics reveal that a large percentage of applications are concerned with immigration cases. Third, although the number of cases has increased greatly in recent years the caseload represents a tiny fraction of decisions taken by public bodies (well under one per cent). It might be concluded from the bare statistics that there is uneven access to judicial review, and that, if government administration is taken as a whole, its impact is apparently not of central importance. On the other hand, the possibility of judicial review lurking in the background almost certainly has a deterrent effect and encourages decision-making bodies to act lawfully.

The common law recognised the prerogative remedies (recently renamed: original names in italics) of a quashing order (*certiorari*), a prohibiting order (*prohibition*) and a mandating order (*mandamus*) which, together with the equitable remedies of the declaration and injunction, could be used to control an excess of legal authority. The effect of a quashing order is to invalidate a decision and make the decision-maker take the decision again lawfully. A prohibiting order prevents the decision from being taken. A mandating order requires the public body to act in a particular way. A declaration sets out the legal position between the parties without imposing a remedy. Injunctions are usually granted to prevent a public body from acting. However, the private law remedy of damages, while sometimes available, is rarely granted in judicial review proceedings. General exposure to financial compensation would have far-reaching implications for the funding of public bodies (see the discussion of liability of the Crown in contract and tort in chapter four).

DISTINGUISHING PUBLIC LAW FROM PRIVATE LAW

A series of procedural innovations introduced in the late 1970s greatly simplified the process for applying (now claiming) for judicial review, and contributed to the increase in cases coming before the courts. The House of Lords decided unanimously in *O'Reilly v Mackman*[38] that the application for judicial review procedure[39] had been set up specifically to deal with public law issues and to impose, in the public interest, safeguards against, in Lord Diplock's words: 'groundless, unmeritorious or tardy attacks upon the validity of decisions made by public authorities in the field of public law.' The public interest was therefore given priority over the private. The normal route would be by way of the judicial review procedure, with a number of limited exceptions being made to this general rule. A public law issue might be defined by reference to the authority making the decision: if it is a 'public' authority, then it should be subject to 'public' law regardless of the actual power being exercised. However, the exclusivity principle is subject to certain exceptions, for example, if the conduct of a public body impacts on private law rights as well as public law rights, an action can be brought in the ordinary civil courts.[40]

Apart from recognising that the judicial review procedure was directed at the control of public as opposed to private power, it has been necessary to find a method of distinguishing the public from the private—a task made more difficult by the increasing overlap between the two. For example, in what has been termed the 'contract state' not only has there been widespread privatisation and regulation, but also many governmental services, ranging from prisons to street cleaning and refuse disposal, are performed by private companies. The Court of Appeal in *R v Panel on Takeovers and Mergers, ex parte Datafin*[41] was faced with the dilemma of deciding whether it was the source of the powers of the organisation which was the crucial factor, or the nature of the body itself and the public consequences of its decisions. In this instance, the Panel on Takeovers and Mergers took the form of an entirely non-statutory, self-regulating association, set up by persons having a common interest, which had devised and operated a code of conduct to be observed in the takeovers and mergers of public companies. The court held that, bearing in mind that the panel did have government backing and was exercising public duties in the public interest, it should be subject to the control of public law. However, there has been a succession of cases where qualifications in the application of this functions test have seen charitable organisations, regulatory bodies, and religious organisations falling beyond

---

[38] [1983] 2 AC 237.

[39] Introduced by Rules of the Supreme Court, Ord 53, later enacted under s 31 of the Supreme Court Act 1981 and revised under the Civil Procedure Rules, Part 54 (in 2000).

[40] See, eg, *Roy v Kensington and Chelsea and Westminster Family Practitioner Committee* [1992] 1 AC 624.

[41] [1987] 1 All ER 564.

the ambit of judicial review.[42] As will be apparent in the section below, distinguishing between public and private bodies is relevant to cases with a human rights dimension, as the HRA 1998 applies directly only to public authorities.[43]

THE REQUIREMENTS OF STANDING

In order to proceed with a claim for judicial review the claimant must have *standing*, which is defined as having 'sufficient interest' (under Rules of the Supreme Court (RSC) Order 53, rule 7) in the contested matter. This hurdle has a useful function in that it deters frivolous or vexatious claims, but if the rules are too narrowly drawn worthy cases might also be excluded. The extent to which standing has to be a direct personal interest has been a matter of discussion in a number of important cases. For example, in *Inland Revenue Commissioners v National Federation of Self-Employed and Small Businesses Ltd*[44] the Federation objected to a decision taken by the tax authorities, who had reached a deal with a completely unconnected group of casual workers from the newspaper industry. Although it was held that this group representing small businesses did not have standing as ordinary taxpayers to mount a challenge, in an influential judgment Lord Diplock set out a more 'open' approach to standing:

> It would . . . be a grave lacuna in our system of public law if a pressure group, like this federation, or even a public-spirited taxpayer, were prevented by outdated technical rules of locus standi [that is, standing] from bringing the matter to the attention of the court to vindicate the rule of law and get the unlawful conduct stopped.

Such an approach, which also recognises 'group' standing, has been in evidence in many subsequent cases. For example, the Child Poverty Action Group was recognised as a representative charitable organisation for poor families and thus was able to challenge changes to the benefits system using judicial review[45], and the World Development Movement, an international pressure group, was allowed to challenge the government's decision to devote a substantial proportion of the overseas aid budget to the Pergau Dam project in Malaysia.[46] On the other hand, in another well-known case,

---

[42] For example, see *R v Disciplinary Committee of the Jockey Club, ex parte Aga Khan* [1993] 2 All ER 853.

[43] See *Aston Cantlow and Wilmcote with Billesley Parochial Church Council v Wallbank* [2003] UKHL 37.

[44] [1982] AC 617.

[45] *R v Secretary of State for Social Services, ex parte Child Poverty Action Group* [1990] 2 QB 540.

[46] *R v Secretary of State for Foreign Affairs, ex parte World Development Movement Ltd* [1995] 1 WLR 386.

R v Secretary of State for the Environment, ex parte Rose Theatre Trust Co,[47] in which standing was denied to a charitable trust which comprised members of the public and well-known figures in the theatre and the arts, it was held that the mere gathering together of people with a common interest did not achieve standing. It appears then that while there is a case for facilitating access to justice, it has also been recognised that, if no individual rights are at stake, granting unrestricted access to groups claiming to be representational runs the risk of allowing judicial review to become a means of political lobbying. As Professor Harlow puts it: 'the legal process is transmut[ed] into a freeway [and is in danger of becoming] a free-for-all.'[48] Lastly, it is worth noting that the rules of standing under the HRA 1998 depend on a narrower 'victim' test[49] which suggests that an action is open only to a person who is personally subject to a violation of rights. However, in practice, this requirement has not proved a significant impediment to claimants.

GROUNDS OF JUDICIAL REVIEW

The basic principle is that a public authority cannot act outside the power (ultra vires) conferred on it or abuse that power. The power often derives from a statutory source; sometimes it is a prerogative power which is challenged, and abuse of power through failure to adhere to procedural rules is another familiar ground in judicial review cases. If power is exceeded the courts have the capacity to intervene by awarding a remedy. For example, a quashing order will have the effect of invalidating a decision taken by a public body. The body concerned is required to act lawfully when taking the decision in the future. On the other hand, the courts should not intervene when public bodies are acting within their powers unless Parliament has specifically given them the authority so to do, usually by way of granting a statutory right of appeal. In *Associated Provincial Picture Houses v Wednesbury Corporation*[50] Lord Greene MR was concerned to emphasise that the courts only interfere with an act of an administrative authority if it has contravened the law. Even when the action is found to be ultra vires the court must not substitute itself for the decision-making authority. The court is acting in a supervisory capacity, not as an appellate body able to change the outcome.

---

[47] [1990] 1 QB 504.
[48] C Harlow, 'Public Law and Popular Justice' [2002] *MLR* 1–18 at 17.
[49] See HRA 1998, s 7.
[50] [1948] 1 KB 223.

The terminology used to describe the main grounds of review was explained by Lord Diplock in *Council of Civil Service Unions v Minister for the Civil Service*:[51]

> The first ground I would call 'illegality', the second 'irrationality" and the third 'procedural impropriety' . . . By 'illegality', as a ground for judicial review, I mean that the decision maker must understand correctly the law that regulates his decision making power and give effect to it. Whether he had or not is *par excellence* a justiciable question to be decided, in the event of a dispute, by . . . the judges, by whom the judicial power of the State is exercisable. By 'irrationality' I mean what can now be succinctly referred to as '*Wednesbury* unreasonableness' . . . It applies to a decision which is so outrageous in its defiance of logic or of accepted moral standards that no sensible person who had applied his mind to the question to be decided could have arrived at it . . . I have described the third head as 'procedural impropriety' [which includes] failure to observe basic rules of natural justice or failure to act with procedural fairness towards the person who will be affected by the decision . . . this head covers also failure by an administrative tribunal to observe procedural rules that are expressly laid down in the legislative instrument by which its jurisdiction is conferred, even where such failure does not involve any denial of natural justice.

Additional sub-grounds of review exist under each of these main categories referred to by Lord Diplock.[52] Looking at the development and application of the grounds and sub-grounds under the common law, it becomes clear that for the decision-making process of public bodies to be lawful, it has to take place within a framework of rules. To take a few commonly occurring sub-categories associated with illegality (see Lord Diplock above), improper purpose/motive is clearly related to exceeding lawful authority, since it refers to the fact that the decision-taker may have acted outside a statutory purpose, while the idea of relevance suggests that a body in exercising discretionary power must have regard only to legally relevant considerations. By the same token, it may have acted unlawfully by taking irrelevant considerations into account. Under the fettering principle, it can be unlawful for a decision-making body to form an over rigid policy in advance which prevents it from exercising the discretion granted to it. Improper delegation occurs when a decision-making body acting under statutory authority gives away the power to act to another body.

An equally important aspect of judicial review has been the recognition of procedural protection under the rules of fairness/natural justice, for example

---

[51] [1985] AC 374 (known as the *GCHQ* case) at 410–11B.
[52] M Fordham 'Surveying the Grounds: Key Themes in Judicial Intervention' in P Leyland and T Woods (eds) *Administrative Law Facing the Future: Old Constraints and New Horizons*, London, Blackstone, 1997.

the right to a fair hearing. Furthermore, legitimate expectation, which is closely related to the doctrine of legal certainty, has become an important part of domestic administrative law, both in a procedural sense, and as a matter of substantive law. The first signs of renewed judicial activism emerged in the 1960s. The scope of fairness/natural justice in procedure was extended in *Ridge v Baldwin*.[53] Limits were set on the exercise of ministerial discretion in relation to subjectively worded clauses in statutes in *Padfield v Minister for Agriculture, Fisheries and Food*.[54] The concept of jurisdictional error and the status of statutory ouster clauses appearing to exclude judicial review were considered in *Anisminic v Foreign Compensation Commission*.[55] In a famous assertion of its constitutional role the House of Lords held that statutory provisons appearing to limit the jurisdiction of the court were invalid. In the *GCHQ* case Lord Diplock acknowledged the potential for further developments by predicting that the principle of proportionality would be adopted by the common law. (Proportionality is now accepted as part of human rights jurisprudence. See the section below on the HRA 1998.)

THE QUESTION OF MERITS

We have already noted that, according to the 'red light' view, the courts operating under the rule of law have, what we have called, a supervisory jurisdiction. They perform a control function but the scope of this jurisdiction is crucially important. Many writers have observed that even before the introduction of devolution and the HRA 1998 the reformulation of the grounds of judicial review coincided with a period of greater judicial activism.[56] The constitutional effect of widening the scope of judicial review represents a rebalancing of power between Parliament and the courts. *Roberts v Hopwood*[57] can be cited as an early twentieth-century case which demonstrates the implications of judicial intervention. Poplar Council had been empowered under the Metropolis Management Act 1855 to pay its employees such salaries and wages 'as . . . the council may think fit.' Although the statute appeared to confer a broad discretion when a socialist local authority chose to use these wide discretionary powers to pay female and male workers equally and also a wage above the market rate, its policy was deemed to be unlawful by the House of Lords.

[53] [1964] AC 40.
[54] [1968] AC 997.
[55] [1969] 2 AC 147.
[56] See, eg, S Sedley, 'Sounds of Silence: Constitutional Law without a Constitution' (1994) 110 *LQR* 270.
[57] [1925] AC 578.

Looking back to the post-World War II period, it is clear that a restricted role for the courts is envisaged in Lord Greene's landmark judgment in *Associated Provincial Picture Houses v Wednesbury Corporation.*[58] He stated:

> The court is entitled to investigate the action of the [public] authority with a view to seeing whether they have taken into account matters which they ought not to have taken into account, or, conversely, have refused to take into account or neglected to take into account matters which they ought to take into account. Once that question is answered in favour of the local authority, it may still be possible to say that, although the local authority have kept within the four corners of the matters which they ought to consider, they have nevertheless come to a conclusion so unreasonable that no reasonable authority could ever have come to it. In such a case, again, I think the court can interfere.

The example of a red-haired teacher dismissed for no other reason than the colour of her hair was used to illustrate how absurd a decision needed to be before the courts would be prepared to overturn it. To keep the courts a step removed from political decision-making, the concept of *Wednesbury* unreasonableness/irrationality deliberately erects a high hurdle to overcome before a court will be prepared to intervene on *Wednesbury* grounds alone. For example, a challenge to what was alleged to be an unfair rate-capping policy directed by central government (which was under Conservative control) at high-spending Labour local authorities was rejected by the House of Lords in *Nottingham City Council v Secretary of State for the Environment.*[59] Lord Scarman made it clear that in cases of this type a high threshold had to be overcome. *Wednesbury* unreasonableness/irrationality meant that the decision of the minister would have to have been so absurd that he must have taken leave of his senses for a remedy to be granted.

JUDICIAL REVIEW CASES

There are important decisions which demonstrate a greater judicial willingness than was previously discernible to intervene in policing the activities of central and local government, often with controversial results. In *Bromley v Greater London Council*[60] the courts were called upon to decide on the legality of a policy decision by the Greater London Council (GLC) (later abolished). In line with a local election commitment the Council wanted to reduce fares on London transport. The Transport (London) Act 1969 placed the authority under a duty to develop policies, and to encourage, organise and, where

---

[58] [1948] 1 KB 223.
[59] [1986] AC 240.
[60] [1983] 1 AC 768.

appropriate, to carry out efficient and economic transport facilities and services for Greater London. This section of the Act appeared to give the GLC considerable discretion in the way it chose to run the transport system and allocate resources, but on final appeal to the House of Lords, it was held that the new policy was unlawful. The fiduciary duty owed to ratepayers (local taxpayers) had not sufficiently been taken into account when making the decision. The word 'economy' used in the Act was given a narrow interpretation in the House of Lords. The council was not acting irrationally, and an alternative approach to interpreting the statute would have recognised that the GLC had the scope to reallocate funding in the form of grants to underpin its reduced fares policy.

A ministerial decision to grant aid to Malaysia for the Pergau Dam project under section 1 of the Overseas Development and Co-operation Act 1980 was successfully challenged as unlawful in *R v Secretary of State for Foreign Affairs, ex parte World Development Movement Ltd*[61] (referred to above in relation to standing). It was held by Rose LJ that 'Whatever the Secretary of State's intention or purpose may have been, it is . . . a matter for the courts and not for the Secretary of State to determine whether, on the evidence before the court, the particular conduct was, or was not, within the statutory purpose.' The judge's reading of the statute identified an abuse of power, but it is arguable that the court has come close to interfering with ministerial discretion in the sensitive area of the formulation foreign policy.

In an entirely different context it was held in *R v Lord Chancellor, ex parte Witham*[62] that the introduction by the government of a flat rate court fee which applied to the unemployed and individuals on income support through a form of delegated legislation was ultra vires the Supreme Court Act 1981. The fee had the effect of preventing certain categories of individuals who were poor from having access to the courts and thereby interfered with a presumptive constitutional right. The court ruled that such a change to the Supreme Court Act could be made only by way of primary legislation. It has been suggested that a new jurisdiction of constitutional rights has been emerging from such decisions.

In *M v Home Office*,[63] as was pointed out in earlier chapters, clear limits were placed on governmental powers in the field of immigration and asylum. A political asylum seeker on the point of being deported obtained an order from the court requiring his immediate return to the United Kingdom. The Home Secretary ignored the court order and the asylum seeker was duly deported. The minister's actions were successfully challenged. The House of

---

[61] [1995] 1 WLR 386.
[62] [1997] 2 All ER 77.
[63] [1994] 1 AC 377.

Lords held that the minister had acted in contempt of court and that injunctions were available against officers of the Crown.

The courts have redefined the scope of prerogative powers exercised by ministers when these powers appear to conflict with statutory powers. As we noted in chapter four, the House of Lords had to decide in *R v Secretary of State for the Home Department, ex parte Fire Brigades Union*[64] the legality of a revised compensation scheme for victims of crimes of violence which was to be introduced using the minister's prerogative powers. This scheme was entirely different in its effect to the provisions of the Criminal Justice Act 1988, which had been enacted by Parliament for the same purpose. However, the minister, instead of using his discretion to bring the relevant sections of the 1988 Act into force, had decided to change the system for awarding compensation by the prerogative route. The court held unanimously that the minister was not in breach of his statutory duty by not bringing the statute into force, but it was held by a 3:2 majority that the revised scheme was an abuse of the Secretary of State's power. The prerogative had been used in a manner which was inconsistent with the statutory scheme, and this decision had frustrated the will of Parliament. The case raised significant constitutional issues. The judges for the majority viewed the matter as a narrow question of legality. For them, on a reading of the legislation the minister was acting inconsistently with a statutory duty. The dissenting judgments argued that the courts were overstepping the boundary and trespassing on political territory by setting aside the decision of the Secretary of State.

PART III: THE COURTS AND THE HUMAN RIGHTS ACT 1998

The HRA 1998 marks a new departure for the UK constitution because it has the effect of incorporating the European Convention on Human Rights (ECHR) into domestic law. Prior to the enactment of the HRA, the ECHR enjoyed the status of an international treaty. In the absence of any statute or domestic authority to the contrary, the courts endeavoured to interpret domestic law in a way that was consistent with the ECHR, but, in general, a citizen who considered that his or her Convention rights had been breached had to take the case to the Court of Human Rights in Strasbourg for resolution, and this process often took in excess of five years. In contrast, the rights set out in the Convention might now be regarded as being equivalent to a domestic bill of rights. Since the Act came into force it is unlawful for a public authority to disregard an individual's Convention rights. (The ECHR

---

[64] [1995] 2 All ER 244.

includes rights to: life; freedom from torture; freedom from slavery; freedom of thought, conscience, and religion; privacy; freedom of expression; and freedom of peaceful assembly and association.)

The idea of positive rights was not part of the Diceyan constitution. The rule of law operated on the basis that all conduct would be regarded as lawful unless it happened to conflict with a particular law. For example, UK citizens have enjoyed freedom of speech to the extent that what they uttered did not defame the reputation of another citizen contrary to the laws of libel and slander, divulge an official secret contrary to the Official Secrets Act 1989, or incite a person to racial hatred contrary to the Public Order Act 1984, and so on. The HRA approach requires a marked change in legal culture. This is because public authorities have been forced to comply with the Act from the time it came into force in October 2000. Any action by government or other public bodies that does not comply with the ECHR can be challenged as being unlawful. It should also be pointed out that the Human Rights Act may be used as a defence by a public authority in an action taken against that authority. A defence might be raised by the authority in circumstances where the authority is acting to uphold Convention rights and a claim is made against the authority.

It is stressed once again that the HRA 1998 seeks to prevent judicial supremacy from replacing Parliamentary supremacy. If the courts are called upon to determine whether legislation or delegated legislation is in conflict with Convention rights, section 3 provides that 'So far as it is possible to do so, primary legislation and subordinate legislation must be read and given effect in a way which is compatible with the Convention rights.' This section confers an interpretative power which allows the courts to consider legislation and transform it by stretching its meaning, where it is possible to do so, in order to achieve Convention compatibility. This marks a significant shift of power from Parliament to judges, since the courts are able to rewrite sections of Acts by reading into them words that are not there, and by doing so, remove potential conflicts with the Convention. For example, in *R v A (No 2)*[65] Lord Steyn held in respect to the Youth Justice and Criminal Evidence Act 1999 which, among other things, changed the rules for the conduct of rape trials:

> It is therefore possible under section 3 [HRA 1998] to read section 41, and in particular section 41(3)(c), as subject to the implied provision that evidence or questioning which is required to ensure a fair trial under Article 6 of the Convention should not be treated as inadmissible.

[65] [2002] 1 AC 45.

The judicial insertion of words has a substantial impact on the application of the section and, in consequence, on the balance between prosecution and defence in rape trials. Section 3(1) of the HRA 1998 was arguably given an even wider interpretation in *Ghaidan v Godin-Mendoza*.[66] In this case the House of Lords interpreted the term 'spouse' under schedule 1 to the Rent Act 1977 to allow surviving same-sex partners to enjoy equal tenancy rights to heterosexual couples. The majority of their Lordships were mindful of achieving a correct separation between the courts and Parliament in fulfilling their interpretative obligation, and it is possible to view this case as acceptable judicial legislation:

> [T]he courts were interpreting existing statutory words as opposed to filling in gaps, no procedural modifications were required, there were no wide-ranging practical ramifications of the Convention compatible interpretation and the modification was an incremental addition to previous legislative amendments.[67]

The courts are not given power to invalidate primary legislation. If they find it impossible to interpret legislation in a Convention-friendly way, they can issue a declaration of incompatibility under section 4. This does 'not affect the validity, continuing operation or enforcement' of the Act in question. The effect of a declaration of incompatibility is to refer the matter back to Parliament. The Act introduces a fast-track procedure for the purpose of amending any offending legislation (there have been examples of this procedure being used). After a declaration of incompatibility has been issued, section 6(2) stipulates that until such time as any offending legislation is amended it will not be unlawful for a public authority to act in a way which is incompatible with the Convention. To achieve the compatibility of prospective legislation there is a procedure at the drafting stage under section 19 requiring the relevant minister to 'make a statement of compatibility'.

VERTICAL OR HORIZONTAL EFFECT

The HRA 1998 has a 'vertical' effect by requiring *public* bodies such as government, local government, the courts, and the police in their dealings with the public to adhere to the Convention. The courts are required to determine what constitutes public functions for these purposes, and, since the Act has been in force, it has been necessary to determine how far its provisions extend. This task is complicated by the fact that the *private* sector frequently carry out high-profile *governmental* services that are publicly funded (eg, in the

---

[66] [2004] UKHL 30; [2004] 3 All ER 411.
[67] A Young, '*Ghaidan v Godin-Mendoza*: avoiding the deference trap' [2005] *PL* 23–35 at 27.

realms of health, education, housing, prisons, and so on). It would appear that ECHR rights are not only directly enforceable against public bodies in respect of *all* of their activities, but may also be directly enforceable against some private companies and organisations in respect of their *public* functions.

In determining the extent to which the Act can be applied there are already some indications that the courts will give a narrow definition to what constitutes a public body and such an approach could limit the scope of the Act. In *Heather v Leonard Cheshire Foundation and HM Attorney-General*[68] a claimant sought to argue that a decision to close one of its homes by the Leonard Cheshire Foundation, a charitable organisation, infringed Article 8 of the Convention, but it was decided that this decision was not amenable to review since the foundation was not exercising a public function. Further analysis of this issue is provided in *Poplar v Donoghue*,[69] which was a claim involving a housing association. The Court of Appeal came to the conclusion that, while activities of housing associations need not involve the performance of public functions, in this case, in providing accommodation for the defendant and then seeking possession, the role of Poplar was so closely assimilated to that of Tower Hamlets London Borough Council that it was performing public and not private functions. The House of Lords provided a further definition of public authority in *Aston Cantley and Wilcote with Billesley Parochial Church Council v Wallbank*,[70] which concerned a dispute over the liability for church repairs that were required under the Chancel Repairs Act 1932. The claim of discrimination under the HRA 1998 against the church council failed. It was held that although the Church of England had special links with central government and performed certain public functions, it was not a core public authority (or a hybrid body) under section 6(1) but essentially a religious organisation. It was acknowledged that in other capacities the Church of England has governmental functions (eg powers of general synod, religious schools). Lord Nicholls explained that a public authority is a body whose nature is governmental in the broad sense of that expression.

Section 6 of the HRA 1998 is directed primarily at public authorities, but it is clear that there are ways in which Convention rights apply 'horizontally' under the Act. The HRA 1998 gives no direct right to sue in the civil courts for an alleged breach of a Convention right by another individual or private company, but the courts are a public body to which the Act applies. Therefore, if an action is taken to sue in the courts on a private law matter which involves interpreting a statute affecting Convention rights, the courts are now required to interpret that statute according to section 3 in a way that

---

[68] [2001] EWHC Admin 429.
[69] [2001] 3 WLR 183
[70] [2003] UKHL 37; [2003] 3 WLR 283.

is compatible with Convention rights. The same obligation attaches to the common law, which must be interpreted in a compatible manner.[71] In sum, the HRA 1998 places no *direct* obligations in regard to the conduct of private citizens and private organisations.

PROPORTIONALITY REVIEW

It is clear that the HRA 1998 establishes a new statutory type of illegality by requiring ministers and public officials at all levels to exercise their powers in ways that are compatible with Convention rights. Judicial review proceedings may be taken by victims to contest any violation of Convention rights by a public authority. The standard of review which is applied in cases involving ECHR rights is proportionality (rather than *Wednesbury* unreasonableness/ irrationality). In essence, the administrative court has to determine whether the interference with Convention rights has been proportionate In the first place, the proportionality test is a *balancing* exercise, which usually ends up deciding whether the means employed, involving interference with fundamental rights, are justified by the end, which is nearly always associated with considerations such as pressing social need, public policy, national security, or public good. Second, the court decides between competing interests (often those of an individual against those of a public authority). Therefore, it would appear that there is a danger of the court being sucked into the decision-making process itself, which should be regarded as the province of the executive (see discussion of the *Prolife Alliance* case below, and the divergence of views between the Court of Appeal and House of Lords). However, it might be argued that this question of proportionality is decided as a question of law, just as matters are determined under the ultra vires principle. The court decides the boundaries of discretion according to familiar grounds of judicial review; similarly, under proportionality the central issue is not the correctness of the decision or action taken by the executive branch, but simply whether the decision-maker is operating within the bounds set by the ECHR and the HRA 1998. A further point is that the approach of the courts will vary according to the ECHR Articles which are at issue, since the intensity of review will depend upon the subject matter in hand. Certain Convention rights are set out in absolute terms with no exceptions and cannot be balanced against a public interest. These are Article 2 (right to life),

---

[71] See *Douglas v Hello! Ltd* [2001] 2 WLR 992 and *Campbell v MGN* [2004] 2 WLR 1232. For example, Baroness Hale said in *Campbell* that the courts could not invent a new cause of action to cover types of activity not previously covered. But where there is a cause of action, the court, as a public authority, must act compatibly with both parties' Convention rights.

Article 3 (prohibition of torture), Article 4(1) (prohibition of slavery), and Article 7 (no punishment without law). On the other hand, the rights in Article 4(2), Article 4(3) (forced labour), and Article 5 (liberty and security) are subject to a long list of exceptions, while Articles 8–11 and the First Protocol of the ECHR permit a public authority to claim that the interference was necessary in the interests of a democratic society.

The House of Lords confirmed that the proportionality test would apply to HRA 1998 in *R v Secretary of State for the Home Department, ex parte Daly*.[72] The case concerned a challenge to regulations under section 47(2) of the Prison Act 1952 which affected the rights of prisoners. In this situation there was a conflict between the need to protect the rights of individuals in prison who might be exposed to regulations that could be regarded as oppressive and unnecessary, and the state having a legitimate interest in interfering with certain rights to ensure that prisons can be a secure and safe environment. It was pointed out by Lord Bingham that the prison population includes a core of dangerous, disruptive, and manipulative prisoners, hostile to authority and ready to exploit for their own advantage any concession granted to them. The question was whether new prison rules permitting staff to read the correspondence of prisoners when searching cells without the prisoner being present constituted a breach of Article 8 of the Convention. In a unanimous judgment the House of Lords accepted the view that the policy contained in this rule constituted a breach of the Convention and that a prisoner should be entitled to be present when privileged correspondence is examined.

Lord Steyn stated that proportionality should now be used in cases of this type. He was in no doubt that the differences in approach between the traditional grounds of review and proportionality may sometimes lead to different results:

> The starting point is that there is an overlap between the traditional grounds of review and the approach of proportionality. Most cases would be decided in the same way whichever approach is adopted. But the intensity of review is somewhat greater under the proportionality approach. Making due allowance for important structural differences between various Convention rights . . .'

Proportionality operates as 'a *balancing* exercise':

(1) it usually ends up deciding whether the means employed, involving interference with fundamental rights, are justified by the end, which is nearly always associated with considerations such as pressing social need, public policy, national security, or public good.

---

[72] [2001] 3 All ER 433.

(2) the court decides between competing interests (often those of an individual against those of a public authority).

In the section that follows we will look more closely at three significant cases decided under the emerging HRA jurisprudence.

THE *PROLIFE ALLIANCE* CASE

The case-law revealed a marked divergence of opinion among senior judges over the scope provided by the HRA 1998 for judicial intervention. The difference between the approach of the Court of Appeal and that of the House of Lords in this case[73] provides a good example of two distinct conceptions of the judicial role. The claim involved a challenge to a decision by the BBC and other broadcasters not to transmit in Wales a party election broadcast which had been made by the ProLife Alliance. The Alliance contended that this was in breach of its Convention rights to free speech under Article 10 of the ECHR. The broadcast used material that the broadcasters considered to be sensational and disturbing. Prior to this refusal it had been pointed out to the ProLife Alliance (as would be the case with others proposing to make election broadcasts) that a significant proportion of their programme would not comply with the relevant provisions of the Producers' Guidelines of the BBC and the Programme Code of the Independent Television Commission in respect of matters of taste and decency. It was held by the Court of Appeal that freedom of political speech enjoyed by an accredited party at a public election, especially a general election, must not be interfered with save on the most pressing grounds. It was argued by Laws LJ that the courts owed a special responsibility to the public as the constitutional guardian of the freedom of political debate. While it was acknowledged that broadcasters enjoyed wide editorial discretion in entertainment and news reporting, it was argued that they did not have such a discretion where political free speech was concerned.

The majority in the House of Lords rejected this approach, and their Lordships believed that the court had taken on the role Parliament had given to broadcasters. For example, Lord Nicholls stated:

> As it was, the Court of Appeal in effect carried out its own balancing exercise between the requirements of freedom of political speech and the protection of the public from being unduly distressed in their own homes. That was not a legitimate exercise for the courts in this case. Parliament has decided where the balance shall be held.

---

[73] *R (on the application of the Prolife Alliance) v BBC* [2002] 2 All ER 756, CA; *R v British Broadcasting Corporation, ex parte Prolife Alliance* [2003] UKHL 23; [2003] 2 WLR 1403.

The majority concluded that there was nothing to indicate that the BBC had applied an inappropriate standard in assessing whether the broadcast was offensive. Their Lordships held that:

(1) There was no challenge to the statutory or quasi-statutory requirement for exclusion of offensive material. The judgment of such matters required a value judgment by broadcasters and, by implication, not by the courts.

(2) In making the decision whether to reject the programme the primary relevant consideration for the decision-maker was the power and persuasiveness of television, which still prevailed over the human rights considerations.

(3) The decision had been taken in a responsible manner with account taken of the implications for freedom of speech.

(4) Although free speech is particularly important for elections, party political broadcasts were subject to the requirement not to broadcast offensive material.

Lord Scott contributed a powerful dissenting judgment, which explained and developed many of the points made by Laws LJ in the Court of Appeal. However, the decision of the majority places clear limits on the capacity of the courts to intervene where Parliament has set out a clear statutory framework for the determination of such issues. The Court of Appeal decision comes close to a merits review, with the court, rather than the statutory body/regulatory authority, deciding what was fit for transmission. The court had no hesitation in expressing its opinion on whether the broadcast met the relevant criteria of taste. The question comes down to whether this is the court's prerogative, or that of the decision-maker.

THE *BELMARSH DETAINEES* CASE

This *Belmarsh* case was a landmark decision which has vividly illustrated the potential and, at the same time, the limits of the HRA 1998. The government had been accused of eroding individual rights by introducing the Anti-Terrorism, Crime and Security Act in 2001,[74] which permitted the indefinite detention of foreign nationals suspected of terrorism. The challenge was mounted by a group of suspects who had been kept in Belmarsh prison for three years. In recognition of the importance of the case, a nine-judge panel

---

[74] See A Tomkins, 'Legislating against terror: the Anti-Terrorism, Crime and Security Act 2001' [2002] *PL* 205.

of the Judicial Committee of the House of Lords (rather than the normal five judges) in *A and Others v Secretary of State for the Home Department*[75] overturned delegated legislation and issued a declaration of incompatibility in respect of the Anti-Terrorism, Crime and Security Act 2001.

First, it was argued by the Belmarsh detainees that the derogation from the Convention under Article 15 was unlawful. This was on the grounds that the threshold test of reliance, which requires proof of public emergency threatening the life of the nation, had not been satisfied. On this point alone the judges in the House of Lords, with the exception of Lord Hoffmann, sided with the government and accepted that great weight should be given to the judgment of the Home Secretary, his colleagues and Parliament. This approach was justified because the government was called on to exercise a pre-eminently political judgement requiring the advice of the security services. Moreover, it was acknowledged that the European Court of Human Rights had taken a fairly expansive view of what could constitute a threat to the life of the nation.[76] (On the other hand, it was ruled that the derogation from Article 5 did not satisfy the condition of being 'strictly required': see below.)

Second, the House of Lords rejected the government's contention that the discrimination in the treatment of non-nationals was allowed on the grounds that the case was a matter of immigration law, which was placed beyond the reach of the courts. The detention was not an issue decided at the point of entry, rather the detainees' treatment was a matter of security. The court held that this group of detainees was now being regarded differently from British citizens or those with a right of abode in the United Kingdom who were suspected terrorists.

Third, a related question for the court to resolve concerned the lawfulness of the scheme under the Act, which selectively allowed for the detention of foreign nationals. Lord Bingham held:

> Assuming, as one must, that there is a public emergency threatening the life of the nation, measures which derogate from Article 5 are permissible only to the extent strictly required by the exigencies of the situation, and it is for the derogating state to prove that that is so.

It is a matter of established principle that aliens should enjoy Article 5 protection 'in accordance with domestic law and subject to the relevant international obligations of the state in which they are present.' Such protection of course includes 'the right not to be deprived of liberty except on such

---

[75]   [2004] UKHL 56.
[76]   *Lawless v Ireland (No 3)* (1961) 1 EHRR 15.

grounds and in accordance with such procedures as are established by law and the right to be equal before the courts.' Lord Hope explained that:

> Put another way, the margin of the discretionary judgment that the courts will accord to the executive and to Parliament where this right is in issue is narrower than will be appropriate in other contexts.

It came down to whether persons in a similar situation to the detainees were subject to preferential treatment without objective justification, and the difference of treatment was on grounds of nationality or immigration status (which are proscribed grounds under Article 14). It was reasoned by the Law Lords that if measures short of detention were sufficient to deal with suspected terrorists with a right of abode in the United Kingdom, it was not possible to maintain that such measures were 'strictly required' under the derogation from Article 5 for foreign nationals similarly designated in terms of threat posed. At the same time it was held that indefinite detention without trial constituted a wholly disproportionate response to the problem.

In reaching this conclusion the House of Lords was, in effect, required to consider the limits of judicial deference. Lord Bingham (the senior Law Lord) assessed the respective roles of Parliament, the executive, and the judiciary and decisively rejected a distinction which the Attorney-General had attempted to draw between democratic institutions such as the Immigration Service and the courts. It was

> wrong to stigmatise judicial decision-making as in some way undemocratic. It is particularly inappropriate in a case such as the present in which Parliament has expressly legislated in section 6 of the 1998 Act to render unlawful any act of a public authority . . . incompatible with a Convention right . . .

Moreover, he stated:

> [T]he greater the legal content of any issue, the greater the potential role of the court, because under our constitution and subject to the sovereign power of parliament it is the function of the courts and not of political bodies to resolve legal questions.

It was observed above that the House of Lords issued a declaration of incompatibility under section 4 of the HRA 1998 but this, of course, could not nullify the legislation directly. The suspects remained in prison. However, the judicial condemnation of the legislation in such comprehensive terms prompted the government to respond. It was persuaded to replace the incompatible provisions of the Anti-Terrorism, Crime and Security Act 2001 with a revised approach to controlling terrorist suspects under the Prevention of Terrorism Act 2005 involving arguably less Draconian 'non-derogating control orders' and 'derogating control orders' issued by the Secretary of State under judicial supervision.

THE *DENBIGH HIGH SCHOOL* CASE

Another important case concerning religious freedom which raised the issue of the respective roles of courts and decision-makers was *R (on the application of SB) v Head teacher and Governors of Denbigh High School*.[77] The United Kingdom has a general policy of multi-culturalism which gives religious communities scope to wear dress associated with their beliefs. A contrast can be drawn with France, which under Article 2 of its constitution has a secular state. A controversial law was introduced in 2004 banning the wearing of headscarves and other religious symbols in French state schools. Supporters argued that this new law was necessary to uphold the constitutional commitment to secularism, while opponents of the change viewed the new law as a veiled attack on the Islamic community and more generally on their right to manifest their religious beliefs.

Denbigh High School in Luton is situated in a locality with a high proportion of Muslim students (about 80 per cent) and the school had a uniform policy for Muslim students which included a headscarf and coverage of the arms. The case arose because an Islamic student changed to a type of Islamic belief which required the wearing of a *jilbab* (full-length dress covering the arms). This was not acceptable to the school, and she was not allowed to attend school wearing this form of dress. In her claim for judicial review it was argued that there had been a violation of her right to manifest her religious beliefs under Article 9. In other words, the school as a public body under section 6 of the HRA1998 was, in effect, acting unlawfully by not respecting her right to express these religious beliefs in this way. Could the HRA 1998 be used to gain legal recognition of this right by challenging the process of decision-making by the school? Although the administrative court rejected her claim, the Court of Appeal found against the school. In the leading judgment, rather than commenting directly on the school's policy on uniforms, Brooke LJ suggested that the school should have taken the decision by employing a legal test of proportionality in forming its policy.

Lord Bingham, giving the leading judgment in the House of Lords, entirely rejected the approach adopted by the Court of Appeal. He explained that proportionality is a test to be applied by the court when reviewing decisions by public authorities after the decision has been taken. The obligation under the HRA 1998 lies in relation to formulating the substance of a policy, which now needs to be Convention compatible, but public authorities (eg

---

[77] [2005] EWCA Civ 199; [2005] 2 All ER 396; [2006] UKHL 15; see T Poole, 'Of headscarves and heresies: the Denbigh High School case and public authority decision-making under the Human Rights Act' [2005] *PL* 685.

schools) should not themselves adopt a proportionality approach to their decision-making process.[78] Further, not only was his Lordship unable to find Strasbourg authority for following the sort of reasoning process laid down by the Court of Appeal, but he also believed that such an approach would introduce 'a new formalism' and be 'a recipe for judicialisation on an unprecedented scale.' In any situation of this kind, it is the practical outcome that matters, not the type of the decision-making process that led to it. The school in laying down its rules, which were acceptable to mainstream Muslim opinion, had acted in an 'inclusive, unthreatening and uncompetitive' way.[79]

ASSESSING THE IMPACT OF THE HUMAN RIGHTS ACT 1998

What has been the impact of the HRA 1998? The practice of public authorities has been affected by the imposition of a duty under section 6 of the HRA 1998 which requires that they conform with the ECHR. Public bodies, including the police, prison service, Immigration Service, and the courts, have been forced to modify many of their procedures to make sure that they perform their duties in a manner which is compliant with Convention rights. Turning to the courts, the proportionality principle gives judges a more sensitive tool to consider whether the restriction of a right can be justified (are the means used to impair the right or freedom no more than is necessary to accomplish the objective?). In cases such as *Prolife Alliance* and *Denbigh High School* the courts have been cautious about straying into the territory of administrative decision-making by public authorities. However, in the *Belmarsh Detainees* case the House of Lords was willing to issue a declaration of incompatibility in a situation where it considered that fundamental rights had been contravened in a disproportionate manner. Parliament responded by amending the offending legislation. In a period where there is a perceived increase in the threat of terrorism, the HRA 1998 has not prevented repressive legislation from reaching the statute book. Most recently, for example, the Prevention of Terrorism Act 2005 allows the detention of terrorist suspects without trial for periods of up to 28 days.[80]

---

[78] T Poole, above n 77, at 690.
[79] Some doubts over aspects of the policy were expressed in a thoughtful partly dissenting judgment by Baroness Hale.
[80] The Patriot Act 2001 in the United States gives enormous powers to the authorities to combat terrorism, effectively suspending important rights under the Constitution.

CONCLUSION

Against a backdrop of the manifest limitations in parliamentary scrutiny of primary legislation and delegated legislation and the ever-increasing powers handed over to the executive, we have seen in this chapter that judicial review has emerged as one important counterweight to executive dominance, with a growing recognition of the role of the courts. The jurisdiction under the HRA 1998 and the devolution legislation represent a further shift of power to the judiciary, who must now adjudicate on alleged breaches of Convention rights, inter-governmental disputes, and the validity of legislation emanating from the Scottish Parliament and the Northern Ireland Assembly. In turn, this much higher judicial profile raises a number of further and, as yet, unresolved issues about the role of the courts at the highest level. It may be widely accepted that these developments have resulted in a significant 'constitutionalisation' of public law,[81] but there is much less agreement on whether the new Supreme Court should also act as a constitutional court, in the sense of being able to determine the limits of powers under the constitution. Certainly, it would be a drastic step to dispense with the core principle of parliamentary sovereignty and allow the courts to invalidate legislation. The courts are not directly accountable, except through the appellate process. This would mean that unelected judges would have the capacity to undermine the legitimacy of decisions made by democratically elected politicians. Finally, it is doubtful whether members of a judiciary schooled in specialist areas of law have the training and background to equip them to act as guardians and regulators of an uncodified constitution.

FURTHER READING

Introduction to the Courts System

Barnett H, *Britain Unwrapped: Government and Constitution Explained* (London Penguin, 2002) chs 7, 9, 10.

Harris P, *An Introduction to Law*, 6th edn (London, Butterworths, 2002).

Le Sueur A, 'Judicial Power in the Changing Constitution' in J Jowell and D Oliver (eds), *The Changing Constitution* (Oxford, Oxford University Press, 2004).

Twining W and Miers D *How to do Things with Rules*, 4th edn (London, Butterworths, 1999).

Supreme Court Reforms

Hale B, 'A Supreme Court for the United Kingdom?' (2004) 24 *Legal Studies* 36.

Le Sueur A, 'Developing mechanisms for judicial accountability in the UK' (2004) *Legal Studies* 73.

Le Sueur A (ed), *Building the UK's New Supreme Court: National and Comparative Perspectives* (Oxford, Oxford University Press, 2004).

Malleson K, 'Modernising the constitution: completing the unfinished business' (2004) 24 *Legal Studies* 119.

Woodhouse D, 'The Constitutional and Political Implications of a United Kingdom Supreme Court' (2004) 24 *Legal Studies*, 134.

Judicial Review and Administrative Law

Bamforth N, 'Courts in a Multi-Layered Constitution' in N Bamforth and P Leyland (eds), *Public Law in a Multi-Layered Constitution* (Oxford, Hart Publishing, 2003).

Craig P, *Administrative Law*, 5th edn (London, Sweet & Maxwell, 2003).

Elliott M, *Administrative Law: Text and Materials*, 3rd edn (Oxford, Oxford University Press, 2005).

Griffith J, 'The Political Constitution' (1979) *Modern Law Review* 1.

Griffith J, *The Politics of the Judiciary*, 5th edn (London, Fontana, 1997).

Harlow C and Rawlings R, *Law and Administration*, 2nd edn (London, Butterworths, 1997).

Leyland P and Anthony G, *Textbook on Administrative Law*, 5th edn (Oxford, Oxford University Press, 2005).

Loughlin M, *Sword and Scales: An Examination of the Relationship between Law and Politics* (Oxford, Hart Publishing, 2000).

Oliver D, *Common Values and the Public Private Divide* (London, Butterworths, 1999).

Stevens R, 'Government and the Judiciary' in Bogdanor V (ed), *The British Constitution in the Twentieth Century* (Oxford, Oxford University Press, 2003).

Civil Liberties and the Human Rights Act 1998

Campbell T, Ewing K, and Tomkins A (eds), *Sceptical Essays on Human Rights* (Oxford, Oxford University Press, 2001).

Ewing K, 'The Human Rights Act and Parliamentary Democracy' (1999) *Modern Law Review* 79–100.

Ewing K, 'The Futility of the Human Rights Act' [2004] *PL* 829.

Feldman D, *Civil Liberties and the Human Rights Act in England and Wales*, 2nd edn (Oxford, Oxford, University Press, 2002).

Gearty C, 'Reconciling Parliamentary Democracy and Human Rights' [2002] *Law Quarterly Review* 248.

Hunt M, 'Sovereignty's Blight: Why Contemporary Public Law Needs the Concept of Due Deference' in Bamforth N and Leyland P (eds), *Public Law in a Multi-Layered Constitution* (Oxford, Hart Publishing, 2003).

Irvine of Lairg, Lord, 'The Impact of the Human Rights Act: Parliament, the Courts, the Executive' [2003] *PL* 308.

Klug F and Starmer K, 'Standing Back from the Human Rights Act: how effective is it five years on?' [2005] *PL* 716.

Lester A and Clapinska L, 'Human Rights and the British Constitution' in Jowell J and Oliver D (eds.) *The Changing Constitution*, Oxford, Oxford University Press, 2004.

Tomkins A, 'Readings of *A v Secretary of State for the Home Department*' [2005] *PL* 259.

Wadham J, Mountfield H, and Edmundson A, *Blackstone's Guide to the Human Rights Act 1998*, 3rd edn (Oxford, Oxford University Press, 2003).

8

Devolution, Regional Government, and Local Government

INTRODUCTION

THIS CHAPTER EXAMINES the relationships between central government and the layers of devolved, regional, and local government charged with governing at a local level. Until the introduction of devolution the United Kingdom could be categorised as a centralised unitary state. However, the devolution legislation which was introduced in 1998 conferred varying degrees of autonomy to Scotland, Wales, and Northern Ireland, and a Mayor and Assembly for London have also been introduced. The effect of these changes has been to set up a new set of democratically elected bodies and to confer substantial powers on devolved executives. It will soon be apparent as the extent and implications of these reforms are discussed that the constitutional balance between central government and the regions has been significantly modified. In fact, the unequal treatment of England prompted the government to introduce proposals for a form of English regional government (Discussed below).

An underlying tension between devolution of power and the centralisation of power can be identified. If the UK trends in devolution and regional government are viewed from a wider European angle, the principle of subsidiarity set out in the Treaty of the European Union (TEU) can be regarded as having far-reaching significance in encouraging decentralisation and regionalism. The principle itself is set out under Article 5:

> In areas which do not fall within its exclusive competence, the Community shall take action, in accordance with the principle of subsidiarity, only if and in so far as the objectives of the proposed action cannot be sufficiently achieved by the Member States and can therefore, by reason of the scale or effects of the proposed action, be better achieved by the Community. Any action by the Community shall not go beyond what is necessary to achieve the objectives of the Treaty.

Subsidiarity addresses the difficult question of what is best achieved in the application of European law and policy at European level, and what is best achieved at national level, but the principle is not prescriptive of the internal organisation of member states. Indeed, subsidiarity is not clearly defined and has been interpreted in different ways by different nations.[1] For example, the UK Government interpreted Article 3B of the TEU as representing decentralisation in the sense of power being exercised at the level of the nation state in seeking to achieve Community objectives. The Germans saw the principle applying to a federal system with Community objectives being implemented at the level of the individual states (which are called *Länder*). Notwithstanding these differences, the crucial point is that subsidiarity has legitimised claims for decentralisation in Europe. As one commentator puts it: 'No longer must arguments be made for the devolution of power from the nation-state. Instead the nation-state itself must defend its legitimacy against claims from communities demanding greater controls over decision making.'[2] Also, the EU has been influential in encouraging devolved and regional government in a different context, namely, the capacity for the regions to be eligible for EU regional funding. To put it simply, it might appear that there has been a momentum building up giving rise to the weakening of the nation state, and a consolidation of the position of the EU which has had the effect of promoting the cause of devolved forms of government. At the same time, a

---

[1] See P Craig and G De Burca, *EU Law: Text, Cases and Materials*, 2nd edn (Oxford, Oxford University Press, 2002) p 127ff.

[2] J Hopkins, *Devolution in Context: Regional Federal and Devolved Government in the European Union* (London, Cavendish, 2002) pp 29–30.

wider trend towards recognition of smaller nation states in Eastern Europe has been encouraged by the collapse of the Soviet Union in 1991 and the resurgence of nationalism.

Despite the fact that varying degrees of power have been given away as part of the devolution, it would be a mistake to underestimate the continuing role of central government. Central government based at Westminster retains sovereignty and retains control over the purse strings. Only Scotland has been granted limited tax-raising powers which, to date, have not been used. Moreover, the arrangements are co-ordinated by a network of soft law agreements, called concordats, which tend to reflect the dominance of Whitehall over the devolved administrations. If we turn to local government, we find a different picture. Local government operates under powers granted by Parliament under statute. Far from extending the autonomy of local authorities, we will see that legislation has been introduced by governments of both Conservative and Labour persuasion to constrain the activities of local authorities and to reign back their spending powers. The effect of these policies has been to concentrate power at the centre. Local government has been in decline. Public involvement in the political process at a local level has atrophied, with turnouts at local elections dropping to extremely low levels. The Labour government has responded with an attempt to encourage wider participation by introducing new models for decision-making by local councils, and by setting up more transparent accountability mechanisms.

PART I: DEVOLUTION

BACKGROUND TO DEVOLUTION

Devolution developed into an important political issue in the 1970s. Support for the Scottish Nationalist Party (SNP) had risen between 1964 and 1974, and the Welsh Nationalist Party also emerged as a force in domestic politics. However, the original devolution legislation for Scotland and Wales introduced by the Labour government of 1974–79 failed to attract the popular support in referenda required for its implementation. Subsequently, the Conservative Party was in government for 18 years. During this period political power was concentrated at Westminster, and South-East England boomed economically. This success was perceived to be at the expense of Scotland, Wales, and the English regions, which resulted in a build-up of pressure for change. There was a spectacular decline in political support for the Conservatives in Scotland and Wales, and the party failed to win a single Scottish or Welsh parliamentary seat at Westminster in the elections in 1992 and 1997. In 1997 the Labour Party was elected with a manifesto commitment to introduce devolution for Scotland and Wales. Labour also promised a directly elected Mayor and Assembly for London. Legislation was introduced immediately in the form of the Scotland Act (SA) 1998, and the Government of Wales Act (GWA) 1998. The electors of Scotland and Wales were required to approve the legislative measures passed by the Westminster Parliament in order for devolution to be put into effect, and referenda were successfully held in 1998. In contrast, the new form of devolution for Northern Ireland was intended to settle the conflict between the main communities. It was based on the 'Good Friday' peace agreement reached in April 1998. Devolution was introduced following a referendum on this agreement, which then formed the basis of the Northern Ireland Act (NIA) 1998.

Devolution was not part of a grand constitutional design; rather the approach in each case needs to be understood in relation to the distinct history of each nation. Scotland has been united with England since the Act of Union of 1707, but aspects of the system were not fully integrated. For example, Scotland retained its own legal system and different system of education. In contrast, Wales is closely linked to England, for example, through the Act of Union of 1536, sharing institutions (except certain quangos) but with a strong separate cultural identity and language. Northern Ireland has two distinct and conflicting traditions that the power-sharing system seeks to reconcile. The extent to which power has been devolved varies markedly with each statute. The devolution legislation has produced an asymmetrical distribution of powers because the extent of the powers given to the Scottish Parliament and the Assemblies in Wales and Northern Ireland are different.

The handover of power from Westminster to the devolved executives was relatively straightforward. The smooth transition was possible because, for the most part, the functions previously administered by the Scottish Office, Welsh Office, and Northern Ireland Office were conferred on the devolved executives, and the civil servants from central government formed the core administration as part of the new scheme. Moreover, the mechanisms of accountability that have been set in place as part of devolution are in several ways different from those at Westminster. The Labour government sought to bring democracy closer to the people by introducing these reforms. The devolution arrangements not only provide the electorate in each nation with the right to vote on the basis of proportional representation, but each piece of legislation introduces its own brand of democratic institutions and processes.

SCOTTISH DEVOLUTION

The strongest support for devolution has been in Scotland, which has its distinct system of law, education, and church allied to a tradition of nationalism, with a minority seeking independence. In the wake of the discovery of reserves of oil and gas offshore in the 1960s, nationalists in the 1970s maintained that Scotland could claim economic self-sufficiency. The cause of nationalism was further reinforced by UK membership of the European Economic Community in 1973. A case has been made for an independent Scotland within Europe, which would not only expect to reap the benefits of EU funding provision, but would also be protected from the imposition of tariffs from England. Furthermore, an independent Scotland would possess a veto in Europe, which could be used if its interests were threatened. The Republic of Ireland served as a model of a successful small independent state, which had managed to establish itself within the EU. The Kilbrandon Commission, which reported in 1973, recognised that the system of government was over-centralised and recommended an elected assembly for Scotland and a lesser form of legislative devolution for Wales.

The SA 1998 confers more powers than the other devolution statutes. Scotland has a Parliament which has been empowered to pass primary laws but this power is limited to matters under the scope of its legislative competence. Functions conferred on the Scottish Parliament and Executive include: education, law, courts, prisons, judicial appointments, economic development, agriculture, fisheries, local government, the environment, housing, passenger and road transport, forestry, and the arts. Matters reserved for Westminster are listed in some detail in the Act.[3] This provision means that the interpretation of the SA 1998 under section 29(2)(b) is important constitutionally, since it provides that a matter is outside the competence of the Scottish Parliament if it relates to any of these reserved matters. If this section were to be given a narrow definition, it would restrict the Scottish Parliament's legislative capacity. The Judicial Committee of the Privy Council may be required to determine whether the Scottish Parliament enacts legislation which is outside its powers, and it is empowered to set aside such legislation.[4] The Judicial Committee of the Privy Council, comprising Law Lords and other senior judges, mainly retains a residual jurisdiction relating to appeals from Commonwealth nations. Devolution cases will come under the jurisdiction of the Supreme Court when it takes over from

---

[3] SA 1998, sch 5.
[4] SA 1998, s 98, sch 6.

the House of Lords in 2009.[5] The Scottish Parliament can determine its own procedures for passing legislation and for executive accountability. A system of subject committees has been introduced which combines the oversight function of select committees with the role of standing committes in scrutinising legislation.

The additional member system selected for Scotland is based on the election of a constituency member for each of the 73 pre-existing Scottish constituencies, with a total of 56 additional regional members.[6]. Each elector is entitled to cast two votes, one for a constituency candidate and the other for a regional candidate. A member is returned for each constituency on the basis of first past the post, and the additional member system operates on a top-up basis which allows a party that has won disproportionately fewer seats in relation to their overall level of support to be allocated additional seats from the party list of candidates. The system is designed to make sure that the outcome will be approximately proportional to the popular votes cast for each party. The Scottish system of devolved government has a single-chamber Parliament of 129 members (MSPs), which normally meets for a four-year term.

Following an election to the Scottish Parliament, a government is formed after Parliament has nominated a Scottish First Minister.[7] If MSPs cannot agree on a suitable candidate as First Minister, the Parliament's Presiding Officer is required to enter into negotiations with the parties to facilitate the selection of a candidate. After a nomination has been accepted the First Minister is empowered to appoint ministers from the MSPs to form a Scottish Executive. The executive is roughly equivalent to the Cabinet, and the ministerial appointments are made subject to formal approval by the Queen. The First Minister and Scottish Executive are directly accountable to the Scottish Parliament for the policies pursued by the devolved administration.

Scottish Legislation

The Scottish Parliament can pass primary legislation in areas within its legislative remit.[8] Bills can originate from ministers (executive bills), MSPs (members' bills), or parliamentary committees (committee bills). The process is designed to be open and participatory with a formalised process of pre-legislative consultation. The first parliamentary stage allows discussion

[5] Constitutional Reform Act 2005, s 40, sch 9.
[6] SA 1998, ss 5–8.
[7] SA 1998, ss 45 and 46.
[8] SA 1998, ss 28–39.

by the full Parliament of the general principles of a Bill. The second stage is designed to provide detailed scrutiny. The Bill is normally referred to the relevant subject committee, which takes evidence as the 'lead' committee (eg from Scottish ministers and officials) and then compiles a report. Unlike the standing committees at Westminster (see chapter five), these specialist subject committees, which are formed for each main policy area, perform an important role in regard to the passage of legislation, as well as being responsible for scrutinising the executive. At the third stage, the full Parliament decides whether to accept or reject the final amended version of the Bill.

Although not part of the SA 1998 or parliamentary rules, it was agreed as part of the new arrangements that the UK Parliament would not normally legislate in areas devolved to Scotland without the consent of the Scottish Parliament. This agreement, which is commonly referred to as 'the Sewel Convention', was considered necessary to prevent the role of the Scottish Parliament from being undermined by the Westminster Parliament. However, in practice, the situation has not worked out quite as originally envisaged, because Scotland's Parliament and executive have regularly consented to the Westminster Parliament legislating on devolved matters, so that Westminster legislation continues to be of importance in relation to certain devolved areas of competence. Despite the number of Sewel motions in terms of its overall output, the Scottish Parliament has still produced a substantial amount of 'home grown or self-generated legislation.'[9]

Tax-raising Powers

The conferment of tax-raising powers on a Scottish Parliament featured prominently in the discussion that preceded the introduction of the legislation. The referendum in Scotland to approve devolution had a second question, asking for the endorsement of a Parliament with tax-raising powers. Despite the attention devoted to this issue when devolution was under discussion, the financial powers actually conferred by the SA 1998 are limited. The Scottish Parliament is empowered under Part IV of the SA 1998 to vary the rate of income tax in Scotland by up to 3p in the pound by means of a Scottish income tax which could provide extra revenue totalling around £450 million. However, this was a relatively small amount when set against an annual budget of £14 billion from Westminster. The size of the budget for Scotland has risen significantly. The Draft Budget reports significant increases in public expenditure from £22.7 billion in 2003–04 to £25.7 billion

---

[9] A Page, 'A Parliament That Is Different?' in R Hazell and R Rawlings (eds), *Devolution, Lawmaking and the Constitution* (Exeter, Imprint Academic, 2005) p 12.

in 2005–06, which is equivalent to an increase of around £700 million in real terms for 2004–05; and a further £1 billion in real terms for 2005–06. These figures continue the pattern of real growth in expenditure since 1999. Moreover, it is doubtful whether these tax-varying powers will be used at all. The prospect of levying higher taxes might result in accusations of profligacy and the risk of losing electoral support for the party in government responsible for increasing the burden of taxation. These additional tax-raising powers were given to the Scottish Parliament and the executive but, as will be pointed out below, the method of funding has been under a pre-existing formula determined by Westminster.

WELSH DEVOLUTION

After the Act of Union of 1707 which combined the English and Scottish Parliaments, Scotland retained a distinctive legal system, educational system, and church. By way of contrast, Wales has been closely integrated with England for the purposes of law and administration since the late Middle Ages. Welsh nationalism has been inspired by a desire to see formal recognition of the Welsh national identity, language, and cultural heritage, rather than being built upon distinctive institutions of law and administration. Although there has been strong nationalist support in some areas, it was not easy to muster a majority in favour of devolution. The referendum in 1998 with a 50.1 per cent vote in favour only just achieved the majority required for the provisions of the GWA 1998 to be activated (the 1978 referendum demonstrated minimal support for devolution).

The electoral system for Wales is similar to that introduced in Scotland.[10] The GWA 1998 set up a single-chamber Assembly for Wales, consisting of 60 members. It must be elected every four years. There is one member for each of the 40 Welsh constituencies (identical to the constituencies for the Westminster Parliament), and four for each of the five Assembly electoral regions. The method used is a mixture of simple majority and proportional representation. Each elector is given two votes. Assembly members for each constituency are returned by simple majority, while the four Assembly members for each region are returned under an additional member system of proportional representation.

The Welsh Assembly is required to form policy and take decisions in its particular areas of responsibility, and through its subject committees it is responsible for executive scrutiny. However, the Welsh Assembly does not

---

[10]   GWA 1998, ss 3–7.

have the power to pass primary legislation. Since the introduction of devolution there have been calls to give the Welsh Assembly the power to pass laws (see Government of Wales Act 2006 below), but to date it has been the responsibility of the Secretary of State for Wales to guide Welsh legislation through the Westminster Parliament. However, the Welsh Assembly does have the power to pass secondary legislation.[11]

The Welsh Executive has taken over by transfer orders most of the administrative functions of the Secretary of State for Wales under the GWA 1998.[12] Cabinet members have the equivalent of departmental responsibility for their given policy areas. But whereas the Scottish Parliament is granted general competence, subject to the reserved matters under the SA 1998, in the case of Wales, powers are conferred in respect of particular areas of policy. The principal matters devolved are: agriculture, forestry, fisheries and food, environmental and cultural matters, economic and industrial development, education and training, health, housing, local government, social services, sport and tourism, town and country planning, transport, water and flood defences, and the Welsh language. The Assembly and executive are also responsible for many Welsh quangos (non-departmental governmental organisations, funded and appointed by government, eg Welsh Health authorities, the Welsh Tourist Board).

The Cabinet style of government is formed following an election. The newly elected members of the Welsh Assembly vote for a First Secretary. Once elected, the First Secretary has the power to appoint an Executive Committee of Assembly Secretaries, which forms the equivalent of a Cabinet. The ministerial portfolios of this Executive Committee (the combinations of policy areas allocated to the individual Assembly Secretaries) determine the areas of competence of the scrutiny committees (subject committees) that are subsequently formed. The appointments to the Executive Committee may be from a single party or a combination of parties.

The Government of Wales Act 2006

The dynamics of devolution have been evident from the outset. It was obvious that there were shortcomings with the original system of devolution in Wales.[13] Not only was there a lack of legislative power, but the institutional arrangements did not quite work out in practice as originally envisaged. In

---

[11] GWA 1998, ss 64 ff.

[12] GWA 1998, s 22(2), sch 2.

[13] R Rawlings, 'Hastening Slowly: The Next Phase of Welsh Devolution' [2005] *PL* 824 at 825.

particular, although the National Assembly of Wales was formed as a single corporate body, a *de facto* division emerged post-devolution between the Welsh Assembly government and the Welsh Assembly as representative body. The Welsh Assembly government has been recognised under the GWA 2006 as an entity separate from, but accountable to, the National Assembly. The Richard Commission was set up in 2002 to look into enhancing the powers of the Welsh Assembly and to consider changes to the electoral arrangements in Wales. The Commission[14] recommended that the membership of the Welsh Assembly should expand from 60 to 80 members and that it should be elected by single transferable vote (STV) rather than the present additional member system. The Labour Party manifesto in May 2005 promised to 'develop democratic devolution by creating a stronger [Welsh] assembly with enhanced legislative powers.' Under section 93 of the GWA 2006, the Assembly has been granted powers to pass a form of law which is to be known as a 'Measure of the National Assembly of Wales'. These 'measures' will be enacted by first receiving scrutiny and approval by the Assembly, and then the measure being referred to the Westminster Parliament for approval by resolution of each House before being recommended as a new form of Order in Council.[15] In effect, this new procedure creates a special form of delegated legislation which potentially could be vetoed at Westminster. However, in practice, the new procedure is expected to overcome the problem of securing the passage of legislation required for Wales through the Westminster Parliament. Previously, Welsh Bills had to take their place in the queue, and then they were shepherded through Parliament by the Secretary of State for Wales.[16] The revised arrangements may prove problematic if there is a strong conflict of wills between the Welsh Assembly and the government at Westminster, for example if Labour retains its majority in the Assembly while a Conservative government is elected at Westminster. In such circumstances the veto powers could be exercised to rein back the Welsh Assembly, or the Secretary of State could use powers granted under the 2006 Act to refuse, with reasons, to lay the measure before Parliament. A referendum will have to take place before the Welsh Assembly formally gains full law-making powers in its own right. The 2006 Act also makes other changes: for example, the electoral system is altered to prevent individuals from standing as candidates in both constituency and regional seats.

[14] *Report of the Richard Commission on the Powers and Electoral Arrangements of the National Assembly for Wales* (March 2004).

[15] GWA 2006, s 94. Orders in Council are usually secondary legislation issued under powers in a parent Act, and they are often used for transferring powers and responsibilities.

[16] R Rawlings, 'Law Making in a Virtual Parliament: the Welsh Experience' in R Hazell and R Rawlings (eds), *Devolution, Law Making and the Constitution* (Exeter, Imprint Academic, 2005).

POWER-SHARING IN NORTHERN IRELAND

It was pointed out in the opening chapter that the culmination of the campaign for Irish home rule came after World War I and led to the formation of an independent Irish Free State in the mainly Catholic South; after first being given dominion status, the new state became the fully independent Irish Republic. For the six counties in the North of Ireland the Stormont Parliamentary system of devolved government was set up by the Government of Ireland Act 1920 in order to avoid direct rule from Westminster. The arrangements conferred considerable powers to the Parliament and executive, but the method of government formation resulted in a permanent Unionist majority. The devolved government at Stormont pursued policies which were regarded as discriminatory by the Catholic minority, and the flaws in the system, particularly the under-representation of Catholics, contributed to the upsurge in violence during 'the Troubles' of the 1970s and 1980s. Stormont was suspended in 1972, and Northern Ireland was governed directly from Westminster by the Secretary of State, Ministers of State, and officials at the Northern Ireland Office (see chapter one).

The NIA 1998 was designed to restore devolved government.[17] It resulted from protracted negotiations between the main political parties which led to the Good Friday Agreement in 1998. The elements of power sharing were agreed by the parties, but the controversial question of disarmament of paramilitary elements were set to one side as a separate process to be realised in stages. The new arrangements have been plagued with difficulties. In particular, lack of progress with the disarmament process led to delays and later repeated breakdowns in the operation of devolved government itself. As well as establishing a system of devolved government, the main objective in Northern Ireland was to accommodate the deep-seated political differences between Unionist and Republican communities. Specialist watchdogs were designed to oversee the wider process of reconciliation. In particular, a Northern Ireland Human Rights Commission was set up under section 68 of the NIA 1998 to promote awareness of the importance of human rights in Northern Ireland. At the same time, the Equality Commission for Northern Ireland was established under section 73 of the NIA 1998 as an independent public body responsible for the elimination of discrimination, and also for promoting good relations between different racial groups.

---

[17] C McCrudden, 'Northern Ireland, The Belfast Agreement and the British Constitution' in J Jowell and D Oliver (eds), *The Changing Constitution*, 5th edn (Oxford, Oxford University Press, 2005).

Northern Ireland is granted a directly elected Northern Ireland Assembly consisting of 108 members elected every four years.[18] These members are elected by Single Transferable Vote (STV) from 18 six-member constituencies. The Assembly is given competence to exercise legislative authority[19] over those matters falling under the responsibility of the shared office of First and Deputy First Minister and the ten Northern Ireland government departments[20] (with the possibility of taking on responsibility for other matters as detailed elsewhere in the Good Friday Agreement). The Presiding Officer of the Assembly examines proposed legislation to ensure it falls within the legislative scope of the Assembly. Legislation passed by the Assembly requires the royal assent,[21] and the NIA 1998 further provides that this law-making power should not affect the sovereignty of the UK Parliament,[22]

The NIA 1998 has created a unique system of compulsory power-sharing at every level of decision-making to ensure joint participation by both communities in the processes of government. In order to accommodate Nationalist aspirations for a united Ireland, the system of government is linked to that of the Irish Republic. To satisfy Unionists' fears that the union could be severed without consent there are links with the United Kingdom. The North–South Ministerial Council brings together members of the executive of the Northern Ireland Assembly and representatives of the Irish government for the purposes of co-operation on issues of common interest. The British–Irish Council is a body to consider broader mutual interests with the United Kingdom. It consists of representatives from the Scottish Parliament, Welsh Assembly, the Channel Isles, and the Isle of Man. To satisfy nationalist aspirations the need for on-going consent to remain part of the United Kingdom is built into the legislation. Devolution has been suspended in Northern Ireland because of political difficulties. Following the elections in November 2003 in which Sinn Fein and the Democratic Unionist Party made substantial gains, there are no immediate prospects for the resumption of devolved government. The Northern Ireland Assembly is empowered to pass legislation but it has no independent tax-raising powers.

---

[18] See Northern Ireland (Elections) Act 1998, s 1, and NIA 1998, Part II.

[19] See G Anthony and J Morison, 'Here, There and (Maybe) Here Again: The Story of Law Making for Post-1998 Northern Ireland' in R Hazell and R Rawlings (eds), *Devolution, Law Making and the Constitution* (Exeter, Imprint Academic, 2005).

[20] The NI government departments are: Agriculture and Rural Development; Culture, Arts and Leisure; Education, Employment and Learning; Enterprise, Trade, and Investment; Environment; Finance and Personnel; Health; Social Services and Public Safety; Regional Development; and Social Development.

[21] NIA 1998, s 5(2).

[22] NIA 1998, s 5(6).

FUNDING DEVOLUTION

Devolution has been underpinned by a secure financial base. In essence, the methods for financial allocation of funds from central government that preceded devolution have been retained without significant modification (apart from the extra tax-raising power given to the Scottish Parliament). The funding parameters for Scotland, Wales, and Northern Ireland are determined by a 'block and formula' system named after Lord Barnett, who was the Chief Secretary to the Treasury responsible for its introduction. The 'Barnett formula' has operated by setting out a ratio by which the total spending is fixed in relation to England. An overall budget is made available annually by the Westminster Parliament in each departmental field and the Barnett formula has determined the allocations for the increase or decrease in expenditure according to a ratio calculated on relative population size. In its original form for every £85 on English services, Scotland received £10, Wales £5, and Northern Ireland £2.75. In 1997 the government introduced an annual revision of the Barnett population weighting based on the latest population estimates for England, Scotland, Wales, and Northern Ireland. The formula relates the levels of spending by the Westminster Parliament to the amounts made available to Scotland, Wales, and Northern Ireland. In effect, it guarantees an amount reflecting a proportion of the spending allocated to England. Each nation has been able to count upon a consistent overall level of funding. The devolved executives are under an obligation to ensure that sufficient funds are allocated to meet statutory requirements in the main policy areas. However, that apart, there is a wide discretion in the allocation of resources, which can be diverted from one policy area to another. Scotland has introduced care for the elderly and support for students; neither of these benefits has been made available to the equivalent groups in England.

Two further points should be noted. First, a general decline in population and variations in patterns of public expenditure determined by central government could prove detrimental to Scotland, Wales, and Northern Ireland. In view of such trends there have been calls to review the Barnett formula, and it will almost certainly require some modification. Any comprehensive change is bound to be controversial because a review of funding introduces complex economic arguments concerning the extent to which Scotland and Wales are net contributors to the UK economy. How can the revenue from oil be offset against the expenditures for health, education, and employment? Devolution has been able to function for several years without having to confront such issues directly. Second, an obvious shortcoming of devolution has been the failure to activate a link between revenue-raising, in the form of local taxation, and the political process, in the form of the provision of public services on offer. Voters do not see a clear relationship between spending and the taxes they pay at a local level. As already mentioned, the Scottish Parliament has the capacity to introduce up to 3p in the pound extra tax but shows no signs of using this power.

INTERGOVERNMENTAL RELATIONS

The co-ordination of administration between central and devolved government has been managed to a large extent without resort to legislation but by means of a series of informal agreements, termed concordats. At an administrative level intergovernmental relations have required a distinct approach and devolution has been incorporated into the existing uncodified constitutional arrangements in an unsystematic and informal fashion. The process has been managed by mechanisms that exist and operate outside the legislative framework. As well as the more familiar device in the United Kingdom of conventions, concordats were drawn up at an advanced stage and amount to a form of bureaucratic law. First, there is a general Memorandum of Understanding (MOU) containing a set of principles. These include: good communication and information sharing, early warning of policy proposals, co-operation on matters of mutual interest, and rules of confidentiality to be applied within the workings of the post-devolutionary system of government. The MOU is supported by a (still) increasing number of bilateral and multilateral agreements (eg 20 with the Scottish executive) between the devolved executives and Whitehall departments, which have been drawn up behind the scenes by senior departmental officials. The concordats have been introduced in a way that has contributed to a lack of openness and transparency, and this in turn raises issues of political accountability. There is evidence to suggest that these agreements have been formulated in a spirit that reinforces an unequal partnership that tends to allow domination from the centre. Another dimension to intergovernmental co-operation relates to the Sewel Convention explained above. This convention was deliberately formed to recognise the respective legislative competencies of the Scottish Parliament and the Westminster Parliament. It introduced an expectation that legislation in devolved areas would be routinely enacted by the Scottish Parliament. Since devolution a great deal of Westminster legislation continues to apply in Scotland, but before Westminster legislates in these devolved areas, consent is given by the devolved administration in Scotland after a Sewel motion has been placed before the Scottish Parliament.[23]

[23] A Page and A Batey, 'Scotland's Other Parliament: Westminster Legislation about Devolved Matters in Scotland since Devolution' [2002] *PL* 501–24.

THE POLITICS OF DEVOLVED GOVERNMENT

Elections are held at four-year intervals and are not triggered by a defeat on a Bill introduced by the Scottish executive. There is more freedom for individual members dissatisfied with proposals to vote against them. Such opposition might threaten the majority of a ruling coalition through the withdrawal of support over the issue under consideration, but a defeat on a policy matter does not trigger an election for the Scottish Parliament as would be the case with the loss of a vote of confidence in the House of Commons. The introduction of a proportional element to the electoral system made it difficult for any single party to obtain an overall majority in the Scottish Parliament or Welsh Assembly. After the first round of elections a coalition was required to secure the majority needed to form an administration in Scotland. The Scottish Labour Party and the Liberal Democrats formed an alliance in 1999. The turnout in 2003 was disappointing compared to 1999 with only 38 per cent voting in Wales and 50 per cent in Scotland. Nationalist parties, which have lacked a clear post-devolution strategy, did badly and lost seats in both Scotland and Wales. In Scotland support for Labour and for the SNP declined in May 2003. The election was followed by protracted negotiations between Labour and the Liberal Democrats over the formation of a new Scottish government. In order to reach a deal, the Liberal Democrats secured a commitment to introduce proportional representation for local government elections in Scotland and the finance portfolio in Scotland. The coalition has a majority of only two in the Scottish Parliament, and this has meant that other parties have a greater impact than previously. The Scottish Socialist Party with seven seats and the Green Party with seven seats have more potential to cause disruption to the legislative process. On the other hand, in Wales, Labour ruled as the largest minority party after the 1999 election and improved their performance in 2003 at the expense of Plaid Cymru.

At the devolved level there have been further trends towards greater democratisation in Scotland. Recently, the Scottish Parliament passed the Local Governance (Scotland) Act 2004, which changes the method of election for local government elections in Scotland from 2007 to the single transferable vote system. After a re-drawing of local boundaries, Scottish electors will return three or four local councillors per ward (local constituency). The change also means that there is a distinct method of voting in Scotland for each form of election (European: Party List PR; Westminster Parliament: first past the post; Scottish Parliament: additional member system; Scottish Local Government: single transferable vote). Another welcome feature of devolution has been the very high ratio of women elected to the Welsh Assembly and to the Scottish Parliament. After the 2003 elections 30 women members were elected to the 60-strong Welsh Assembly, and there were 48 women out of a total of 129 MSPs.

The Scottish Parliament and the Assemblies in Wales and Northern Ireland began work with a strong commitment to more open government, in line with a wider trend towards greater openness. The public has access to the deliberations of committees and more information is placed in the public domain, including minutes of Cabinet meetings, which are published within six weeks of a meeting. The Scottish Parliament has passed a Freedom of Information Act which goes further than its English counterpart.[24]

Since the introduction of devolution, the national party machine based at Westminster has attempted to maintain its control in Wales, in Scotland, and in London, but it has not met with much success. After the Secretary of State for Wales, Ron Davies, who was also due to become leader of the Labour Party in the Welsh Assembly, unexpectedly resigned in 1998 to avoid a scandal, Alun Michael was appointed Welsh Secretary. His subsequent selection as Labour leader in the Welsh Assembly relied heavily on strong pressure exerted from the Westminster Labour Party leadership. After losing support in the Assembly as a result of a perceived failure to stand up for Welsh interests, Michael was forced to resign as leader of the Labour group within a year, in 2000. In the 2003 elections Labour obtained a bare majority in the Welsh Assembly, which allowed the party to govern in Wales without entering into coalition deals with other parties. Under the leadership of First Minister, Rhodri Morgan, the Welsh Assembly government has managed to pursue 'Old Labour' policies in the sphere of education and health with a marked emphasis on social justice and it has carried out a manifesto commitment to abolish Welsh quangos, including the Welsh Development Agency and Education and Learning Wales.

To take another example, the student fees issue in Scotland is interesting because it has illustrated that changes in policy in Scotland have a wider impact in the United Kingdom. In defiance of Labour Party policy in England, the Scottish Parliament decided in 2001 that tuition fees for Scottish university students would be paid for by the Scottish Executive. The disparity of treatment between English and Scottish students has prompted a continuing debate about this issue south of the border. As we have observed, with the acceptance of devolution it is increasingly difficult for the party machine to impose discipline on all parts of the United Kingdom from

---

[24] For example, s 30 of the Freedom of Information (Scotland) Act 2002 introduces a 'substantial prejudice' test to determine whether information will be exempted from disclosure.

the centre. During the Thatcher/Major era (1979–97) local government had been rigidly controlled to reduce the cost of government. Although Prime Minister Tony Blair has retained the centralising instincts of his predecessors, the devolution initiative was designed to move power away from Westminster. If the impression had been conveyed that devolving power made no difference because of the intervention of central government this would have had the effect of undermining the entire initiative. Finally, the introduction of devolved government did not lead to wider calls for independence initially or to any significant advance at the ballot box for the nationalist parties in Scotland and Wales but recent opinion poll evidence (2006) suggests that support for Nationalist Parties is now increasing.

RELATIONS WITH EUROPE

In an era of multi-levelled governance, UK devolution has to address the issue of the implementation of EU law and relations with Europe. Europe is an important issue post-devolution. First, this is because Brussels legislates in the same fields over in which power has been devolved, for example, economic development, agriculture and fisheries, the environment, training and enterprise. Second, it is because Europe is a significant source of regional funding. Turning to the implementation of EU law, there are concurrent powers in existence post-devolution. In Scotland, Wales, and Northern Ireland, the application of community law within the jurisdiction is made a matter for the devolved executives. The legislation further provides that where Scottish/Northern Irish ministers are empowered to use section 2(2) of the European Communities Act 1972 to implement obligations under Community law, a minister of the Crown also retains power to use section 2(2) for the same purpose. This concurrence introduces an element of ambiguity concerning compliance with EU law. It is meant to be resolved by reference to the Concordat on Co-ordination of European Union Policy Issues, and European policy provides an excellent illustration of the practical application of concordats. The legislation and the concordat both emphasise that financial penalties will apply to a devolved administration for failing to meet deadlines. The UK government is ultimately responsible for ensuring that Community laws (eg Directives) are enforced on time.

The EU is of great importance because it offers a potential source of funding within defined limits on a regional basis, and approximately a third of the EU's budget is devoted to its regional policies. A basic criterion for 'objective 1 funding' is to promote the development and structural adjustment of the less well-off regions. It is increasingly apparent that in making such allocations the

Commission favours decentralisation and subsidiarity. Decision-making is encouraged at a level as close as possible to the population that will be affected. Proposals for Scotland were approved in December 1999, and over £1 billion has been allocated for the 2000–06 period. A comparable bid for structural funding in Wales was approved by the Commission in 2000. Such funding is not only conditional on shared responsibility between the different layers of government but brings together the public and private sectors. A drawback with this EU funding is that any allocation requires matching contributions to be provided by the Treasury. The funds have to be found from existing allocations designated for Scotland and Wales (£885 million of matched funding).

Further, it is the national UK government which is still ultimately responsible for negotiations with Brussels. Any such negotiations are conducted by UK rather than Scottish ministers. However, the importance of the EU to regional governance has been recognised in a number of ways. The Scottish Parliament and Welsh Assembly have moulded their institutions to respond to Europe with a European Committee in Scotland and a European and External Affairs Directorate in Wales. A Welsh European Funding Office is dedicated to the task of bidding for and overseeing the spending of European structural funding. Moreover, the case has been accepted for the Scottish Parliament and the Welsh Assembly having a representative office in Brussels. Scotland and Wales are represented as roughly equivalent European regions to the German *Länder*. Scotland has a representative on the EU's Committee of the Regions. In addition, Scottish and Welsh ministers regularly attend meetings of the Council of Ministers.

DEVOLUTION AND THE COURTS

The courts are required to oversee the limits of the powers conferred as part of the devolution arrangements. Although from a UK standpoint Acts of the Scottish Parliament might be regarded as a type of subordinate legislation, the SA 1998 gives the Scottish Parliament the right to pass a form of primary legislation over the areas falling under its competence. (Similar powers have been given to the Northern Ireland Assembly while the Welsh Assembly has recently been granted powers to pass a new form of secondary legislation under the GWA 2006.) Ultimately the job of policing the boundaries of the devolution legislation is given to the courts. The introduction of new procedures involves handing over a new kind of constitutional jurisdiction to judges which, in turn, has important political, as well as legal, implications. Any person or body with *locus standi* can apply to the court for judicial review to determine 'a devolution issue' and this may involve the court declaring an

Act of the Scottish Parliament to be invalid. The court performs this statutory role with the assistance of new interpretative rules which place judges under an obligation to read Scottish legislation and subordinate legislation so as to render any measure under consideration *within* the legislative competence of the Scottish Parliament.

In Scotland 'devolution issues' concern the legislative competence of the Scottish Parliament and the extent of the competence of the devolved Scottish executive. There is a similar provision for the judicial resolution of devolution issues under the GWA 1998 and the NIA 1998. In Wales the Attorney-General can institute proceedings, for example, to determine whether a function is exercisable by the Assembly and comes within its powers, or whether the Assembly has failed to comply with a duty imposed on it.

Certain safeguards are in place to prevent unlawful legislation and delegated legislation from reaching the statute book under devolution. In the first place, the SA 1998 sets express limits on the extent of the Scottish Parliament's power to legislate. Prior to bringing legislation before the Scottish Parliament, the Presiding Officer is under a duty to ensure that legislative proposals fall within the powers conferred on the Parliament, and following Parliamentary approval, but before the royal assent is given, there is a four-week delay to allow the Scottish law officers, if they consider it necessary, to send a Bill to the Privy Council to determine whether the proposal is intra vires. It should be noted that the law officers (that is, the Advocate General, the Lord Advocate and the Attorney-General) have an important role in making sure that this function is properly discharged.

Challenges to Acts of the Scottish executive or legislation passed by the Scottish Parliament can be mounted on the basis of incompatibility with the European Convention on Human Rights (ECHR) (as well as that of being beyond the executive's competence). We observed earlier that in respect of English legislation the Human Rights Act 1998 recognises the sovereignty of the Westminster Parliament and only gives the courts the right to issue a declaration of incompatibility if a provision is not Convention-compliant, but any action of the Scottish Executive or legislation from the Scottish Parliament in breach of the ECHR may be invalidated. For example, not long after the SA 1998 came into force the independence of Scottish sheriffs[25] was successfully challenged in Scotland as a 'devolution issue' in *Starrs and Chalmers v Procurator Fiscal, Linlithgow*[26] because it was successfully argued that the appointment procedure for this class of judges was in breach of Article 6 of the ECHR.

---

[25] Sheriffs perform a judicial function in the lower courts in Scotland, roughly equivalent to that of magistrates in England.

[26] [2000] HRLR 191.

Most legal proceedings in Scotland concerning devolution issues are by way of judicial review in the Court of Session. But in certain circumstances the SA 1998 allows devolution cases to be resolved by direct reference to the Privy Council, although this jurisdiction will be taken over by the Supreme Court in 2009 when the new court replaces the House of Lords.[27] The Judicial Committee of the Privy Council has been called upon to consider the validity of Scottish legislation. In *Anderson, Reid and Doherty v Scottish Ministers*[28] patients at a mental hospital challenged section 1 of the Mental Health (Public Safety and Appeals) (Scotland) Act 1999 on the grounds that the legislation passed by the Scottish Parliament was incompatible with Article 5 of the ECHR. Any such Convention-incompatible legislation would have fallen outside the Parliament's legislative competence and could therefore be declared invalid. After considering the relevant Convention jurisprudence the Judicial Committee of the Privy Council concluded that section 1 of the Scottish Mental Health Act did not infringe the claimant's rights under Article 5 of the ECHR, and the Act remained in force.

R (on the application of South Wales Sea Fisheries) v National Assembly for Wales[29] is an example of the courts determining the limits of a devolved competence under the GWA 1998. On this occasion the devolution issue was in regard to subordinate legislation. It was held that the South Wales Sea Fisheries (Variation) Order 2001[30] was unlawful, because it not only set the precise amounts of contributions by South Wales Sea Fisheries, but also imposed restrictions on this body's discretionary powers. In essence, by adopting this Order the Assembly had been misdirected in law concerning both the membership and the funding of sea fisheries committees, and, accordingly, the Order was quashed so that the Assembly could reconsider its position. Under the GWA 2006, proposed Orders in Council can be referred by the Attorney-General for scrutiny by the UK Supreme Court.[31]

One of the most significant cases to date in terms of its constitutional and political implications for devolution (although not concerning a devolution issue) was *Robinson v Secretary of State for Northern Ireland*.[32] The case arose from the failure of the Northern Ireland Assembly to elect a First Minister and a Deputy First Minister within a six-week period, as required by section 16(8) of the NIA 1998. If the challenge to the election of leader and deputy leader

---

[27] See Constitutional Reform Act 2005, s 40.
[28] [2001] UKPC D5, [2002] HRLR 6.
[29] [2001] EWHC Admin 1162, [2002] RVR 134.
[30] SI 2001/1338.
[31] See GWA 2006, s 95.
[32] [2002] UKHL 32. See also B Hadfield 'Does Northern Ireland Need an Independent Judicial System Arbiter?' in N Bamford and P Leyland (eds), *Public Law in a Multi-Layered Constitution* (Oxford, Hart, 2003) at p 184 ff.

had succeeded, it would have resulted in an immediate dissolution of the Northern Ireland Assembly followed by elections with adverse consequences for the peace process. Lord Bingham, speaking for the majority who rejected the challenge to the validity of the election, considered that:

> [T]he provisions should, consistently with the language used, be interpreted generously and purposively, bearing in mind the values which the constitutional provisions are intended to embody . . . It is difficult to see why Parliament, given the purposes it was seeking to promote, should have wished to constrain local politicians and the Secretary of State within such a tight straitjacket.

On the other hand, the dissenting view is based upon a literal interpretation of the NIA 1998 as a statute with a high constitutional status and without regard to the wider political implications. Lord Hobhouse argued: 'The Act does say what is to happen if the six-week period is allowed to expire. The Assembly is to be dissolved and an extraordinary Assembly election is to be held.'

The *Robinson* decision has drawn attention to the exposed political role of the courts under transformed constitutional arrangements. In having to finally determine the application of the NIA 1998 the House of Lords was making a decision which inevitably would have a direct bearing on the political process. The decision reached offered the possibility of keeping the Assembly and executive operating, while a finding for the other side would have prompted immediate elections at a time that appeared unfavourable for the peace process.

PART II: DEVOLUTION AND ENGLAND

Devolution has changed the nature of domestic politics, but it has also reshaped the constitution by a substantial distribution of powers from Westminster and by the introduction of new political and administrative institutions. In considering how much power has been given away, it will be evident that Scotland comes closest to having the powers which are often conferred under federal constitutions. The Scottish Parliament can pass a form of primary legislation and can raise taxes. The Northern Ireland Assembly has similar law-making powers but over more restricted policy areas. The Welsh Assembly has seen its powers recently upgraded under the GWA 2006. At this point we will consider how devolution brings in its wake a number of implications for England, which is not as well served by current arrangements as Scotland, Wales, and Northern Ireland. Its citizens lack a comparable level of political representation, England receives less generous funding under the Barnett formula, and devolution has an impact on pre-existing governmental and administrative organisation.[33]

THE WEST LOTHIAN QUESTION

First of all, from a constitutional standpoint, devolution has produced an inequality of political representation at Westminster, an issue sometimes referred to as the 'West Lothian question'.[34] As one commentator has put it:

> It raises serious questions about the role of MPs as members of the UK parliament, and about the nature of the Union itself. The Union has traditionally been built on an equality whereby all members can vote on all matters, regardless of territorial extent of their application, as members of a single parliamentary body.[35]

The introduction of a Scottish Parliament and Executive with considerable power plays havoc with the notion of representative government in the United Kingdom. MPs representing English, Welsh, and Northern Irish constituencies are no longer able to vote on devolved matters in Scotland, but Scottish MPs at Westminster retain the right to vote on domestic policy for the rest of the United Kingdom. Furthermore, by the transfer of many domestic functions to the Scottish Parliament, Scottish Westminster MPs have a greatly reduced role to play in relation to their constituents. The obvious line of accountability for the devolved areas of domestic policy in Scotland is through their Scottish representatives (MSPs).

A response to this problem which has been gaining support politically relates to modifying the voting rights of Westminster MPs. The right to vote on Bills could be restricted according to the part of the United Kingdom they represented. In essence, new rules within Parliament would apply which would prevent Scottish and Northern Irish Westminster MPs from voting on legislation not applying in Scotland and Northern Ireland.[36] Introducing such a change would be challenging to parliamentary draftsmen in precisely delineating how policy areas overlap, for example, where there are mixed clauses, some of which apply only to particular parts of the United Kingdom.

---

[33] See P Leyland, 'Post Devolution: Crystallising the Future for Regional Government in England' (2005) 56(4) *Northern Ireland Legal Quarterly* 435–62.

[34] Tam Dalyell, the Westminster MP representing the Scottish constituency of West Lothian, raised this issue as a question in a debate in the House of Commons on 14 November 1977, and it has since been referred to as 'the West Lothian question'.

[35] See M Russell and G Lodge, 'The Government of England by Westminster', in R. Hazell (ed) *The English Question* (Manchester, Manchester University Press, 2005).

[36] See M Keating, 'The UK as a post-sovereign polity' in M O'Neill (ed), *Devolution and British Politics* (Harlow, Longman, 2004) p 323.

There is an obvious political difficulty with reaching such a resolution at Westminster in the immediate future. A Labour government which is heavily dependent on the support of Scottish and Welsh Labour MPs to get its legislation through Parliament is unlikely to agree to a change which has the effect of disabling its political power.[37] On the other hand, it has suited the Conservative Party in opposition to take up the call for 'English votes for English laws'.[38] A change in the rules so as to prevent MPs outside England from voting on English Bills would effectively mean that Labour would no longer have an overall majority in the House of Commons for votes on legislation which concerned England alone, and such a change would be a means of consolidating the power base of the Conservative Party in England where its support is normally at its strongest. In a different sense, the recent measures which enhance the law-making capacity of the Welsh Assembly are likely to have an incidental impact on England. This will mean that, as the revised and distinct procedure for law-making in Wales is introduced, distinctively 'English' legislation in the Westminster Parliament is on the horizon.[39]

ENGLISH REGIONAL GOVERNMENT

While there has been no widespread popular campaign for English devolution, some discontent with the lack of regional representation has been expressed especially in the North-East region. The disadvantages of not having devolution were perhaps felt most strongly in this region which borders Scotland. The Labour government responded with detailed proposals for regional government but only in areas that made a choice in favour of this option.[40] A central problem to overcome with inventing a system of regional government is that England has never historically been organised into geographical regions, but divided into counties, which were administrative units with county councils and the traditional basis for the organisation of other activities, such as representative sport. In 1998 the Labour government passed the Regional Development Agencies (RDA) Act to promote sustainable development and economic competitiveness in nine geographically based English regions. The policy behind the Act was to put the regions in a position to develop their industrial potential and to compete for EU funding. The RDA Act 1998 intro-

---

[37] Russell and Lodge, above n 36.
[38] Both William Hague and Michael Howard as opposition leaders have supported this idea.
[39] See GWA 2006, s 93; R Rawlings, 'Hastening Slowly: The Next Phase of Welsh Devolution' [2005] *PL* 824–52 at 841.
[40] *Your Region, Your Choice: Revitalising the English Regions*, Cm 5511, 2002.

duced RDAs and regional assemblies made up from nominated members of local authorities and local stakeholders (eg nominees of organisations and businesses) to promote the economic interests of these regions.

Under the government's further plans for English regional assemblies, the same regions were to form the basis for the introduction of a new layer of government. The RDAs were to be made accountable to elected regional assemblies, which would also be given other functions formerly in the hands of local authorities and central government. A vote in a referendum in favour of regional government would have resulted in a region having an assembly elected by the additional member system of proportional representation consisting of between 25 and 35 members. After it had been elected, each assembly, funded mainly by central government grant, would itself elect an executive of no more than six members, with the remaining members performing an executive oversight function through scrutiny committees. The new assemblies would not have been given law-making powers, but would have had control over policies such as: economic development, housing, public health improvement, and culture, which are currently under the control of county councils and district councils. Social services, education, and other local services would have remained with existing local authorities. The main objectives of an elected assembly would have been to formulate a number of high-level targets, which would then have to be approved by central government.

The government drew up these proposals as part of an attempt to improve policy delivery by ensuring better co-ordinated government at regional level. Regional assemblies, in those regions where they were introduced, were not intended to add an extra layer of government in relation to specific policy areas, or to result in any additional bureaucracy, as the majority of their functions would have come from existing central government bodies or local government. The initiative was presented as a significant decentralisation of power. In common with Scotland, Wales, and Northern Ireland, many non-departmental public bodies would have been placed under local control but only in those regions where the electorate voted in favour of opting for an assembly. It will be obvious from the brief sketch of powers and functions provided above, that the proposed regional government for England would have been much less powerful than devolution in any of its other forms. Furthermore, the phased introduction, contingent on holding regional referendums, might have led to greater asymmetry in provision between regions voting for and regions voting against. A broader question concerns whether this particular geographical division into regions was a sound basis for establishing a popular system of devolved power, and one likely to restore flagging public confidence in government at sub-national level.

The implementation of the government's proposals for English regional government depended on referendums being held in each of the designated regions to approve the principle,[41] rather than on a single referendum as a test of opinion throughout England. Referendums were initially planned in the North-East, Yorkshire, and the North-West, where support for regional government was believed to be at its strongest, but only one referendum was held, in the North-East region in November 2004. The regional government proposals were emphatically rejected. On a 46 per cent turnout, only 22 per cent of the local electorate voted for the government plans. No further progress on English regional government is likely in the short to medium term following such a negative electoral response, but there continues to be pressure to address the problems caused by the lack of regional government in England.

The introduction of English regional government would have resulted in enhanced accountability mechanisms at an intermediate level of government through elected assemblies, but, as we have seen, these proposals were extremely limited in comparison to other devolved systems in the United Kingdom, and the forms of regional government introduced in other European nations. However, it should be recognised that an important layer of non-elected regional governance set up under the RDA Act 1998 continues to function in the English regions:

> Although major steps in democratising [the English regions] failed in 2004, possibly for a generation, the continued presence of a strong tier of English regional administration should not be doubted. Government offices, RDAs and non-elected stakeholder Assemblies have become the principal building blocks of developing government in the [English] regions since 1997.[42]

AN ENGLISH PARLIAMENT?

A case has been presented for the introduction of an English Parliament.[43] Proposals for an equivalent body to the Scottish Parliament might appear to have some justification, since setting up a Parliament for England could provide the constitutional basis for correcting the glaring asymmetries relating to representation, accountability, and administration which have been raised by

---

[41] Regional Assemblies (Preparation) Act 2003.
[42] J Bradbury, 'Devolution: Between Governance and Territorial Politics' (2005) 58(2) *Parliamentary Affairs* 287–302 at 300.
[43] http://www.thecep.org.uk/.

devolution. However, an English Parliament is unlikely to be introduced in the foreseeable future[44] as there is a lack of the necessary support within any of the mainstream political parties, or more widely among the English electorate. The idea can be objected to for a number of reasons. For example, a Parliament for England, representing more than 80 per cent of the UK population, with equivalent powers to the Scottish Parliament, would be dominant in relation to its Scottish, Welsh, and Northern Irish counterparts, and it would be a strong competitor to the Westminster Parliament, which would no longer have a pivotal role in relation to domestic issues. Also, an English Parliament as an additional elected political body would be expensive to introduce. A fresh cohort of politicians would be required at a time when there is already evidence of voter fatigue with existing elected political institutions. Further, the additional funding needed for an English Parliament would prompt a debate about the financial provisions on which devolution is based. In so doing, this would be likely to open up fresh controversy over the allocation of resources within the United Kingdom. In turn, such controversy might provide further impetus to the devolution process by prompting wider calls for Scottish independence.

PART III: LOCAL GOVERNMENT

INTRODUCTION TO LOCAL GOVERNMENT IN THE UNITED KINGDOM

The Westminster Parliament has introduced a succession of statutes which set the parameters for the structure and operation of local government since the Municipal Corporation Act 1835 established the modern principle of introducing democratic government at a local level (see, for example, the Local Government Acts 1888, 1894, 1933, and 1972). The effect has been to introduce locally elected bodies responsible for a range of different functions. In constitutional theory, Parliament has the power to abolish local government. Such a drastic step, of course, would be most unlikely to occur, although Parliament has, on a number of occasions, re-organised local government. For example, a layer of local government comprising the Metropolitan Councils, and including the Greater London Council, was dispensed with by the Local Government Act 1985. It is also important to remember that central government through the passage of legislation

---

[44] The issue of an English Parliament is discussed in B Hadfield, 'The English and Welsh Questions' in J Jowell and D Oliver (eds), *The Changing Constitution* (Oxford, Oxford University Press, 2004) at p 246ff.

imposes important statutory duties and limitations on local authorities. For example, the Education Act 1944 requires the appropriate authority to ensure that there are sufficient schools in its locality; the Housing Act 1985 imposes a duty on local authorities to maintain council housing in their areas, while the Housing Act 1985, Part III imposes a duty to accommodate certain limited categories of homeless persons. Local authorities are the elected bodies which perform the majority of essential everyday governmental functions, and in a number of policy areas local government has become the means for the implementation of policy by central government at local level.

MAYOR AND ASSEMBLY FOR LONDON

The form of London-wide government first introduced in 2000 seeks to provide a more accountable method for governing the largest urban conurbation in Western Europe. After the abolition of the Greater London Council in the mid 1980s, it was recognised that London lacked a crucial layer of government which was necessary both to provide democratic accountability and to co-ordinate strategic aspects of administration that cut across the remit of the inner and outer London boroughs. The Greater London Authority Act 1999 introduced a Mayor and Assembly for London. The first elections by an additional member system were held in 2000 after a referendum in 1999 approving the principle. The Mayor and Assembly were responsible for spending approximately £4.7 billion in 2002/03, but with the assumption of full responsibility for Transport for London, the projected figure for 2006/07 had risen to in excess of £9.6 billion.

The Greater London Authority Act 1999 restored democracy and accountability for many services and bodies by putting the police, fire service, and a number of non-departmental bodies under democratic control. The main areas coming under the Mayor and Greater London Authority (GLA) are: transport—that is, integrated strategy for London, traffic management, and regulation; economic development—responsibility for London Development Agency; police—creating a new Metropolitan Police Authority, and Fire and Emergency Services; planning—required to develop a land use strategy for London; environment—for example, air quality and waste; culture, for example, museums, library services, and the arts.

The Mayor is placed at the head of the executive and is directly responsible

for the strategies the GLA adopts to achieve its objectives and for the quality and effectiveness of the services which it delivers. The Mayor's functions can be summarised as: devising strategies and action plans on London-wide issues; proposing a budget and submitting it to the Assembly for agreement; co-ordinating action to implement the agreed strategic plans for transport, economic development bodies, police and crime; environmental problems, fire and emergency planning authority; acting as a voice for London; and making appointments to the bodies under the Mayor's control.[45]

A separation of powers is built into the system. The Assembly is responsible for holding the Mayor to account for these strategies and proposals by public scrutiny and criticism. The Assembly is able to question the Mayor and the Mayor's staff, to hold public hearings on issues of importance, and to have access to relevant people, papers, and technical expertise. It also has powers to secure amendments to the Mayor's budget proposals.

A new type of personality politics has developed around the character and style of the candidates seeking mayoral office. The office is professionalised along North American lines with a properly remunerated Mayor and a trimmed-down executive. The Mayor is given a mandate by the London electorate and is placed under an obligation to deliver manifesto commitments. Since the introduction of the Mayor and Assembly, it was suggested that insufficient powers and functions were vested in the office. The government has responded to these calls. For example, in 2004 the Mayor was granted a £5 billion package of capital funding for investment in London Transport. After further consultation, additional powers were granted in 2006 in respect to aspects of policy in the following fields: housing, learning and skills, planning, waste, health, climate change and energy, water, and European structural funds.[46]

THE FRAMEWORK OF LOCAL GOVERNMENT

Local authorities share with Parliament the characteristic of being elected, and in this sense they are representative bodies of the communities on behalf of which they administer services. Councillors represent territorial units called wards, and they normally face re-election every four years, which means that the composition of the authority changes with elections, but the Local Government Act 1972 lays down that each authority is a body corporate that exists in perpetuity. This provision means that authorities are distinct legal entities able to acquire property, enter contracts, and be party to private legal proceedings. Local councillors do not generally receive a salary,

---

[45] White Paper, *A Mayor and Assembly for London*, Cm3897 (HMSO, 1998) para 3.16.
[46] See 'The Greater London Authority: the Government's Final Proposals for Additional Powers and Responsibilities for the Mayor and Assembly', a Policy Statement published by the Department of Communities and Local Government on 13 July 2006.

but they are entitled to claim expenses incurred while performing council business.

The main form of the current arrangements was established in outline by the Local Government Act 1972, which came into force in April 1974. This framework has been subject to ongoing review since 1997.

In rural areas the 1972 Act provides a two-tier division of the main powers between county councils as the upper layer and district councils as the lower layer. In addition, parish councils have responsibility for a very limited number of minor matters. The Act originally created 39 county councils, responsible for education, strategic planning, personal social services, major highways, public transport, consumer protection, and fire and police services (although fire and police services may spread over more than one authority). The county areas were subdivided into 296 non-metropolitan district councils, with responsibility for housing, environmental health, public health and sanitation, and refuse collection. Responsibility for town and country planning is shared with district councils.

The Local Government Act 1992, section 13(1) empowered the Local Government Commission to recommend boundary, structural, or electoral changes 'having regard to the need: (a) to reflect the identities and interests of local communities, and (b) to secure effective and convenient local government.' This re-organisation was essentially completed by 1997 and it resulted in many two-tier authorities becoming single tier 'unitary' authorities. In much the same way, the Local Government (Wales) Act 1994 provided a new unitary structure for local government in Wales. The previously existing counties and districts were abolished and replaced by 22 unitary authorities, known as 'principal councils'. In Scotland the Local Government (Scotland) Act 1994 provided for the creation of 32 single-tier authorities. In Northern Ireland local government comprises 26 district councils and 9 area boards. Responsibility for local government comes under the devolved governments established in 1999.

The situation in the main cities has always been different. The position was modified significantly by the Local Government Act 1985 which (as mentioned above) abolished the Greater London Council and the six metropolitan area councils. This reform left the 32 London boroughs and 36 metropolitan district councils as a single tier of local government in urban areas. These councils are now typically responsible for providing education (with the exception of those schools opting out), personal social services, highways and transportation, refuse disposal, town and country planning, consumer protection, parks and recreations, and libraries.

It has already been stated that the main powers of local authorities are defined by legislation, and section 101 of the Local Government Act 1972 provides that many decision-making powers can be delegated by an authority to council committees, sub-committees, or officers of the authority. However, delegation to individual council members, including committee chairpersons, is unlawful. The title of these committees will correspond to the nature of the functions for which each is responsible. These committees used to draw up and discuss the more detailed questions of policy formation, and their recommendations were usually presented to the main body of the council for ratification, but since the Local Government Act 2000 decision-making is in the hands of the leader/mayor and a cabinet. Once policy is formed, the power to implement it at a local level is by officers of the council. The power under which the officers act is not usually by direct means, but rather through specific forms of statutory provision, by-laws, and compulsory purchase orders.

THE FINANCING OF LOCAL GOVERNMENT

Another reason why local government has limited autonomy is because of its financial dependency on Westminster. (In Scotland and Wales it is the devolved executive which allocates funding to local government. This funding has been made available to the executives under calculations made according to the Barnett formula discussed earlier.) The main slice of local government revenue comes from central government grants (about 60 per cent of total revenue) with a proportion of this revenue targeted for particular services, for example, the fire brigade and police. In addition, central government makes a general contribution to local government funding, which can be allocated by an authority between budget heads. Local authorities make up the remainder of their budget requirements by raising revenue locally. The major component of their income comes from council tax, which is a tax paid on all properties in an area.[47] It is a banded tax calculated according to the market value of the property concerned. As well as taxation, local authorities are allowed to charge for the provision of certain services ranging from rents and repairs, the sale of council houses, recreational facilities, pest control, etc. Finally, local authorities can borrow money by issuing bonds, but this is subject to strict conditions imposed by the Treasury.

Since the early 1980s there have been repeated attempts by central government to impose strict cash limits by 'capping' local government spending. The Treasury used to supplement the budgets of councils by making up a fixed proportion of the requirements of the authority. In order to control public expenditure during the 1980s the government introduced financial

[47] See the Local Government Finance Act 1992.

penalties for councils that failed to operate within the limits set by central government; in its latest form this amount is referred to as Standard Spending Assessment (under Part II of the Local Government Act 1999). If the authority exceeded the amount spent, the contribution from central government would diminish. These capping measures were the product of bitter political controversy between central government and the local authorities (often in different political hands) during the 1980s, and the legality of the schemes was challenged in the courts (mainly unsuccessfully). The imposition of such rigid financial constraints has reduced direct accountability to the local electorate, since many councils have found it necessary to cut their services to meet government financial targets without regard to electoral commitments to continue with them or expand them.

FROM COMPULSORY COMPETITIVE TENDERING
TO BEST VALUE

Central government has been equally concerned, particularly since the 1980s, to achieve value for money and greater efficiency at all levels of government including local government. Market-orientated policies were adopted in pursuit of this objective. Under the local government legislation introduced by the Conservative governments between 1979 and 1997 (see, for example, section 2 of the Local Government Act 1988, which introduced compulsory competitive tendering (CCT)), authorities were required to privatise many services ranging from refuse collection and street cleaning, to maintenance of housing stock if private sector companies could undercut provision by the local authority's in-house services. The authority was required by statute to offer contracts for local government services, either to the lowest tender, or to the one that was the most economically advantageous. This meant that local authorities were heavily constrained in the way in which they were allowed to exercise their contracting powers.

The Labour Government has strongly supported market-driven policies in the public sector and in local government, but it has abolished CCT in favour of a new system. The Local Government Act 1999 requires local authorities to make arrangements for 'best value' in the performance of their functions. Best Value is defined in section 3 of the 1999 Act as 'securing continuous improvement in the exercise of all functions undertaken by the authority, whether statutory or not, having regard to a combination of economy, efficiency and effectiveness.' A number of performance indicators are applied to measure progress, and the relevant standards can be set by the Secretary of State having regard to any recommendations made to him or her by the Audit Commission. Local authorities are further required to provide 'best value' performance plans for each financial year under section 6. This legislation seeks to allow improved efficiency and effectiveness in the use of resources, but also to achieve significant improvements in service quality. The new emphasis on quality means that for contracted services a local authority is able to consider the appropriateness of contracting for that service, and it also provides greater flexibility in the negotiation of different forms of contract and contractual relationship.

Certain statutes provide wide powers for local authorities to use contracts in furtherance of policy. For example, this applies in the area of planning under the Town and Country Planning Act 1971. Local authorities may reach agreements under their planning powers to restrict development. It is not uncommon for local authorities to attach conditions in regard to the development and use of land. These may be inserted as a quid pro quo for the grant of planning permission. Moreover, it should be stressed that if any local authority steps beyond the scope of these powers, judicial review may be available as a method of control. An example is *Hazell v Hammersmith and Fulham London Borough Council*,[48] where a series of interest rate swapping transactions by local authorities was held to be unlawful.[49]

In October 2006 the government published a White Paper which promised to reduce the level of control from central government, provide greater citizen involvement and give local authorities increased flexibility in policy delivery.[50]

THE LOCAL GOVERNMENT ACT 2000

Part I of the Local Government Act 2000 (LGA 2000) allows additional scope for authorities to develop participation with the community taking up the themes of partnership and 'joined-up' government[51] so that it moves from merely being service provider to community leader. This initiative involves:

> A multi-organisational, community-based process, initiated by the council, for creating a shared vision of community identified priorities leading to a programme of actions which demonstrate the commitment and support of the groups involved.[52]

---

[48] [1992] 2 AC 1.

[49] See *Credit Suisse v Allerdale Borough Council* [1997] QB 306.

[50] See 'Strong & prosperous communities—The Local Goverment White Paper', October 2006, CM 6939–1.

[51] See *Modernising Government*, Cm 4310, 1999, and *Modern Local Government: In Touch with the People*, Cm 4014, 1998.

[52] V Jenkins, 'Learning from the Past: Achieving Sustainable Development in the Reform of Local Government' [2002] *PL* 130–52 at 138.

Sections 2 and 3 of the LGA 2000 give local authorities powers to take any steps which they consider are likely to promote the well-being of their area or their inhabitants. Under section 4 they are placed under a duty to develop community strategies, together with other local bodies, for this purpose. These provisions are intended to give local authorities increased opportunities to improve the quality of life of their local communities. Although they were previously able to incur expenditure in the interests of their area under section 137 of the Local Government Act 1972, this was subject to many restrictions which are now relaxed by section 8 of the LGA 2000.

Against a background of voter apathy with turnouts in many parts of the country falling well below 30 per cent in recent years, the government proposed that local government should be radically overhauled.[53] Part 2 of the LGA 2000 seeks to transform the operation of local democracy, to provide greater efficiency, transparency, and accountability for local authorities. It does this by setting out new political management structures. These include local authority executives and executive arrangements which will replace the present committee systems. The effect will be to create a new decision-making framework in which there is a separation of decision-making and scrutiny of decisions by new committees.[54] The Act sets out three initial forms of executive[55] which might be adopted and on which all local authorities must consult by means of a referendum.[56] These models are based on two variants of a cabinet system with a leader elected by the council, or an elected executive mayor and separately elected authority (similar to the current arrangements for London).

The local government reforms for cities are an attempt to bring power closer to the citizen but so far there is little evidence of much support for the new presidential-style personality politics centred upon a directly elected mayor accountable to an elected assembly. Stoke-on-Trent and Middlesborough are two of the cities to have opted for this new type of system. London remains a special case.

ACCOUNTABILITY MECHANISMS

In order to improve the public perception of local government and local councillors Part III of the Local Government Act 2000 establishes a new ethical framework, which includes the introduction of statutory codes of conduct, with a requirement for every council to adopt a code covering the

---

[53] See, eg, White Paper, *Modern Local Government: In Touch with the People*, Cm 4014, 1998.
[54] LGA 2000, s 21.
[55] *Ibid*, ss 11 and 12.
[56] *Ibid*, ss 34–6.

behaviour of elected members and of officers, and the creation of a standards committee for each authority. This approach has many characteristics in common with the Westminster regime for parliamentary standards.

In addition, the Local Government Act 1972, section 151 provides that councils must ensure the proper administration of their financial affairs, and the Local Government Finance Act 1982 set in place the mechanism for external audits by an Audit Commission for local authorities in England and Wales. This introduced commercial accounting methods to the local government sector. (For the auditors' current powers, see the Audit Commission Act 1998.) The district auditor has the duty to see that public money is spent according to the law. If it is found that there has been unlawful expenditure by the authority in the discharge of its public duties, the auditor has the power to enforce financial penalties against named councillors or officials. See *Porter v Magill*.[57] Finally, the Local Government Act 1974, Part III allows a local government ombudsman to investigate complaints concerning questions of local maladministration. These matters are referred to the local government ombudsman directly or through a local councillor.

CONCLUSION

The primary legal objective of setting up modern forms of local government was to vest elected authorities with broad enabling powers, permitting them to respond flexibly to new challenges without being unduly constrained by the fear of legal intervention. As a result, local government in its original form was afforded considerable discretion in its ability to respond to local needs. However, the predominant concern of central government in recent years has been to strictly control public expenditure. The Conservatives while in power (1979–97) were set on a course of reducing the role of local government by privatising services, establishing housing trusts and introducing private sector funding. But while it is clear that the Labour government has been intent on controlling public expenditure by imposing tight restrictions on the spending of local authorities, it is less ideologically driven than its Conservative predecessor, and while it has retained a commitment to public–private partnerships and privatisation in general, it has also relaxed controls and extended certain additional powers of local government. For there to be a genuine extension of local democracy based on a regeneration of interest in local government, new models of decision-making will not suffice on their own. There must also be a loosening of the grip on financial control and the introduction of appropriate methods of tax-and-spend provision at a local level.

[57] [2001] UKHL 67, [2002] 1 All ER 465.

Turning to devolution, the Westminster Parliament has been significantly affected by this redistribution of power. However, there has been no attempt so far to address 'the West Lothian question'. The Conservative Party leadership has stated that, should the Party get returned to power at the next election, they will bring before Parliament proposals to restrict the voting rights of MPs in line with devolution, thereby preventing MPs from Scotland from voting on legislative matters concerning England and Wales. Also, there is a strong case for reducing the number of MPs representing constituencies in Scotland, Wales, and Northern Ireland, and it has been proposed that a reformed second chamber replacing the House of Lords should have an elected element with emphasis on providing a further degree of regional representation in Parliament.[58]

Each devolution statute includes elaborate safeguards to prevent sovereignty from being undermined. There have been several breakdowns of devolution in Northern Ireland giving rise to the restoration of direct rule from Westminster. While in one sense this reassertion of authority illustrates that ultimate control lies with central government, in another sense, devolution has reduced the sovereignty of the Westminster Parliament. On narrow issues of strict legality, devolved bodies must operate legally within devolved powers, but it is now difficult for the government acting through the Westminster Parliament to challenge actions of the devolved bodies, particularly where there is a democratic mandate for any policy that has been adopted. Scotland has a Labour-dominated coalition, Labour is in power on its own in Wales, but the Labour government and the national party machine has not been able to exert control over policy-making. For example, the Scottish Parliament and executive has followed its own independent line on student grants and on providing long-term care for the elderly. The coalition between Labour and the Liberal Democrats has resulted in compromise and a watering-down of policy. Following the 2003 elections the introduction of proportional representation for local government elections was a condition extracted by the Liberal Democrats for joining the coalition with Labour.

In sum, it is important to remind ourselves that the new constitutional framework of devolved government has not been conceived as part of a grand design. Rather, the arrangements set in place have each been a pragmatic response to the particular situations in Scotland, Wales, Northern Ireland, and London. The result is described as asymmetrical because it produces an uneven distribution of powers. But the uneven treatment has led to demands for further reform. For example, in Wales calls to give the Assembly comparable law-making powers to the Scottish Parliament have,

---

[58] See, eg, Royal Commission on the Reform of the House of Lords,

in part at least, been answered. Moreover, devolution has strengthened the case for democratic representation in England at regional level. UK devolution should not be regarded as a settlement, nor as a first step towards a federal system, but as a stage in a dynamic process which will almost certainly lead to further reform. It is consistent with a European trend encouraged by the concept of subsidiarity which aims to combat a perceived democratic deficit. The assumption is that this objective can be achieved by re-allocating centralised authority and power to more local levels of territorial governance. The UK experience can therefore be usefully compared with recent provisions for regional government in Italy, Spain, and other European nations.

FURTHER READING

Bogdanor V, *Devolution in the United Kingdom* (Oxford, Oxford University Press, 1999).

Bologna C, Frosini J, and Leyland P, 'Regional Government Reform in Italy: Assessing the Prospects for Devolution' in Frosini J, Pegoraro L, and Waller T (eds), *Europe, Regions and local government in Italy, Spain and the United Kingdom* (Libreria Bonomo, Bologna, 2003).

Bort E, 'The new institutions: an interim assessment' in M O'Neill (ed), *Devolution and British Politics* (Harlow, Longman, 2004).

Bradbury J and Mitchell J, 'Devolution: Between Governance and Territorial Politcs' (2005) 58(2) *Parliamentary Affairs* 287–302.

Burrows M, *Devolution* (London, Sweet & Maxwell, 2000).

Cornes R, 'Devolution and England: What is on Offer' in Bamforth N and Leyland P, *Public Law in a Multi-Layered Constitution* (Oxford, Hart Publishing, 2003).

Hadfield B, 'Devolution in the United Kingdom and the English and Welsh Questions' in Jowell J and Oliver D, *The Changing Constitution*, 5th edn (Oxford, Oxford University Press, 2004).

Hadfield B, 'Devolution Westminster and the English Question' [2005] *Public Law* 286.

Hazell R (ed), *The English Question* (Manchester, Manchester University Press, 2006).

Himsworth C and Munro C, *The Scotland Act 1998*, 2nd edn (Edinburgh, Sweet & Maxwell, 2000).

Himsworth C and O'Neill M, *Scotland's Constitution: Law and Practice*, (Edinburgh, Lexis Nexis, 2003).

Hopkins J, *Devolution in Context: Regional Federal and Devolved Government in the European Union* (London, Cavendish, 2002).

Leigh I, *Law, Politics and Local Democracy* (Oxford, Oxford University Press, 2000).

Leigh I, 'The New Local Government' in Jowell J and Oliver D, *The Changing Constitution*, 5th edn (Oxford, Oxford University Press, 2004).

Leyland P, 'The Modernisation of Local and Regional Government in the United Kingdom: Towards A New Democratic State?' in Frosini J, Pegoraro L, and Waller T (eds) *Europe, Regions and local government in Italy, Spain and the United Kingdom* (Libreria Bonomo, Bologna, 2003).

Leyland P, 'UK Devolution: Questions of Integration, Accountability and Control' in Frosini J, Pegoraro L, and Waller T (eds), *Europe, Regions and local government in Italy, Spain and the United Kingdom* (Libreria Bonomo, Bologna, 2003).

McCrudden C, 'Northern Ireland, The Belfast Agreement, and the British Constitution' in Jowell J and Oliver D, *The Changing Constitution*, 5th edn (Oxford, Oxford University Press, 2004).

McMillan J and Massey A, 'Central Government and Devolution' in O'Neill M (ed), *Devolution and British Politics* (Harlow, Longman, 2004).

Loughlin M, 'The Demise of Local Government' in Bogdanor V, *The British Constitution in the Twentieth Century* (Oxford, Oxford University Press 2003).

O'Neill M (ed) *Devolution and British Politics* (Harlow, Longman, 2004).

Rawlings R, *Delineating Wales: Constitutional, Legal and Administrative Aspects of National Devolution* (Cardiff, University of Wales Press, 2003).

Rawlings R, 'Wales in Europe' in Craig P and Rawlings R (eds), *Law and Administration in Europe: Essays in Honour of Carol Harlow* (Oxford, Oxford University Press, 2003).

Stevens C, 'English Regional Government; in O"Neill M (ed), *Devolution and British Politics* (Harlow, Longman, 2004).

Vandelli L, *Devolution e altre storie* (Bologna, il Mulino, 2002).

Winetrobe B, 'Scottish Devolution: Aspirations and Reality in Multi-Layer Governance' in Jowell J and Oliver D, *The Changing Constitution*, 5th edn (Oxford, Oxford University Press, 2004).

Your Region, Your Choice: Revitalising the English Regions, Cm 5511 (2002).

WEBSITES

http://www.regional-assembly.org.uk
http://www.emmecidue.net/devolutionclub
http://www.devolution.ac.uk/home.htm
http://www.scottish.parliament.uk
http://www.scotland.gov.uk/Home
http://www.scotland.gov.uk/concordats

http://www.wales.gov.uk/index.htm
http://www.wda.co.uk/index.cfm/wda_home/index/en2
https://www.cclondon.com/index.shtml
http://www.london.gov.uk
http://www.odpm.gov.uk/stellent/groups/odpm_devolution/
    documents/sectionhomepage/odpm_devolution_page.hcsp
http://www.ni-assembly.gov.uk
http://www.nics.gov.uk

9

Conclusion: The UK Constitution Facing the Future

————◦————

THIS CONCLUDING CHAPTER draws attention to two questions which are likely to have an important bearing on the UK constitution over the next few years, each in different ways. The first issue concerns the case for codifying the UK constitution, or for adjusting the balance of the constitution in favour of the judicial branch. We then consider the developing shape of the European Union, and, in particular, the effect of a European constitution, should one eventually be ratified.

(1) A WRITTEN CONSTITUTION OR A LEGAL CONSTITUTION?

What should next be done to modernise the constitution? A decade of radical constitutional reform has changed the complexion of the UK constitution. In many respects it has come to look much more like a codified constitution. From a territorial standpoint, the Scotland Act 1998, the Government of Wales Act 1998, and the Northern Ireland Act 1998 operate as a constitutional framework for devolved government. In terms of citizen rights, the Human Rights Act 1998 approximates to a domestic bill of rights by, in effect, incorporating the rights contained in the European Convention on Human Rights as part of domestic jurisprudence. The reforms relating to the Lord Chancellor, judicial appointments and the introduction of a UK Supreme Court have eliminated some of the glaring anomalies which conflicted with the idea of separation of powers. Finally, the Freedom of Information Act 2000, despite its limitations, has altered the balance in favour of the disclosure of information held by public bodies.

Constitutional reform has generated its own momentum for further reform. To take some obvious examples mentioned in this book, in response to the asymmetry of devolution there is an emerging case for some form of Parliament or regional government for England. A further phase of reform is required for the House of Lords. A Civil Service Act has been proposed to place the civil service on a statutory footing and limit the number and role of special advisers. To address the above issues, and correct other manifest shortcomings in our current constitutional arrangements, the answer for some is to introduce a written constitution. As one commentator explains, this would:

> animate society with a sense of what is right and instil into government an under-standing of the proper limits to the exercise of power; above all it can inform the conversation of politics with a sense of dispersed responsibility[1].

In common with most other nations, the United Kingdom would adopt a codified constitutional text setting in place all aspects of the institutional framework (Parliament; civil service; courts; devolved, regional, and local government) and this would also be allied to a liberal democratic creed of cit-izen rights and a statement of government obligations. In practice, however, any such attempt at codification is unlikely to bear fruit, because it pre-supposes a consensus can be reached between disparate political groups on institutional design and other values to incorporate in a new constitution. For example, already the official opposition are currently proposing (2006) to amend the Human Rights Act 1998 in line with their conception of citizen rights.

The trend towards progressively codifying key aspects of the constitution has redefined the relationship between Parliament, the executive, and the courts in a wide range of different contexts. Perhaps most significantly, the greater visibility of judicial review has meant that the modern judiciary has already assumed a new role amounting to a silent shift in the balance of the constitution. Over the last 40 years or so the courts have reacted to the increase in the powers of government, referred to in our discussion as 'elec-tive dictatorship', and the failings in accountability before Parliament, with a new era of judicial assertiveness.[2] Certain advocates of codification (or par-tial codification) would seek to recalibrate the distribution of constitutional power in favour of the judges as part of a written constitution.[3] This approach rests on the assumption that political questions can be, and should be, separated from legal questions. State powers and individual rights would

---

[1] F Mount, *The British Constitution Now* (London, Mandarin, 1993) p 266.
[2] R Stevens, 'Government and the Judiciary' in V Bogdanor (ed), *The British Constitution in the Twentieth Century* (Oxford, Oxford University Press, 2003) p 350ff.
[3] Lord Lester, 'Human Rights and the British Constitution' in J Jowell and D Oliver (eds), *The Changing Constitution*, 5th edn (Oxford, Oxford University Press, 2004) p 85.

be limited by principles of legality laid down by judges as higher order law.[4] As part of the revised arrangements in a legal constitution (as opposed to a political constitution), the Human Rights Act 1998 would be amended to give the courts power to override legislation which contravened Convention rights (rather than issuing declarations of incompatibility), and a constitutional court would have the task of ultimately deciding political questions which would be considered as matters of constitutional legality.

Opponents of this view reject the idea that the courts can be relied upon as impartial guardians of the law and do not accept that unelected and unaccountable judges are qualified to take political decisions.[5] For example, in resolving the disputed Presidential election in 2000, the US Supreme Court lined up according to the declared political affiliation of its judges. Lord Denning, whose interventions when Master of the Rolls were often controversial, nevertheless recognised that:

> if judges were given power to overthrow sections of Acts of Parliament, they would become political, their appointments would be based on political grounds and the reputation of our Judiciary would suffer accordingly.[6]

Professor Loughlin goes further. Rejecting the enclosure of politics within the straitjacket of the law, he concludes that:

> The project of establishing law as an objective framework of rational principles . . . has not been successful. With the ascendancy of law as right we do not therefore reach the end of history, or an escape from politics. Instead, this legalization of politics has led primarily to a politicization of law.[7]

In sum, shortcomings in accountability and effectiveness will not be cured by adopting a written constitution, or by vesting the courts with the ultimate power over constitutional matters. The answer is to reinvigorate the political process and restore confidence in politicians and political institutions. In regard to Parliament, this calls for the introduction of a reconstituted second chamber. Further improvements to the parliamentary committee system are needed to enable enhanced legislative scrutiny and to achieve improved scrutiny of delegated legislation. The rigorous enforcement of existing restrictions is essential to combat conflicts of interest relating to ministers, MPs, and peers. Also, additional regulation of the funding of political parties is required. Loans as well as gifts should be declared to reveal the influence of

---

[4] See, eg, J Laws, 'Law and Democracy' [1995] *PL* 72–93 at 84ff.

[5] J Griffith, 'The Political Constitution' (1979) 42 *MLR* 1; A Tomkins, 'In Defence of the Political Constitution' (2002) 22(1) *Oxford Journal of Legal Studies* 157–75.

[6] 369 HL Deb, 25 March 1976, cols 797–8.

[7] M Loughlin, *Sword and Scales: An Examination of the Relationship between Law and Politics* (Oxford, Hart Publishing, 2000) p 232.

powerful individuals and business interests. The case for the introduction of limited state funding for parties should also be re-examined. In addition, the emergence of a stronger parliamentary opposition committed to a new agenda is likely to encourage the more effective functioning of Parliament.

(2) THE EU, THE EUROPEAN CONSTITUTION, AND THE UK CONSTITUTION

Finally, we turn to the possible implications of a European constitution on domestic constitutional arrangements. From a constitutional angle we have already noted that the sacrifice of sovereign power in a number of areas to a supra-national economic and political organisation was a consequence of UK membership of the European Economic Community (now the EU). As an important step towards European stabilisation, a European constitution was agreed between member states in 2004.[8] To some extent the impetus for this EU constitution might be regarded as a consolidation process, knitting together the provisions of previous treaties into a more coherent whole. As with national constitutions, a constitution at a European level was drafted to embed a general commitment to core values and objectives, in this case, human dignity, freedom, democracy, equality, respect for human rights, security, justice, as well as economic freedoms—free movement of goods, capital, people, and services.

Of course, before agreement on a constitution, the EU could already pass laws applying in member states relating to external trade and customs policy, the internal market, agriculture and fisheries, and many areas of domestic law, including employment, the environment, and health and safety at work. This European constitution, if it had been ratified, would have extended law-making into additional areas, including aspects of criminal justice, and asylum and immigration law. Further, to facilitate more effective action among the greatly increased family of nations, the principle of voting by qualified majority would be more generally applied, but with a veto for members on foreign policy, defence, and taxation. The European constitution sets out 'rights, freedoms and principles'. These include a long list from the right to life and the right to liberty to the right to strike.

Many advocates of a European constitution share the belief that a reinvigorated Europe under a new constitution would enable Europe, as a collective force, to be better able to stand up to its major competitor, the United States, but also to resist the awesome power of financial markets and of global

---

[8] http://www.unizar.es/euroconstitucion/Treaties/Treaty_Const.htm.

capitalism. For example, where individual nations have been increasingly unable to act to regulate and control the pressures exerted by multi-national companies dominating markets, it might be reasoned that a Europe-wide regulatory system would be much better placed to intervene to protect consumers and to protect the environment.

An obvious problem has been that the negotiation of the treaties (eg Amsterdam, Maastricht, Nice) and the drafting of the European constitution were mainly undertaken as a top-down exercise carried out by officials and by politicians representing member states. Moreover, formidable obstacles had to be cleared in order to reach agreement. In formulating a constitution and thereby setting an agenda for Europe the most influential nations were committed to very different objectives. For example, political leaders in France, Germany, Italy, Belgium, and Holland were keen to strengthen the EU as a political entity (European Super State) committed to public services and social support, while the United Kingdom, with its growing euroscepticism, was content with a mainly economic union comprising a large marketplace. It wished to see a more limited state sector challenged by liberalisation and the introduction of market forces.[9] The European constitution held out the prospect of protecting UK economic interests without the United Kingdom forming one of the core group of integrating states towards greater union.

There has been an emerging legitimacy problem relating to the EU and its institutions. The European Parliament (EP) consists of members elected in member states. Its authority was set to be enhanced, still only marginally, by the new constitution, but the EP has limited powers and often only operates on the fringes of the law-making process. Crucially, government at EU level is unelected. There is no transnational party system capable of rising above national politics, and the European constitution which was agreed subject to ratification does not address the issue of the role of national Parliaments and other accountability mechanisms. The absence of democratic political accountability at EU level helps to explain the general apathy and indifference which pervades European political space.[10] In fact, it is argued that this immunity from accountability has resulted in a gap opening up between national governments and the prevailing public opinion within many of the member states. This problem was graphically illustrated in referendums held in France and Holland in 2005 where the local electorates voted decisively against the constitution, despite strong endorsement from the ruling political elite.

---

[9] C Lambroschini, (2004) *Le Figaro*, February 19.
[10] C Harlow, 'European Governance and Accountability' in N Bamforth and P Leyland (eds), *Public Law in a Multi-Layered Constitution*

The Labour government has promised a national referendum before ratification of this or any future version of a European constitution (or committing the United Kingdom to the Euro currency zone), and this commitment is justified in view of further qualifications to domestic sovereignty. The electorate has not been consulted because of a generally hostile public mood towards the EU and to any increase in power granted to Europe at the expense of domestic institutions. The upshot is that, although 15 states have approved the constitution, ratification has been delayed indefinitely following the referendums in France and Holland, which means that the introduction of important reform, including certain improvements to accountability mechanisms, have been put on hold. At a moment when the EU has increased substantially in size, its credibility has been dealt a severe blow, reflecting growing public disillusionment with the European project.

Index